Advance Praise for DREAMS & DEADLINES

"*Dreams and Deadlines* takes the proven discipline of OKRs and makes them personal. Sebastian and Wolfram apply well-established professional discipline to personal ambitions in a way that's both practical and human. As someone who has spent years helping leaders bring humanity into organizations, I found this book to be a refreshing reminder that the same clarity and rhythm we demand at work can transform our personal lives too. This is a must-read for anyone ready to finally make progress on what matters most."

—**EVAN LEYBOURN**, Co-founder at Business Agility Institute, Australia

"Individuals often excel in their careers, building professional lives with impressive structure and discipline. Ironically, however, this very success often coexists with profound personal challenges—from unhappy marriages and unfulfilled holiday plans to neglected health. This highlights a striking imbalance: the meticulous approach to career advancement rarely extends to nurturing personal well-being and relationships. *Dreams and Deadlines* bridges this gap, guiding us to bring structure, discipline, and rigor into our personal lives."

—**FRANKIE PHUA**, Managing Director at United Overseas Bank; Distinguished Fellow at Institute of Banking & Finance, Singapore

"Turning dreams into reality is a challenge that so often feels out of reach. In this book, Sebastian and Wolfram show us that it doesn't have to be. By transforming proven strategies from the corporate world into practical tools for everyday life—and illustrating them with clear, relatable examples—they offer a guide that is insightful, uplifting, and grounded in humor and common sense. An inspiring resource for all of us who are ready to pursue our most meaningful goals."

—**MIKE BREWSTER**, former Chief Information Officer at Zuellig Pharma, Singapore

"My career has been defined by fast-changing markets—payments, retail, fintech, and tech platforms—where priorities shift by the quarter, sometimes by the week. OKRs have always been useful in those contexts, but I never fully applied them to life outside of work. *Dreams and Deadlines* makes that translation natural. The POKR method keeps the OKR heart—concise Objectives, measurable Key Results, and quarterly cycles—and adds what busy professionals often miss: the need to include your family, the longer-term mission that gives motivation, and the weekly check-in that tie Key Results to immediate action. That bridge between ambition and execution is what makes it powerful. It's as relevant to closing global partnerships as it is to personal health or family commitments."

—**MATTHIAS SETZER**, Director of Corporate
Business Development at Amazon, USA

"I was already practicing an OKR style process in an effort to force a better balance between my professional and personal lives. But the guidance and cadence I found in *Dreams and Deadlines* provided a much better structure to ensure traction and ultimate achievement of my goals, which is incredibly satisfying."

—**ANDY COOPER**, Founder of ComEx Partners;
former executive in S&P500 firms, UK

"In leadership and in life, I've found that impact comes from pairing purpose with discipline. *Dreams and Deadlines* capture this through the 5+1 framework: first, define a five-year mission that embodies your future self and the legacy you want to create. Then, set a one-year goal that translates that mission into a clear commitment for the year ahead. What makes the method truly actionable is how it connects this long- and short-term focus back to OKRs: quarterly Objectives and measurable Key Results that keep you honest, and weekly check-ins that turn intent into action. It's a system that aligns big dreams with everyday choices—and for me, it echoes my belief that making a difference in lives requires both vision and execution."

—**ENG HONG LIM**, Chief Commercial Officer at Deloitte ASEAN; board member at Trailblazer Foundation, Singapore

"*Dreams and Deadlines* is both insightful and refreshingly candid. What sets it apart from other publications in this area is not only the authors' experience in the field, but also their willingness to confront the reader with common shortcomings that are too often overlooked. They critically examine where things frequently go wrong, providing readers with a more balanced and realistic perspective.

The combination of clear structure and well-funded information with a sense of underlying dry humor makes it not only informative but also entertaining to read."

—**FLORIAN MAYER**, Head of Technology at neoimpulse, Germany

"*Dreams and Deadlines* is a thought-provoking book that explores the ways to help everyone achieve more dreams in their private life. The book offers a well-thought approach and a set of tested tools to encourage everyone to try—and ultimately realize—more dreams within deadlines.

Both authors are seasoned professionals in their own fields. They have gained ample experience in how to achieve ambitious targets in the business world. Now they have transferred their experiences into the private world, which is often neglected by many of us, as we are so busy with fulfilling the targets set by the companies.

This book has triggered thoughts on what is really important for me in my life. Is it all about a successful career? What if I could not have it in the end? How about those dreams I once had in my mind? Are they secondary to my career? When will I have time to get them done? After I'm retired? No, this book has opened another door to demonstrate that we can achieve more than what we thought and imagined. I strongly recommend reading this book. You will find your own paths to your dreams with a deadline you set."

—RONG LIN, Vice President and Head of Marketing
Transportation at HUBER + SUHNER, Switzerland

"I've spent years in consulting and now lead an AI startup, so OKRs are second nature in my professional world. They align teams, drive focus, and keep ambition grounded in results. Yet when it comes to my personal life, it's a different story. Juggling health, family, and personal growth often feels like spinning plates, with no system to keep them from crashing.

Dreams and Deadlines closes that gap. It takes the discipline of OKRs and reframes them for real life: a five-year mission, a concrete one-year goal, quarterly Objectives with measurable Key Results, all grounded in simple weekly rituals. For me, it's the first system that provides the same clarity I use at work to anchor the rest of my life."

—LESLIE CHACKO, Co-founder and COO of AI/Fintech Startup;
former Managing Director of Marsh McLennan Companies, USA

"We've been conditioned to think of productivity as something that belongs only to the workplace. But most of life happens outside of the office—in terms of time, meaning, and what matters. For too long, we've tried our hardest to optimize work and neglected the rest. Not only does this book flip that script, it also lays out a system to help us achieve our personal goals."

—SIDDHARTH PODDAR, journalist and editor;
Co-founder at StoneBench, Singapore

"*Dreams and Deadlines* offers a pragmatic approach to adopting the Objectives & Key Results (OKR) framework for the achievement of personal goals. It serves as an excellent hands-on tool kit for anyone looking to better understand and pursue their life's ambitions.

I was particularly impressed by the application of corporate strategies to personal development, complemented by the author's direct and engaging style. The numerous real-life examples make the concepts very relatable!"

—**EMANUELE PRANDI**, Finance Project
Manager at Holcim, Switzerland

"Grounded in solid evidence and research, *Dreams and Deadlines* reimagines the corporate OKR framework for personal use. Wolfram and Sebastian achieve a rare balance—making goal setting feel at once strategic and humane. As someone who teaches sustainable finance and believes in impact through intentional frameworks, I found this book refreshing, insightful, and deeply practical. It equips readers not just to dream ambitiously but to shape goals—and deadlines—with clarity, purpose, and meaning."

—**PROF. LIANG HAO**, Associate Professor of Finance,
Ho Bee Professorship in Sustainability Management, and
Co-director of Singapore Green Finance Centre, SMU, Singapore

"Having spent over three decades transforming financial services technology across Asia-Pacific, from leading billion-dollar banking mergers to building digital platforms from scratch, I understand firsthand how challenging it can be to apply professional discipline to personal aspirations. The POKR Method brilliantly bridges this gap, offering the structured approach that helped me navigate complex transformations at DBS, UOB, and CIMB, but tailored for life's most important goals outside the boardroom.

As someone who has managed teams of five-hundred-plus professionals while pursuing personal passions like watercolor art and writing, I found this book's practical framework invaluable for achieving meaningful progress across all areas of life. Wolfram and Sebastian have distilled decades of consulting wisdom into an accessible system that actually works in the real world. This book will transform how you approach personal goals. I only wish I'd had it thirty years ago when I started my journey."

—**ONG WHEE TECK**, Former Partner at EY and Fellow at Singapore Computer Society, Singapore

"In a world where professional success often seems to come at the expense of personal life and self-fulfillment, the authors introduce a concept for achieving both: self-leadership through OKRs for personal and professional goals and ambitions.

By adopting a familiar framework from the 9-to-5 to the 5-to-9, Wolfram and Sebastian have developed the compelling, practical, and easy-to-adopt POKR Method—a concept proven effective in countless corporate success stories and one that stands out in today's crowded self-improvement space."

—**SEBASTIAN SOHN**, Director at Aurexia Consulting, Singapore

"As a cancer researcher, OKRs are familiar territory to me. I define them in every grant application and use them together with my team to plan our experiments, both short- and long-term. However, my personal life was never as organized, and I hadn't considered using the same familiar methods to structure my goals outside of the lab. Long-term goals often remained dreams, since they seemed far away and (too) hard to reach. That changed when I read *Dreams and Deadlines*. This book provides the clear, systematic approach I was looking for.

The POKR Method is highly effective in showing a direct strategy on how to get from the long-term objectives (the 'Mission') to the daily execution to get closer to the objectives. The authors have done a great job to adapt the corporate OKR model for the realities of personal life.

On a personal level, it's finally helping me tackle goals I've been delaying for years. I'm finally learning to fly-fish by setting Key Results that ensure I'm regularly out on the water. At the same time, I'm using it to get fit and train for a multiday ski trip in the Norwegian mountains in the coming spring, breaking the preparation down into manageable, quarterly objectives.

For any professional, this book is an invaluable guide to building a more intentional—and effective—personal and professional life. A practical and highly recommended resource!"

—KAY OLIVER SCHINK, PhD, Associate Professor
for Biochemistry at University of Oslo, Norway

"As an actuary, I like structured approaches to problem-solving both professionally and in my personal life. *Dreams and Deadlines* helps you do just that and define what success looks like, review it often enough to learn, and then adjust. Things sometimes go off script no matter how well planned you are, and this book will help you navigate such situations as well."

—JUNAID IQBAL, actuary and risk expert with
leadership experience spanning across some of
the top Fortune 500 insurers, Malaysia

"After decades in banking risk management, I've learned that discipline works best when it is practical and humane. This method keeps things simple: be clear about direction, choose a few priorities, and review them regularly. It can sit quietly beside our daily obligations—family, faith, community—and still help us move forward."

—PARDI SUDRADJAT, former banking executive
and risk management enthusiast, Indonesia

"Being a busy professional in a global firm often means juggling international teams, tough targets, and demanding stakeholders. Add a young family in a bustling city, and life quickly becomes a balancing act.

What makes the difference is approaching it consciously—giving it structure instead of drifting. That's exactly what *Dreams and Deadlines* offers: clarity, focus, and a way to balance competing priorities while making things happen. In the end, it's not just about managing stress but about finally turning bucket-list ambitions—like climbing that mountain in Southeast Asia—into real, tangible achievements."

—UMBERTO PRANDI, Head of Business Strategy, APAC,
Global Asset Management Firm, Singapore

"Strategy is clarity; execution is cadence. *Dreams and Deadlines* nails both. The POKR Method keeps the OKR core intact—concise Objectives, three to five Key Results, and evidence of progress—then adds the piece most of us skip: a weekly commitment ritual that ties KRs to concrete next actions. You review, choose what moves the needle, and ship. Every quarter, you reset with data, not wishful thinking. It's rigorous without being rigid, and it respects the limits of a busy leader's week. After twenty-five-plus years driving transformation, I recognize a system that will hold up under pressure. This is one I can keep."

—STEVEN LEE, Managing Partner and Asia-Pacific
Financial Services Markets Leader at EY

"Over the years I've seen many frameworks for performance and change. Most are either too abstract to use or too rigid to last. What I appreciate about *Dreams and Deadlines* is its quiet practicality. It encourages you to define direction, make a modest yearly commitment, and then return to it in short, regular cycles. This rhythm creates progress that is sustainable and respectful of the different roles we all hold—at work, in family, and in community. For me, that humility and adaptability make the framework accessible to anyone, no matter their background."

—JOHN LAW, board member at RCBC, Khan Bank, and Far East Horizon; former senior banker at Citi, JPMorgan, and IFC

"This book tackles a topic we all know and experience—sometimes even with a touch of humor. Its refreshing, informal style makes it an easy and enjoyable read. Packed with practical examples, it helps spark ideas and guides you toward achieving personal goals. Focused and concise, it highlights what truly matters. Most importantly, it shows how to break down big dreams into small, manageable steps, making progress feel achievable and motivating.

It's a fun, motivating read that gets your brain buzzing and helps you turn wild dreams into real steps you can actually take.

Looking for a witty guideline to help you break down your big dreams into small, manageable steps? Here you go! And now: focus, focus, focus!"

—BENEDIKTA PFITZNER, CTO/COO
Management Assistance at Gedia, Germany

DREAMS & DEADLINES

USING PERSONAL OKRs to Achieve
What Matters Most in **Your Life**,
in Finance, Family, Health, or Career

**WOLFRAM HEDRICH &
SEBASTIAN VOSS**

DREAMS & DEADLINES
Using Personal OKRs to Achieve What Matters Most
in Your Life, in Finance, Family, Health, or Career
First Edition

ISBN   978-1-5445-5085-5   *Hardcover*
       978-1-5445-5084-8   *Paperback*
       978-1-5445-5086-2   *Ebook*

CONTENTS

WHY DREAMS NEED DEADLINES

JONATHAN IS LOST

Jonathan stared at his laptop screen, the glow illuminating his face in the predawn darkness of his home office. Another early Monday morning start: his preferred time to catch up on work before the kids woke up and the daily whirlwind began. At 38, he had what many would consider a successful life: a rewarding career as a department head at a multinational company, a loving family with two young children and a happy spouse, a comfortable home in the suburbs of a major city.

Yet something gnawed at him. His eyes drifted to the drawer where he kept his *ideas notebook* filled with business concepts, half-written book outlines, and plans for personal projects. And he had quite the number of diverse ideas there, ranging from building that shed in the garden, learning Spanish for the next South America vacation, and finally getting that motorbike license for a cross-Canada trip (early midlife crisis coming, it seemed). Some of these dated back 5 years. None had progressed beyond those initial excited scribbles.

The trigger had come during his annual performance review. His boss had praised his ability to consistently deliver results, manage complex projects, and inspire his team. "You have a real talent for turning stuff into reality," she had said. The words echoed in his mind as he drove home that evening, creating an uncomfortable contrast. Why couldn't he apply these same skills to his personal aspirations?

The complications are probably familiar to any busy professional like yourself: constant work demands, family responsibilities, and the endless stream of daily obligations. Time seems to slip through your fingers like sand. Despite reading countless productivity books, listening to podcasts, and trying various planning systems, you can't seem to bridge the gap between professional excellence and personal achievement, the things that should truly matter in your personal life.

The question that kept Jonathan awake that night was deceptively simple: How could he harness the goal-setting and execution skills that made him successful at work to finally make progress on his personal ambitions?

The answer would require more than just another productivity hack or time-management system. As we will see, it would require a fundamental shift in how to approach personal target setting and execution.

WE'VE BEEN THERE, TOO

Jonathan's frustration highlights a shared experience: New Year's resolutions often fall flat. They've turned into a cultural joke due to their consistent failures. Many people give up on their January goals by February, even after starting with real excitement and resolve.

But this isn't just a New Year's problem; it's how we approach personal goals year-round. We get inspired; set ambitious targets for health, relationships, or creative projects; and then life happens. Work intensifies, responsibilities multiply, and our aspirations get pushed to "someday" once again. The problem isn't motivation, it's that we're using goal-setting approaches prone to fail under pressure. What if we could flip this pattern entirely?

We know Jonathan's story intimately because we've lived versions of it ourselves: Sebastian's career spans close to 30 years. He worked as a project manager, tech entrepreneur, startup mentor, and later a trainer and coach. Across all these roles, one thing was clear: Systems and people matter. But what worked great in a professional setting didn't translate to his private life. In the office, systems worked. At home, they unraveled, because you can't "manage" a young family like a team. Spoiler alert: Toddlers don't respond well to KPI discussions.

Wolfram, meanwhile, spent decades as a partner in strategy consulting, thriving in the high-pressure world of financial services. He coached new consultants, tested many productivity tools, and hit big goals. But his personal interests—like learning Chinese, playing guitar, and writing a book—kept getting sidelined by the demands of work and all that life admin. Even a rare three-month sabbatical turned into an overbooked scramble.

Like Jonathan, we were ticking all the professional boxes but felt stuck when it came to making progress on goals that mattered to us. We knew there had to be a better way.

Our backgrounds taught us the power of structured goal setting, especially our experiences with implementing Objectives and Key Results (OKRs) for clients. We'd seen how this specific goal-setting approach helped companies achieve big things. And we started wondering: What if we could use those same tools to get our *personal* lives on track, too?

This book is our answer. We adapted the concept of OKRs for personal life, complete with its surprises, interruptions, and messy middle bits, and turned them into something new: Personal OKRs, or POKR for short.

This book itself is a testament to the approach we'll share with you. We used the POKR Method to transform a vague idea into the reality of this book that you're reading right now. What began as another entry in our own "someday" lists became a structured project with clear Objectives, measurable results, and, most importantly, real, actual progress.

THIS BOOK'S PROMISE TO YOU!

The POKR Method will help you to:

1. **Achieve clarity on what truly matters.** Instead of chasing too many things, you'll focus on a small set of meaningful goals.

2. **Make consistent progress.** No more setting goals that get abandoned after a few weeks. Our iterative process helps foster a growth mindset, as you continuously learn from your efforts and apply those lessons moving forward.

3. **Be in control.** By applying simple, structured habits, you'll gain confidence and momentum in achieving your Objectives.

4. **Achieve balance.** Finally, a system that helps you thrive in all areas of your personal life: career, relationships, health, personal finance, and other passions.

The reality is life doesn't slow down for us. Work demands will always be there, unexpected events will happen, and distractions will never cease. But with the POKR Method, you'll have a system that helps you stay on track with your personal goals outside work, no matter what life throws your way.

Think of it as your *personal "Life Operation System (Life OS)."* It's not about replacing corporate OKRs, but a method to bring your personal *Dreams* into focus and give them *Deadlines* that stick.

THE JOURNEY AHEAD

We've designed this book to be practical, actionable, and easy to follow. We want POKR to be as pragmatic as it can be. Consequently, the book is organized into six parts to guide you through implementing the POKR Method in your life:

Part I: The Fundamentals of the POKR Method

Introduces the basics, explaining why OKRs work for personal use and how the POKR Method brings everything together in one consistent approach.

We build this in part on learnings from corporations that have had "challenging" OKR implementations in the past, and our own experiences with successful ones.

This part is an executive summary of the entire method if you will.

Part II: Mission

The POKR Method begins with its top layer. It provides a clear, step-by-step guide to help you discover your personal Mission.

We keep this brief, but it's an important steppingstone that will enable you to craft powerful yearly goals that in turn will allow you to focus, focus, and focus throughout the year on a small set of critical targets.

Part III: Strategy

The "meaty" part of POKR is all about crafting meaningful personal Objectives and selecting Key Results that measure progress in a proper way. They are the means to deliver on your goals.

We'll explore effective practices for implementing powerful OKRs in a personal context, covering various aspects of everyday life. Additionally, you'll discover strategies to maintain accountability by creating a supportive network that keeps you honest and ensures successful execution.

Part IV: Execution

Strategy without Execution is pointless, so a core premise of POKR is the end-to-end integration into *your* ways of working. In this part, we focus on making the POKR Method stick by incorporating it into your daily routines, with the right cadence of planning and review.

We'll explore different tools and techniques, from simple to-do lists to slightly more advanced visualizations like Kanban Boards, helping you find the approach that works best for you. We aren't forcing anything on you here but making suggestions on what we've seen working really well out there.

Furthermore, we offer a way to, finally!, have the right mechanics in place to make new behavior patterns work: using POKR to successfully establish new habits!

Part V: Beyond the Mechanics

Having a good vision, a proper strategy, and good execution mechanics is great, but not everything is always going to go to plan. So, addressing the human side of personal goal achievement is important: balancing ambition with family time, overcoming the inevitable setbacks, and maintaining momentum over the long term.

By the end of Part V, you'll have the confidence to achieve your goals without sacrificing what matters most!

Part VI: Additional Resources

At the end of the book, you'll find sections full of additional resources, including ready-to-use templates and tools to help you get started right away. It's optional reading, but full of deep-dive opportunities for those who want to know more and includes a useful glossary for quick reference. We'll refer to those sections throughout the book, when appropriate.

To make our subject matter come to life, we use concrete examples from ourselves, friends, family, and clients to illustrate their experiences throughout the chapters. We took the liberty to change names though, and, on occasion, exhibit some artistic creativity to illustrate our points.

IS THIS BOOK FOR ME?

We understand the possible apprehension for embracing a new method of organizing your life. We've done that plenty of times (largely unsuccessfully) before POKR was around. The importance is to take it one step at a time, to not shoot for perfection but to be willing to experiment a bit.

We've paced the method in a way that it is easy to embrace, being as pragmatic yet as prescriptive as it can be. It shouldn't take more than a cycle (being 3 months of time) to be familiar with the approach and get really good at it thereafter. All it takes is around 1 hour a week to start: not too bad for a method that can change the way to live your life, right?

Can I use it in my working life, too? The focus of the POKR Method is on your private life, not the corporate world. Even though we took inspiration from that space, we don't advocate using POKR one-for-one in the enterprise space. The professional world tends to be a lot more team-focused, which introduces different complexities than when focusing on yourself and possibly your family.

What if I am not as "advanced" as Jonathan? We all come from different starting points but tend to struggle with similar issues. Jonathan is one typical case: someone who has tried stuff to get out of the uncomfortable feeling of not being in control of his private life.

You might have a different set of experiences or might not even have thought about any of this, yet. That's cool, too. POKR will take you on a journey, step-by-step. Jonathan might have some practices he likes to take along; you might be more of a fresh canvas. Both are OK to get going with POKR!

READY, SET...

Whether your personal Mount Everest is writing a book, starting a side business, improving your health, or simply being more present with your family, the POKR Method can help you achieve what matters most in your life.

Our hope is that this book serves not just as a guide but as a catalyst for transforming your personal aspirations into reality.

Let's begin!

PART I

THE FUNDAMENTALS OF THE POKR METHOD

"A goal without a
plan is just a wish."

WHY OBJECTIVES AND KEY RESULTS FOR PERSONAL USE?

FROM MICROCHIPS TO GLOBAL ADOPTION: ORIGINS OF OKRS

It all started with a PROBLEM at intel in the 1970s. Andy Grove, Intel's legendary CEO, needed a way to align his rapidly growing company around clear goals. His solution? An innocent-looking, deceptively simple framework called Objectives and Key Results (OKRs).[1]

The idea was straightforward: Set ambitious Objectives (*what* you want to accomplish) and measure progress through Key Results (*how* you know you're getting there). This framework helped transform Intel from a scrappy semiconductor company into a global powerhouse.

But the real magic happened when John Doerr, a former Intel executive, introduced OKRs to a tiny startup called Google in 1999. At the time,

Google had fewer than 40 employees and a wild dream of organizing the world's information. Google embraced OKRs with characteristic enthusiasm, making them transparent across the company and using them to drive their meteoric rise.[2]

The success stories spread! LinkedIn used OKRs to grow from 33 million to over 700 million users.[3] Spotify leveraged them to balance creativity with structure.[4] Even nontech organizations like the Bill & Melinda Gates Foundation adopted OKRs to tackle global challenges.[5]

OKRs are seen as one of the most popular frameworks in the corporate world to implement a strategy: to set a direction and execute toward it, with the ability to pivot, if need be. Your dear authors have helped several organizations to get on board with the OKR framework, so we have some context in the matter.

Here's the thing: The principles that make OKRs effective in business also work well in your personal life. Agata Krzysztofik, who once worked at Google, used OKRs to focus on her personal growth in a fast-paced job. She noted how the framework kept her grounded and allowed her to track her progress toward learning new skills and improving her health.[6]

Like Agata, we will focus on how to apply these techniques to personal goals. So, we won't spend much time on the corporate side. If you want to learn more about the history of OKRs, John Doerr's classic book *Measure What Matters* is a great place to start.

WHAT ARE "PERSONAL OKRS"?

"Personal OKRs" are a flexible goal-setting system, much like those used in enterprises. They help you align your daily actions with your bigger dreams. This approach takes successful corporate ideas and adapts them for regular people, us mere mortals.

They include:

- Personal Objectives: Inspirational targets that show what you want to achieve in the next quarter (e.g., "Become a healthier, more energetic version of myself").

- Personal Key Results: Specific, measurable milestones that indicate progress toward the Objective (e.g., "Ran a 5K in under 30 minutes by the end of June").

The magic of Personal OKRs lies in their simplicity and adaptability. They turn big dreams into small steps. They hold you accountable and let you change your goals as life changes.

WHY DO "PERSONAL OKRS" WORK?

Here's why Personal OKRs work and why we chose this framework for the core of the POKR Method: Life can feel like a whirlwind of competing priorities. Let's say you want to deepen connections with loved ones. Rather than a vague intention to "spend more time with family," you might set specific Key Results: "Take one weekend day trip with the family each month," or "Organize a monthly game night where phones are banned and dad jokes are mandatory." It's about making the important measurable, not just making the measurable important.

By setting clear, inspiring Objectives, you create a roadmap for your personal growth. These Objectives guide us, lighting the way even when life is chaotic. As James Clear would say, "You do not rise to the level of your goals. You fall to the level of your systems."[7] Personal OKRs provide that system.

A clear Objective gives you a sense of direction. It helps you learn a new language, improve your health, or advance your career. With this focus, you can prioritize actions that move you closer to your goals. Christina Wodtke, a Silicon Valley expert and author of *Radical Focus*, shared how OKRs changed her life.[8] After leaving Zynga, she felt burned out. But using OKRs helped her become a bestselling author and a Stanford lecturer.[9]

But what about those big, audacious dreams that seem about as achievable as teaching a cat to fetch? You know the type: like running a marathon even though you get winded on stairs. Or starting a side business while handling a full-time job. Personal OKRs excel at breaking down these mountains into manageable molehills. Instead of gazing at Mount Marathon in despair, you concentrate on your 5k training goal for the week. You can also celebrate finishing your first 10k run.

Aaron Aiken, a Medium author, explained his use of Personal OKRs. They helped him keep track of his health goals and career ambitions. He set Objectives like "Get a 100% remote job." Then, he measured his success with Key Results, such as "Completed 30 hours of remote work training." This helped him make steady progress toward his targets.[10]

Life, however, has a funny way of throwing curveballs when you least expect them. Unlike New Year's resolutions that shatter at the first sign of disruption, Personal OKRs bend but don't break. If your Objective is to improve fitness, but you injure your knee, the Key Result of "ran a marathon" may need to be replaced with "completed a 30-day upper-body workout program." The Objective remains the same, but the path to achieving it adapts. This flexibility helps maintain momentum even when life has suddenly different plans for you. The ability to pivot is a core tenant of the POKR Method!

The power of Personal OKRs is that they change big ideas into specific actions. They help you focus on what really matters. Rather than a nebulous target to "save money," you might aim for an Objective like "achieve financial freedom to spend more time with family" with specific Key Results like "automated 20% of my income into investments" or "built a 6-month emergency fund." It's the difference between playing not to lose and playing to win.

As John Doerr, the author of Measure What Matters, put it: "OKRs motivate us to excel by doing more than we'd thought possible. By testing our limits and affording the freedom to fail, they release our most creative, ambitious selves."[11]

This balance between ambition and realism is crucial for personal growth. As the saying attributed to Norman Vincent Peale goes, *"Shoot for the moon. Even if you miss, you'll land among the stars."* Personal OKRs capture this philosophy. They push you to set ambitious goals and give a clear path to achieve them.

People who set clear, measurable goals are much more likely to achieve them than those who just make resolutions. Personal OKRs assist you in directing your time, energy, and attention to what truly matters.

Remember, the idea isn't perfection; it's progress. Personal OKRs aren't about making your life a spreadsheet. They help you stay focused on what truly matters, even when life gets chaotic. The POKR Method helps you achieve your goals, whether it's running a marathon, starting a business, or spending more time with family. It offers a solid foundation to turn your dreams into reality, step-by-step.

THE POKR METHOD: OKRS EVOLVED!

As we've seen, OKRs are wildly popular in the corporate world. But here's the thing: Your family dinner table isn't a conference room, your friend group isn't a project team, and your weekend pottery hobby doesn't need to generate quarterly cash flows. Personal life requires a different approach, one that captures the power of structured goal setting without turning your living room into a corporate boardroom.

To make enterprise-grade strategy frameworks work in your private life requires some tuning. As lightweight as OKRs are conceptually, they can be surprisingly difficult to implement without structure. And unless you're hiring a personal strategy consultant (which we assume you're not), you'll need more guidance.

Strategy's great, but without a clear *why*, you might sprint efficiently...in the wrong direction. And even when you *do* know where you're going, success depends on sticking with it.

That's where the *POKR Method* comes in. Think of POKR as your life's operating system ("Life OS"), optimizing what programs are worth running in the first place. In our hyperconnected world, notifications ping like persistent woodpeckers and to-do lists breed like rabbits. This efficient operating system makes a big difference. It helps you go from struggling to living with purpose.

POKR makes OKRs work in real life (yours) by focusing on four core principles:

1. Tie Personal OKRs to a compelling Mission (your longer-term Goal, your *why*).

2. Follow solid Personal OKR mechanics, particularly around prescriptive yet lean routines (*inspect and adapt* as a concept, the ability to pivot).

3. Bring it into your everyday life by linking it to your preferred task and time-management tools and approaches (the *what*, Task-level details).

4. Develop an ability to form new habits (that's what we often try to do, but fail at it without proper "mechanics").

POKR ties your long-term Mission to quarterly Objectives and Key Results. Then, you can carry them out with your preferred task-management tools. These can range from simple to-do lists to Kanban Boards.

You might wonder, why not "just" use the standard OKR framework, without the bits about long-term mission and day-to-day execution? Glad you asked. And we tried that, initially. It didn't work: OKRs as a strategy formulation framework is great, but not good enough to move the needle. It tends to lack a strong layer of visioning above, and execution-level details below.

That's actually why a lot of OKR implementations fail in the corporate world. And we didn't want to take those chances for our private lives. Hence, we took the OKR framework and made it a core element of POKR but enhanced it with the missing elements, to make it a truly end-to-end method.

Think of Personal OKRs as the juicy meat patty in a tasty burger. That's the core of the burger. But without the top (your overall Mission) and the bottom buns (your Task execution), not only does the burger not taste as good, but it also gets messy to eat.

Figure 1 expresses that thought as a visually appealing, delicious-looking POKR Burger:

Figure 1. The POKR Method as a Burger

Here's a real-world example:

Sebastian, one of your authors, decided to run a marathon (in Singapore's lovely tropical heat, because why make things easy?). At the same time, he managed an important work project and contributed to this book. Without POKR, that would have been a recipe for burnout. With POKR? It became more manageable, even if it was still difficult. This was due to everything being integrated into a clear end-to-end method.

The beauty of POKR is that it turns what could be weaknesses into strengths. Companies often face issues with individual OKRs leading to silos. POKR, however, values individual focus. This focus is essential for achieving personal goals.

Think about it: If these methods can sort the world's information, create successful businesses, and help someone complete a tropical marathon, they can likely help you reach your personal goals too. The question is: Are you ready to take a bite out of the POKR Burger?

WHAT'S NEXT?

In the upcoming chapter, we'll explain, step-by-step, the essential elements of POKR: The importance of a crisp Vision and/or Mission Statement, the role that Yearly Goals play, and the nature of Objectives and their Key Results, all the way down to execution-level Tasks. You'll learn the power of standardized routines across the board as well as how to ensure that various Categories of your life are covered sufficiently.

Essentially: a quick run-down of the entire method, end-to-end, top-to-bottom, in less than 2,000 words.

Once we have that settled, we'll share what we learned from corporate OKR implementations in the next chapter. This is important for your Personal OKR journey.

Let's dig in!

KEY TAKEAWAYS

As a quick summary of what we alluded to previously:

1. OKRs are a popular framework for implementing strategies. Companies like Intel and startups like Spotify use them widely.

2. Personal OKRs on an individual level can work great as well, *if*:
   a. The simple OKR idea grows into the POKR Method, which becomes your Life OS!
   b. POKR provides a complete approach. It begins with your Mission at the top. OKRs are in the middle, and execution details are at the bottom. You can choose from best practices at every level.

TWO

THE ESSENTIALS FOR MAKING POKR WORK

THE YEAR BEFORE WE BEGAN THIS BOOK, WOLFRAM FACED A common problem. He set big personal goals but saw them fade away within weeks. He wanted to write a book, improve his fitness, and spend more quality time with his family. Each day, work, life, and distractions pulled him in many directions. It wasn't that he lacked motivation; he didn't have a system to turn his ambitions into progress.

Picture waking up each day with clear purpose. You know what to do to reach your most important goals. Imagine moving forward toward your dreams with purpose. You have a simple, powerful system that keeps you focused and motivated. This is the promise of POKR.

In this chapter, we'll cover the various parts of the POKR Method. The goal is to give you a clear overview, without getting into the details right now. Once we have all the parts ready and know their purpose, we'll review each one in Parts II through V of the book.

FROM VISION TO ACTION:
DO YOU NEED A GRAND LIFE VISION?

Let's face it, setting and reaching personal goals can feel like trying to nail jelly to a wall. But what if there were a way to make them stick? That's where POKR comes in. Before we dive into the nitty-gritty rules, though, let's address the elephant in the room: Do you really need to have your whole life planned out before starting with POKR?

Short answer? Nope.

Imagine this: You're juggling 10 priorities (work deadlines, family duties, fitness goals) and you're not seeing progress. Is it because you lack a grand life vision? Not necessarily.

Having a vision or mission for our life is, of course, desirable. Some grand purpose that can guide our pathway through it all. As visions go, they can be fuzzy, fluffy, and not exactly precise. But that is their purpose: Having a North Star that serves as your compass. That's why the top of our POKR Burger starts with it (Figure 2):

Figure 2. The POKR Method, Mission Layer

Many books and approaches cover this topic. They range from the esoteric to the spiritual. In Chapter 4 we give you an overview of different schools of thought, so you can place those in context. And in Chapter 5 we describe a simple approach (we call this the 5+1 Approach) to get you started. But given that the search for meaning in life can be a rabbit hole without end, we keep this very simple here.

You should have at least two elements defined to get started:

- First, a 3- to 5-year expression that can serve as your personal mission, your 5-Year Goal. Something to guide your prioritization. To quote Yogi Berra: "If you don't know where you are going, you might wind up someplace else."

- Second, linked to your Mission, there's usually a detailed version. This one focuses on the important year ahead. We refer to this goal henceforth as the 1-Year Goal. The 12-month runway creates a more manageable and clear time frame and a more concrete goal.

This is the 5+1 Approach: Your Mission consists of a larger 5-Year Goal plus a smaller 1-Year Goal.

Sebastian uses the 5+1 Approach. His 5-Year Goal exhibits his core values: He prioritizes family, aims to grow as an amateur athlete, seeks financial independence, and values open-minded friendships.

His 1-Year Goals focus on several key areas thereafter:

- Aims to create family harmony by spending quality time together
- Explores new career opportunities that match his values
- Works on improving his athletic performance with specific training targets
- Dedicates time to meaningful personal projects, such as writing this book

Then, he breaks his 1-Year Goals into quarterly Personal OKRs. This helps him make steady progress in all areas of life. It shows that even productivity experts need systems to handle competing priorities.

While having a mission or long-term vision will help, it's not a deal-breaker. You don't need to know your "life's purpose" to start using POKR. In fact, the beauty of Personal OKRs is that they can help you uncover what truly matters as you go. Consider POKR a tool for exploration. It acts like a compass, helping you find your way as you figure out your final destination. Start with what matters to you now. It might be about getting healthier, boosting your career, or writing that novel you've had in mind. The journey itself often reveals the destination.

Now, let's get to the meat and pickles of the POKR Burger: the core rules that make POKR work. These aren't just theoretical concepts; they're battle-tested principles that separate successful target-setters from those still stuck in the New Year's resolution cycle of shame.

CRAFTING OBJECTIVES: THE ART OF CLEAR GOALS

Have you ever made a New Year's resolution and dropped it by February? You're not alone. Objectives, the "what" in Personal OKRs, can turn short-lived intentions into motivating commitments. They are high-level and qualitative targets designed to inspire, challenge, and make an impact. These Objectives answer, "What do we want to achieve?"

Figure 3. The POKR Method: Strategy with Personal Objectives

Here are the essential rules to get them right:

1. Make It Personal and Inspiring

A great Objective lights a fire in you. Ditch vague goals like "Get fit." Instead, aim for something specific, like "Run my first half-marathon to prove to myself that I can push boundaries." Connect your Objective to a deeper purpose; it's this emotional resonance that turns ideas into action.

2. Focus on Less, Achieve More

"Focus, focus, focus!" You've heard it before, but it's critical here. Limit yourself to no more than three main Objectives per quarter. Too many priorities dilute your energy and lead to burnout. Treat OKRs like a spotlight, not a floodlight.

3. Set Short Time Frames

Three-month time frames work wonders. They strike the perfect balance between urgency and achievability. It is an inspect-and-adapt approach. Each quarter is a timebox. This helps you get closer to your 1-Year and your 5-Year Goal. A continuous improvement loop, a virtuous cycle. True Kaizen in action, for the Lean freaks out there. Figure 4 illustrates that concept.

Figure 4. 1-Year Goal Meets Quarterly Objectives

4. Discipline Comes from a Good Process!

When you have a few effective routines, it's much easier to succeed with Personal OKRs. POKR sets itself apart from other target-setting methods. It provides a clear and prescriptive approach with established routines. All it takes is about 1 hour per week to get started. The overhead is minimal; every routine serves a laser-sharp purpose.

Figure 5 outlines how POKR creates a set of standard routines for a quarterly cycle.

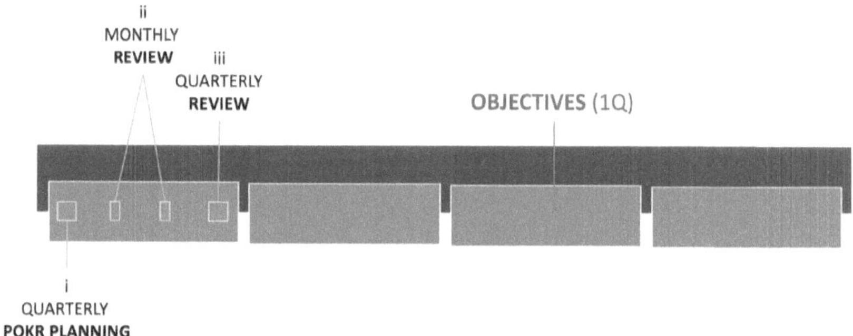

Figure 5. Standard Routines for a Quarter

5. Push Yourself, but Keep It Real

Your Objectives should stretch you but not break you. If you're certain you can achieve it, it's too easy. If it feels impossible, it's demoralizing. Good practices suggest that you want to hit 70% achievement to consider it a success. Failing on an Objective is not the end of the world, assuming you learned the appropriate lessons from it for the next cycle.

6. Write It Down: Apps Optional

Turning your goals into words on paper (or an app or spreadsheet) makes them real. It's like signing a contract with yourself.

Many of these ideas fit well into standardized templates, and we'll provide those for you. But there is no need to get all fancy with technology. It is perfectly OK to go about a POKR implementation via good old paper and pen. A whiteboard in your den can be more powerful than high-tech gadgets. Sliding a physical Post-it note between columns on a Kanban Board can be really satisfying. For tech-addicted users, we'll also explore tools that provide a comprehensive integrated experience.

7. Adapt to Your Life: Categories

Life is complex, so we can't assume you can express everything with just one OKR. This may work for startups or small teams, but not for everyone. Hence, we introduce "Life Categories" for different goals:

- **Family and Other Relationships**: Investing in Your Social Capital
- **Health and Fitness**: Transforming Vague Goals into Personal Missions
- **Personal Finances**: Building Your Path to Financial Freedom
- **Career Development**: Charting Your Professional Path
- **Personal Development**: Pursuing Passion Projects with Purpose

Think about the POKR Burger as being "sliced" via these categories. Figure 6 illustrates this:

Figure 6. POKR Method: Life Categories

These can also overlap, for example, in building a healthier work–life balance. Put differently: You can take multiple bites of the burger, because life is...delicious. Let's take it one bite at a time. Here are some examples of inspiring Objectives:

[o] Establish a consistent fitness routine and improve overall health.
[o] Achieve a healthy work–life balance within the next 12 weeks.
[o] Strengthen connections with family and friends.
[o] Win a gold medal in freestyle swimming in my age group in my swimming club.
[o] Finish the first draft of the POKR book by the end of the quarter.

MEASURING SUCCESS: YOUR KEY RESULTS

Key Results are specific, measurable, achievable, relevant, and time-bound outcomes that define success and indicate whether an Objective is being achieved. This is oftentimes referred to as SMART.

If Objectives are your destination, then Key Results are the signposts showing if you're on track. They answer the question, "How do we measure success?"

Figure 7. POKR Method: Strategy with Key Results

Here is how to craft them in a way that achieves the desired results:

1. Be Specific and Measurable

A Key Result is meaningless if you can't measure it. Instead of "Spent more time outdoors," go for "Hiked 50 miles by the end of the quarter."

You can use different types of metrics:

- Quantitative, like "Lost five pounds."
- Qualitative, such as "Felt energized 5 days a week."
- Binary, for example, "Completed an online course."

2. Focus on Outcomes, Not Activities

Avoid busywork. Instead of "Spent 10 hours studying," aim for "Passed the beginner-level Spanish exam by March." The idea here is to measure real progress, not list the tasks.

3. Own Your Key Results

Each Key Result should have a single owner: you. Each Key Result should be something you directly control. No blaming your coworkers, the weather, or Mercury in retrograde!

4. Limit to Three to Five per Objective

Too many Key Results dilute focus. Stick to a handful of well-defined, measurable outcomes that align with your Objective. Key Results must align with their Objectives in terms of time frame, scope, and level of ambition.

Here are more OKR examples with Key Results that are clear, measurable, and have deadlines:

[O1] **Establish a consistent fitness routine and improve overall health.**

[KR1] Exercised for at least 30 minutes, 5 days a week

[KR2] Processed food intake reduced to two meals per week or less

[KR3] Seven hours of sleep per night on average achieved

[KR4] 5k run in under 30 minutes by the end of the quarter completed

[02] **Strengthen connections with family and friends.**

[KR1] Found and started a new shared activity or hobby with my partner/spouse

[KR2] Had a meaningful conversation (30+ min.) with a family member once a week

[KR3] Planned and executed three social activities with friends (in-person or virtual)

[KR4] Sent personal messages to five people I haven't contacted in over 6 months

THE DON'TS: FOUR COMMON PITFALLS TO AVOID

1. Avoid Overcomplicating Your OKRs

It's tempting to overload your Personal OKRs with endless details. But simplicity is key. Keep your Objectives inspiring and your Key Results clear.

2. Don't Confuse Activity with Progress

Tracking hours spent on a task might feel productive, but it's not the same as achieving results. Focus on meaningful outcomes.

3. Don't Skip Check-Ins

Reviewing progress is key. Weekly or monthly check-ins help you adjust your course and keep moving forward.

4. Don't Be Too Hard on Yourself

Remember, Personal OKRs are meant to inspire and motivate, not to make you feel inadequate. It's okay if you don't reach 100% of your Key Results. This often means you're setting goals that are challenging enough. Aim for progress, not perfection.

STAYING ACCOUNTABLE: WHY YOU NEED A SUPPORT SYSTEM

Even the most motivated people falter. That's where accountability comes in. Regular check-ins with a spouse, friend, mentor, or coach can greatly improve your chances of success. It's not just about support; it's about creating social pressure to follow through.

If you tell your best friend you're training for a marathon, will you be more or less likely to hit snooze on your morning run? (Hint: more likely to lace up.) It's like having a spotter at the gym: They're there to cheer you on and keep you from dropping the weight on yourself.

EXECUTION: FROM RULES TO REALITY

Personal OKRs help clarify goals and measure progress. Yet, they are just one piece of the puzzle. Even the best-crafted OKRs can fall flat if they're not embedded in your daily routines. Execution matters. Personal OKRs work best when they connect easily with your time and task management.

The bottom of the POKR Burger represents the execution dimension, as shown in Figure 8:

Figure 8. POKR Method: Execution with Tasks

Here's the good news: You don't need to overhaul your entire life or adopt some rigid new system. Whether you're a bullet journal devotee, a *Getting Things Done* (GTD) practitioner, a Kanban follower, or someone who lives and dies by their digital calendar, POKR can adapt to work with your existing tools.

But we do need to link Personal OKRs with task management. It is here where a lot of other approaches fall flat: They simply don't provide sufficient "wiring," which leads to a lack of daily "commitment." We address that head-on, by specifying a layer below the Key Results simply called "Tasks." These are standard action items that break a Key Result into smaller, manageable Tasks. You can put these on your calendar or to-do list.

Effective cadences are key to any successful change effort, especially with the POKR Method. Think of cadences as the heartbeat of your productivity system. If you skip regular check-ins, your goals might flatline faster than a smartphone battery at a music festival!

The POKR Method integrates these routines into your daily, weekly, and quarterly life. This creates a practical and powerful rhythm. Each routine is short yet impactful. You only need to commit 1 hour a week, less than the time most spend choosing what to watch on Netflix. These routines take the best ideas from Lean, Agile, and startup methods but skip the Silicon Valley jargon and pricey consultants.

Getting started is better than being perfect. You don't need to get your productivity system right on the first try. Just like you won't master yoga in your first class! The POKR Method shines because it creates a learning loop. Each cycle teaches you something new about what works for you. Your OKR metrics act as helpful guides, not strict taskmasters. They help you handle changes without getting lost in constant adjustments. Think of them as your goals' GPS. They will recalculate when necessary. But they won't have you making U-turns every 5 minutes just because another route seems better.

If you are relatively new to time and task management, don't worry. We'll show you different techniques, from easy to advanced. You can choose the one that fits your style. Whether it's time blocking, Kanban Boards, or the trusted to-do list, there's a way to make POKR work for you. Chapter 9 goes into the specifics.

JONATHAN'S EXAMPLE

Now you have a first overview of the end-to-end POKR Method, and the basic rules on how to set Personal OKRs. But theory is like getting dating advice from your single friend. So let us illustrate this with an example:

Remember our friend Jonathan from the beginning? Back in the Introduction, we met him, with a drawer full of half-finished ideas and the nagging sense that his personal life was being left behind in the rear-view mirror. Despite his track record of getting big things done at work his personal ambitions, like learning Spanish, building that garden shed, or finally getting his motorcycle license, never made it past the planning stage. Now, let's walk through how Jonathan could use the POKR Method to bring clarity, structure, and momentum to his personal aspirations across the year.

After going through the 5+1 Approach, he might articulate a 5-Year Goal such as:

> I want to live a life that feels fully aligned: with how I show up at work, care for my health, support and enjoy my family, grow personally, and use money as a tool for freedom, not stress. I see myself as energized, purpose-driven, physically active, emotionally connected, and financially confident. I'm not just reacting to what life throws at me; I'm building a version of life that reflects who I want to be.

Rearmed with this Mission, he then sets out what he wants to achieve in his first year on this journey. So now we need to get more specific and try to cover various categories in life, particularly important for Jonathan, since his Mission is all about balancing and aligning the different personas that he plays in various parts of his life.

His 1-Year Goals read:

Family and Other Relationships

I will deepen quality time with my children through regular shared activities and milestone projects, because these years with my kids are flying by, and I want to create memories and skills that last longer than any weekend chore list ever could.

Health and Fitness

I will prepare to rejoin competitive amateur tennis through structured training and injury-prevention work, because I want to feel strong, agile, and alive again, like the player I used to be, to reclaim the confidence and joy of competing, not just exercising.

Personal Finances

I will start building financial stability by developing and executing a sustainable investment plan, because I want to stop feeling like financial planning is a mystery and instead build a system that lets me sleep easy, knowing our future is secure.

Personal Development and Passion Projects

I will start reactivating my creative and travel-related goals by learning conversational Spanish and completing one personal DIY project, because it's not just about travel or building stuff; it's about proving to myself that I can still start new things, grow, and enjoy the process.

Career Development

I will establish myself as a visible thought leader by publishing a high-quality article and presenting it at a professional conference, because it's time to step out from behind the scenes and share the insights I've been quietly accumulating, to shape the conversation in my field instead of just following it.

This is already much more specific and spells out the motivation he has for each of the elements. Now we need to plan his first Personal OKRs on the back of this.

Or here as a single paragraph, for those of us who like it short and memorable:

I'm focused on growing with purpose: creating lasting memories with my kids, rebuilding strength through tennis, and securing our financial future. I'm reigniting my creativity with new challenges and stepping into thought leadership to share insights that shape my field.

Following the rules for setting Objectives (O) and Key Results (KR), Jonathan might begin with only two Objectives for the first quarter of the year. Let's start with something fun, yet something that also helps us build muscle memory for the approach, i.e., establishes new cadences and habits:

Family and Relationships: Q1
- [O1] **Build a garden shed as a creative father–son project to create lasting weekend memories.**
- [KR1] Final design and budget agreed together (involve son in process) by Jan. 20
- [KR2] All materials purchased by Feb. 5
- [KR3] Spent eight Saturday mornings building the shed together
- [KR4] Completed shed by Mar. 30, documented with a father–son time-lapse video

Personal Development: Q1

[02] Speak basic conversational Spanish to prepare for our South America family trip.

[KR1] Completed 90 Duolingo lessons (one per day, Jan.–Mar.)

[KR2] Held 10 live practice conversations with native speakers (≥15 min. each)

[KR3] Watched five Spanish-language movies without subtitles

[KR4] Passed entry-level Spanish test with ≥80% score by Mar. 31

The remaining Objectives Jonathan might distribute across the year. He doesn't necessarily need to have them spelled out in detail yet but broadly plan what he will focus on throughout. This might change in the course of the year, but it forces Jonathan to prioritize and focus.

As a quick outlook for the remainder of the year:

Health and Fitness: Q2

[03] Train and compete in the tennis club championship.

Personal Finances: Q3

[04] Create a resilient family investment strategy by fully automating basic financial management.

Personal Development: Q3

[05] Start motorcycle license training as the first milestone toward a cross-Canada dream ride.

Career Development: Q4

[06] Deliver a passionate keynote presentation on my favorite professional topic!

For those of us who are visual thinkers, imagine this as a simple one-pager that showcases your Objectives in the various Life Categories by quarters, with the ones closer to today being more detailed than those further away. Figure 9 depicts that thought.

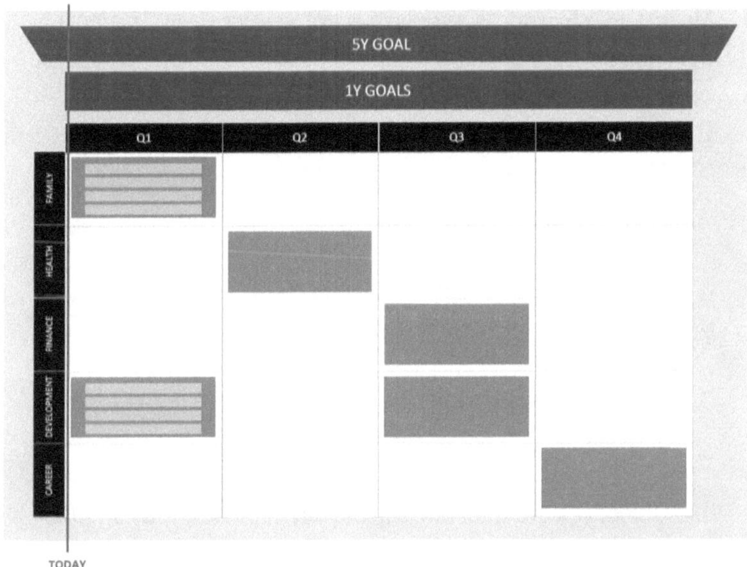

Figure 9. POKR Canvas Concept

WHAT'S NEXT?

To finish Part I and grasp the basics of the POKR Method, we'll explore the history of OKRs next, by examining how different companies used them. Our focus will be on the challenges they faced, and what we can learn from those for our Personal OKR journey. It will show why we need more than the standard OKR framework.

This leads us to Part II, III, and IV thereafter. In these, we will explore the Mission, Strategy, and Execution layers of the POKR Method, one layer at a time.

Ready to learn about the experiences of various enterprise giants with OKRs? Let's see what we can learn from their (mis)adventures!

KEY TAKEAWAYS

Making POKR work is simple but not always easy. The essentials boil down to this:

1. Personal OKRs are effective when they connect the Mission "at the top" to execution "at the bottom." The POKR Burger offers that seamless integration.

2. A Mission is very useful to guide you (5Y), and so is a Yearly Goal (1Y): The 5+1 Approach.

3. Life Categories let you take several bites of the burger, showing its rich complexities.

4. Objectives are qualitative goals set quarterly. They should challenge you and guide you toward a specific target. Aim for no more than three Objectives each quarter.

5. Key Results are specific and measurable targets that define success. They help you know if you're achieving your Objective. Three to five max per Objective, please.

6. Tasks under the Key Results are your action plan for getting work done. They link to your daily tasks and match your time- and task-management style.

7. Prescribed cadences give you rhythm to produce consistent outcomes over time.

8. Patience is key to get you to the finish line, one cycle at a time, making room for regular inspection and adaption.

Think of these rules as your POKR starter kit. Master these basics, and you'll be ready to dig into each topic in the next chapters. Remember, POKR isn't about perfection; it's about progress. Focus on these key points, and you'll see how rapidly you can turn your goals into real results.

THREE

WHAT WE LEARNED FROM CORPORATE OKRs

A QUICK DETOUR BEFORE WE CONTINUE

THIS CHAPTER IS A BRIEF AND DELIBERATE PAUSE IN OUR Personal OKR journey, and a short side trip into the corporate world. Before we move forward, it's worth looking at where OKRs have already been tested on a much larger stage: in companies.

Corporate successes, and particularly failures, provide valuable perspective, showing both the power of the method and its pitfalls when misapplied. By understanding these patterns, we can make more informed choices about how to adapt OKRs to our own lives. In the next part, we'll be firmly back on the road toward applying OKRs in your own life. So, feel free to skip over this chapter if you want to fast-track here.

NOT A SILVER BULLET

When we think of successful companies, we often think of Amazon, Intel, Google, LinkedIn, Spotify, and Netflix. These companies didn't just succeed by chance. They used a strategy framework to focus on what mattered most: Objectives and Key Results (OKRs).[1]

If you work at a company using OKRs, you may know what comes next. Hopefully, this will explain how Personal OKRs differ. We also aim to avoid common challenges companies face when implementing them.

This simple but strong framework has changed how companies and their people set goals. It drives focus and alignment, helping them achieve great results. But like many great innovations, OKRs didn't appear overnight. Their story is one of evolution, adaptation, and the relentless pursuit of excellence.

While OKRs have become widely adopted, they are not without their detractors. Critics say that when OKRs are misused or poorly implemented, they can cause confusion, burnout, and slow progress.[2] OKRs may prioritize short-term numbers over long-term strategy, restrict creativity with rigid Key Results, create misaligned goals across units, complicate goal setting, and overlook interdependencies between Objectives.[3] By examining these critiques and failed OKR cases, we can gain valuable insights for our own personal use.

One of the most common criticisms of OKRs is that they can become overly complex. When teams set too many Objectives or try to track too many Key Results, the focus that OKRs are meant to create is lost. Instead of clarity, teams are left juggling numerous goals, which can result in burnout and diminished performance. They can quickly turn into micromanagement and misuse, which is part of the reason Spotify doesn't use OKRs anymore for individual performance.[4] Overcomplicating OKRs weakens the system's main value: focusing on what really matters.

WHAT CORPORATE FAILURES CAN TEACH US FOR PERSONAL USE

Using OKRs for personal goals can be very effective if done properly. Corporate failures teach us important lessons, but we need a different approach for our lives. Here are some lessons from corporate mistakes that can help you improve your Personal OKRs and achieve real growth.

Ensure Alignment with Your Long-Term Vision

Uber's rapid rise to global dominance is often cited as a success story, but it came at a cost. The company set aggressive OKRs to achieve quick growth. However, this sometimes compromised ethics and long-term sustainability. The focus on short-term results created a culture of poor decision-making and internal conflict.[5]

Your Personal OKRs should go beyond just a checklist. They need to connect with your values and long-term goals. Chasing quick wins can hurt well-being and integrity. This often results in lasting unhappiness. A career goal, for example, should not come at the expense of relationships or health. When your goals match what matters to you, they become meaningful and lasting.

In Chapter 4, we will look at how long-term vision and values link to setting OKRs.

Avoid Overloading Yourself with Too Many Objectives

Microsoft Teams provides a good case study for challenges with erstwhile OKR implementation, largely due to trying to track too many Objectives at once. The overwhelming number of goals diluted focus and made it difficult to prioritize, ultimately undermining the effectiveness of the entire system.[6] Broader studies highlight goals inflation as one of the most frequent mistakes by companies, besides not setting stretched-enough Objectives.[7]

When it comes to goal setting, simplicity is key. Taking on too many Objectives at once can lead to overwhelm and burnout, ultimately hindering progress in all areas. Juggling too many Objectives at once is like taking on five new hobbies in a month. You'll feel exhausted and end up with half-knitted scarves, unread books, and a dusty ukulele.

Narrowing your focus to a few key goals can boost your progress. This approach helps you achieve more in fitness, career, or relationships. You'll feel a greater sense of accomplishment.

How to set good Objectives will be covered in detail in Chapter 6.

Encourage Stretch Goals, But Be Realistic

General Motors and Zynga offer two cautionary tales when it comes to goal setting. In *Car Guys vs. Bean Counters*, former General Motors Vice Chairman Bob Lutz describes how the company's focus drifted from building great cars to ticking off safe, incremental goals. At one leadership review, "product excellence" appeared as just one of 25 equal-sized boxes on a performance grid, buried between targets like "increase market share" and "reduce LTI count." The core problem, Lutz wrote, was that excellence wasn't the goal; it was just another item on a checklist.[8]

When goals become too safe or narrowly defined, especially when tied to bonuses and reviews, it encourages sandbagging: employees aim low to guarantee success, while innovation and ambition quietly exit the building. Companies note that setting Objectives that are not "stretched enough" is the most common learning experience.[9]

Zynga, on the other hand, focused heavily on performance metrics. This obsession made them lose focus on innovation and opened the firm to critique of being too demanding of employees.[10]

In your own life, it's important to find balance. Setting a goal to write a book in 6 months might be an ambitious but achievable target. But expecting to finish it in a month? That's setting yourself up for disappointment. Aim high but be honest with yourself about what's realistic. Stretch goals should push your limits without leading to frustration or burnout.

Again, Chapter 6 is your friend for avoiding too-high ambition.

Don't Focus Solely on Metrics

Under CEO Eddie Lampert, Sears was reorganized into separate business units that had to compete with each other, with an extreme focus on profit metrics for each division. The pressure to meet these numbers led to a competitive culture among different business units, with employees working in silos and trying to outperform each other rather than collaborating toward the company's overarching Objectives.[11] When numbers become the sole focus, the bigger picture often gets lost.

Numbers can provide valuable feedback, but they shouldn't be the only measure of success. An overemphasis on metrics can lead to losing sight of the bigger picture. Focusing too much on numbers can lead to poor choices. Just ask anyone who has tried to hit 10,000 steps before midnight by pacing their living room like a lost tourist. A balanced approach looks at both qualitative and quantitative progress. For example, focusing only on weight loss might overlook gains in strength, energy, and well-being.

Chapter 7 is all about getting the right set of metrics to keep you on the straight and narrow.

Foster a Collaborative Mindset

Microsoft's earlier years were plagued by internal silos, where teams worked independently and often at odds with each other.[12] This lack of collaboration hindered progress and innovation. Eventually, the company learned that success depends on cross-departmental cooperation.

For Personal OKRs, collaboration is key, even if you're not in a department. Involving others helps with accountability, support, and new ideas. Asking friends, mentors, or family for input can keep your goals realistic and meaningful. Remember, success is hardly ever a solo act. Even Batman had Alfred, and Iron Man had J.A.R.V.I.S. If superheroes need help, so do you.

In Chapter 8, we'll explore how to build a supportive environment. This environment will also keep you accountable for your OKR progress.

Ensure an End-to-End Integration with Your Daily Reality

Companies that fail to link their strategic goals with their daily operations can struggle to succeed. Nokia is such a case. The company's vision was clear, but execution fell short because those goals weren't part of everyday processes. Despite recognizing the smartphone revolution early and even developing touchscreen technology three years before the iPhone, this foresight never translated into effective action. Organizational silos and poor internal communication hindered collaboration, while management failed to prioritize key development efforts.[13]

Fab.com, an e-commerce startup, pursued extremely aggressive growth Objectives, essentially an objective to double revenue year over year, without the operational capacity to support it. This oversight led to missed delivery deadlines, customer dissatisfaction, and employee burnout. This underscores the risks of setting strategic goals without ensuring operational readiness.[14]

Translated to our own personal OKR journey, this means we need to a have a way to connect our Objectives and Key Results to actual Tasks. Wanting to spend more time with loved ones is great. But without scheduling visits to the zoo, IMAX movie nights, or regular dinner dates, it won't happen.

Goals that don't connect to daily routines often get forgotten. To make Objectives real, they should fit into your schedule and habits. For example, if you want to exercise more, start with small steps like a daily walk. This makes it easier to be consistent. Setting goals that don't blend into your routine is like signing up for a 6:00 a.m. yoga class when you're not a morning person. It sounds good, but it usually fails in practice.

In Chapter 9 we highlight the importance of linking OKRs to your everyday tasks. In the next chapters, we'll explore tools like Kanban Boards and to-do lists, and their connection to "habit formation."

Cadence Creates a Rhythm for Success

Toyota's famous lean manufacturing system relied on cadence. This means regular check-ins and adjustments kept their production smooth and efficient.[15] In contrast, companies that fail to adjust their goals to changing markets, like Blackberry did, face challenges.[16]

Consistent check-ins keep goals alive and achievable. Just like in business, regular evaluations refine strategy. Personal OKRs also need frequent reflection to align with changing priorities. Tracking progress weekly or reviewing quarterly helps keep a steady pace for ongoing success.

A great example is marathon training. Runners follow a structured plan with regular milestones. They adjust their pace and goals based on performance and recovery. Without cadence, it's easy to lose momentum.

We discuss the need for embedding OKRs with your day-to-day reality in Chapter 10.

WHAT'S NEXT?

Now, we wouldn't have told you all the above if we weren't going to do something productive with it, would we? Every failure is a chance to learn. So, we designed POKR to tackle these challenges directly.

Details will start in Part II, titled "Mission." This section focuses on personal mission and Life Goals. It's the first layer of the POKR Method. Part III is about "Strategy." It looks at Personal Objectives and Key Results. It also explains how to stay accountable. Finally, Part IV discusses "Execution" best practices to help make POKR a part of your daily life.

Imagine a pyramid. We begin at the top and move down, layer by layer, until we reach the foundation.

Ready for an exciting excursion?

KEY TAKEAWAYS

We can learn from these corporate failures to improve our personal OKRs. These lessons help us focus, stick to our values, and make our goals part of our daily habits. They lay out a path for achieving long-term success.

As we reflect on the journey of OKRs from Intel to Google and beyond, several key lessons emerge:

1. Align Your Goals with Your Values and Vision: Don't chase short-term wins at the expense of your long-term well-being and integrity. Your OKRs should support what truly matters to you.

2. Less Is More: Avoid overwhelming yourself with too many Objectives. Focus on two to three meaningful goals at a time to make real, sustainable progress.

3. Challenge Yourself, but Stay Realistic: Set goals that push you, but don't go too far. Unrealistic targets can cause frustration and burnout. Find the right balance.

4. Metrics Matter, but So Does the Bigger Picture: Numbers alone don't define success. Ensure your OKRs focus on a holistic progress, not just easy-to-measure indicators.

5. Success Is a Team Effort: Involve others (friends, family, or mentors) to provide support, accountability, and encouragement on your journey.

6. Embed Goals into Your Daily Life: Make your OKRs an integral part of your routine to ensure they translate into consistent action.

7. Consistency Beats Intensity: Regular check-ins and adjustments will help maintain momentum and keep your goals aligned with changing circumstances.

Using these lessons, you can create Personal OKRs that lead to real growth. This way, you can avoid the same mistakes made by many big corporations. In the end, OKRs are about more than just achieving goals. They're about building a system for continuous improvement.

MISSION

"Your priorities aren't
what you say they are.
They are revealed
by how you live."

FOUR

SETTING YOUR DIRECTION
From Personal Mission to Objectives

WHAT DO YOU WANT TO BE WHEN YOU GROW UP?

SARAH STARED AT HER QUARTERLY PERSONAL OKRS, FEEL-ing disconnected. Despite hitting her targets on improving her social media and digital engagement skills, increasing her workout frequency, and expanding her professional network, something felt off. "I'm ticking boxes," she realized, "but I'm not sure why these boxes matter." "If only I had a clear vision or mission like at work," she wondered. The company she works for has a clear mission statement, after all; why couldn't she?

Meanwhile, her colleague Jin was thriving with his Personal OKRs. The difference? Jin had both a clear mission statement ("Inspire positive change through education and mentorship") and a specific goal ("Build a global education platform"). His OKRs weren't just checkboxes; they were steppingstones toward his bigger vision.

Sarah's story captures a dilemma many busy professionals face when trying to make meaningful progress in their personal lives. In the last chapter, we saw how Personal OKRs can make long-term goals actionable. How can you set Personal OKRs if you're unsure about your life vision or mission? Do you need a Why Statement or Mission Statement to succeed? Or can Personal OKRs work for you even if you're still figuring out your ultimate purpose?

In this chapter and the next, we will dive into these questions. We'll explore how Life Goals, Mission, and Vision Statements can support your Personal OKR journey. You'll see how these elements, even if still developing, can add structure and motivation. The POKR Method will give you the guidance needed to reach your goals.

Alternatively, feel free to skip forward to Chapter 5, where we discuss what you need as a minimum to make POKR work, which is a combination of a long-term goal (where you want to be in the next 5 years), and a more concrete, 1-year milestone (a yearly goal). We call this the 5+1 Approach.

No matter if you have a clear life vision, Personal OKRs are a flexible tool. They grow with you and help you focus on the goals that matter most, one Objective at a time. So, let's dive in.

DECODING THE ALPHABET SOUP OF SELF-DIRECTION

Imagine you're at a bookstore, or more realistically, doomscrolling Amazon at midnight, trying to decide between *Live with Purpose* or *Find Your Why* (secretly hoping to discover *Unleash Your Inner Cactus*). It's overwhelming. Are you building a mission? A vision? A brand? Or just a mildly inspirational Instagram bio? Welcome to the alphabet soup of self-help.

Just to manage your expectations: This book is *not* about how to find your vision, mission, or raison d'être in life.

There is an entire library of guides out there to help you on that journey, some of which we included here for reference. Every generation brings forth their own popular guides illuminating different aspects of how we can find meaning, purpose, value, and long-term worthy goals in our lives, reflecting the surrounding socioeconomic situation.

In this chapter, we will briefly cover five concepts that are often used interchangeably: Personal Mission Statements, Personal Vision Statements, Why Statements, Purpose Statements, and Life Goals.

All these concepts help us shape our long-term goals and daily habits. They are key starting points to think about as we begin our Personal OKR journey. POKR is completely agnostic regarding which option you choose, like that one friend who refuses to take sides in the "pineapple on pizza" debate. It's just like using a different syntax to express a similar direction. So, just think about this section as a selection of different direction setting approaches, and just pick the one that resonates most with you.

Let's explore their subtle distinctions:

Stephen Covey, in *The 7 Habits of Highly Effective People*, describes a Personal Mission Statement as an ethical compass, an articulation of your core values and guiding principles.[1] It serves as a high-level declaration of who you want to be and how you want to live. They help us navigate decisions by grounding them in our fundamental beliefs and values. For instance, Covey's mission, "to live, to love, to learn, to leave a legacy," provided a stable foundation for both his professional and personal life.[2]

Why Statements, popularized by Simon Sinek's *Start with Why*, clarify our core motivations: the emotional fuel that drives us forward.[3] It answers the question: Why do you do what you do? Sinek's own Why Statement, "to inspire people to do the things that inspire them so that, together, we can change our world," serves as the foundation for all his work.[4] This is closely linked to the Japanese concept of Ikigai (生き甲斐), meaning "a reason for being." It's what gets you out of bed in the morning. It's a blend of what you love, what you're good at, what the world needs, and what you can be paid for. When those four elements overlap, you've found your Ikigai.

A Purpose Statement is the bridge between a Mission Statement and a Why Statement. While a mission defines how you live, and a why defines what drives you, a purpose statement defines what you contribute to the world. Dr. Martin Luther King Jr.'s purpose, to nonviolently work toward racial equality, was clear in both his speeches and his actions.[5]

A Personal Vision Statement is aspirational. It paints a vivid picture of the future you want to create. Unlike a Purpose or Mission Statement, which focus on principles and contributions, a Vision Statement is about where you're headed. Consider Oprah Winfrey, whose vision to "be a teacher, and to be known for inspiring my students to be more than they thought they could be" shaped her journey from talk show host to philanthropist. Her vision captured an idealized future and provided a direction that helped steer her decisions and career choices.[6]

If you're wondering whether your Why Statement is secretly a Mission Statement wearing a fake mustache, don't worry. You're not alone. These terms overlap more than Marvel multiverses, and trying to separate them perfectly is about as useful as debating whether Baby Yoda is technically a Jedi.

Life Goals are the most pragmatic and actionable of these concepts. They are concrete, specific, and time-bound milestones that mark progress toward a larger achievement. For example, author Rachel Hollis set a

Life Goal to "run a half marathon before I turned 40 and a full marathon before I turned 50."[7] Unlike a vision or mission, which are broad and ongoing, Life Goals are measurable and finite. Life Goals are particularly effective when integrated into Personal OKRs, as they can be broken down into smaller Objectives and measurable Key Results.

A Bucket List falls under the umbrella of Life Goals. It centers on experiences and achievements people hope to accomplish during their lives, often with a sense of adventure or personal fulfillment. In contrast, Life Goals cover a wider range of aspirations. These include personal growth, relationships, career targets, and contributions to others. If Life Goals are your long-term dating profile (*looking for someone to build an empire, raise plants, and max out our retirement accounts*), then Bucket Lists are your cheeky bio line: *also down to cage-dive with sharks and fire-dancing in Bali.*

Practically, the above approaches often form a mini cascade.

Let's look at these subtle differences with an example. Remember Jin's Mission Statement ("Inspire positive change through education and mentorship") from above? If we were to translate this into the other statements of direction, it would look like this:

- Mission Statement: "Inspire positive change through education and mentorship."
- Why Statement: "Everyone deserves the opportunity to reach their full potential."
- Purpose Statement: "Create accessible learning opportunities for underserved communities."
- Vision Statement: "Build a world-class educational platform reaching millions."
- Life Goal: "Launch an online learning platform serving 10,000 students within one year."

Notice how each statement approaches the same fundamental direction from a different angle, yet all align toward the same ultimate aim? Obviously, we have yet to meet someone who actually uses all these concepts at the same time. That never happens. So don't be a unicorn here.

Practically speaking, these elements act like a personal compass, guiding both our long-term dreams and daily steps toward the future we want. Whether you're creating a Vision Statement or defining Life Goals, clearly stating your desired future improves both clarity and motivation.[8]

If you want to get (even more) fancy, there is also the trifecta of Principles, Purpose, and Passion. In the interest of time and space, we cover those in our blog. Briefly though: Think of Principles (our core values), Passion (what energizes us), and Purpose (our reason for being) as building blocks underpinning the other direction-setting concepts, as shown in Figure 10:

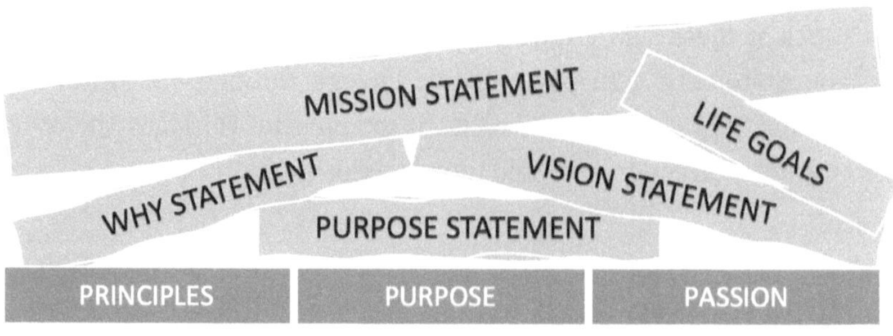

Figure 10. Various Direction-Setting Concepts, with Principles, Purpose, and Passion as a Possible Foundation

PERSONAL DIRECTION-SETTING IS GOOD FOR YOU

Research shows that having clear personal direction is valuable for health. Shocking, we know. Turns out that knowing where you're headed in life is better for you than a kale smoothie with extra chia seeds. This holds true regardless of which framework you pick or how you define it.

It's like how exercise is good for you whether you're doing CrossFit, yoga, or just chasing your toddler around the house: The specific flavor matters less than simply showing up and doing something intentional.

The Japanese concept of Ikigai (finding the intersection of what you love, what you're good at, what the world needs, and what you can be paid for) provides compelling evidence for the health benefits of purpose-driven living.

Studies show that individuals with a clear sense of purpose experience:

- Increased life expectancy
- Reduced risk of cardiovascular issues
- Lower rates of functional disability
- Enhanced overall well-being[9]

Dr. Yasuhiro Kotera is a Japanese psychologist and a father of four. Two of his sons have autism. He shows the health benefits of embracing Ikigai.[10] While raising children with special needs, Dr. Kotera discovered purpose in researching and teaching about Ikigai and mental health. This purpose gave him emotional strength. It helped him handle personal challenges and boosted his overall well-being.

This aligns with Martin Seligman's PERMA model in positive psychology. It outlines five core elements of well-being: Positive Emotions, Engagement, Relationships, Meaning, and Accomplishment.[11] The research equally suggests that by cultivating these elements, individuals can experience greater life satisfaction and long-term well-being.

Creating a Mission Statement, defining your *Why*, or setting Life Goals all help clarify your direction. This clarity brings many benefits. What matters is not the framework you pick. It's about having a clear purpose guiding your Personal OKR journey.

THE POWER OF ALIGNMENT

When concrete goals and actions link to a higher purpose, they are more likely to succeed.

It's like the difference between randomly throwing ingredients into a pot versus following a recipe: You might get lucky with the random approach, but you're more likely to create something edible (and potentially delicious) with a plan. Your Mission Statement is your kitchen philosophy ("farm-to-table" or "whatever doesn't require washing more than one pan"), while your Life Goals are your signature dishes.

Together, they shape your Personal OKRs: your regular cooking adventures that eventually transform you from someone who burns toast to someone who confidently says, "I'll bring the soufflé" to dinner parties. And yes, we've· absolutely stretched this cooking metaphor to its breaking point.

Mission Statements and other guiding tools, along with specific and time-bound Life Goals, work together to shape Personal OKRs. For example, we can look at the Mission Statement, but the same applies to Purpose, Why, and Vision:

- A Personal Mission Statement clarifies your values and how you want to live, helping filter out misaligned goals.
- Life Goals provide concrete long-term targets, making day-to-day Objectives meaningful.

People with both elements show much higher achievement rates than those without.[12] Connecting a higher purpose to specific actions through tools like Personal OKRs creates an "upward spiral" of positive momentum.

Continuing with Jin's example from the beginning, this is how his Mission, longer-term goals, and Personal OKRs align:

[G]   **Launch an online learning platform serving 10,000 students within 1 year.**

[O]   **Launch pilot online learning community.**

[KR]   100 beta users recruited

[KR]   80% completion rate achieved

[KR]   Qualitative feedback from 50 users gathered

By aligning Personal OKRs with your core values and aspirations, you're more likely to follow through on Key Results since each one serves a purpose beyond itself. Here are the main benefits from linking Mission and goals:

- **Enhanced Prioritization**: Individuals with clear Mission Statements make decisions faster when choosing between competing goals. The combination provides two filtering questions:
    - "Does this align with my Mission?" (values check)
    - "Does this advance my Life Goals?" (practical check)

- **Increased Motivation**: Alignment between actions and personal values increases persistence significantly.[13] The synergy occurs because Mission Statements provide emotional connection while shorter-term goals offer tangible targets.

- **Better Goal Achievement**: When your Personal OKRs flow from your Mission and Life Goals, you avoid "goal scatter," which is the tendency to pursue multiple unrelated Objectives that lead to burnout. Instead, each objective becomes a meaningful step toward your larger Vision.

For Sarah, crafting both elements transformed her approach. Her Mission Statement ("To create connections that spark positive change") guided her daily choices. Her Life Goal ("Build a multicultural community center by 2028") set a clear target. Her Personal OKR for improving her social media and digital engagement skills now include Key Results focused on community engagement (learning how to amplify the mission, recruiting supporters, and sharing progress online). Her networking goals aim to create positive change and rally support for the center.

In reality, people have multiple Life Goals, of course. Our 5+1 Goals Approach encourages picking goals from different areas of life. Focus on family, finances, health, personal projects, and career for a balanced life. We'll explore this more in the next chapter.

SETTING PERSONAL OKRS
WITHOUT A MISSION STATEMENT

Can Personal OKRs be set without having a personal Mission Statement or Life Goal? Can I use this even if I don't know yet what I want to be when I grow up, despite technically already being a grown-up with a pension plan and strong opinions about kitchen appliances? Yes, absolutely! Personal OKRs can be set without them.

Personal OKRs focus on action, helping you make real progress without a big *why*. They are effective for short-term goals, such as getting fit, learning a new skill, or completing a project. You can succeed at these without a larger direction. Focusing on short-term goals helps beginners stay consistent and adapt to change. This is especially helpful during fast-moving life stages.

This approach supports flexible growth and quick improvements. Also, it encourages gradual discovery. Personal OKRs are a versatile tool. They can adapt as your purpose and direction become clearer over time.

WHAT'S NEXT?

It's up to you to choose your direction-setting methods, dear reader. From what we've observed, having a long-term direction (5 years) can be very effective. It serves as your guiding light, a North Star of sorts. Plus, set goals for each year, next.

We follow that exact approach, which we call the 5+1 Approach, in the coming chapters, as a good practice, if you will. We'll explain how the 5+1 Approach works in practice, and how you can use the POKR Method to help you find your Vision and Mission in life.

KEY TAKEAWAYS

1. Though overlapping, each direction-setting approach plays a unique role, covering different time horizons, and serves slightly different ends:
    a. Mission Statements serve as ethical compasses
    b. Why Statements clarify our core motivations
    c. Purpose Statements outline our unique contributions
    d. Vision Statements motivate us with future aspirations
    e. Life Goals focus our efforts on specific milestones

2. These approaches support one another. They help clarify your life path by detailing what you want, why you seek it, how you pursue it, and who you wish to be along the journey.

3. A clear Mission or Vision makes Personal OKRs more meaningful and easier to achieve.

4. Having a clear sense of purpose, like a Mission, Vision, or Why Statement, can boost well-being and help you live longer.

5. You don't have to have a larger direction in place to start using POKR, though. It might actually help you to discover the bigger picture.

FIVE

POWER OF PURPOSE
The 5+1 Approach

SIMPLIFIED DIRECTION POWERS PERSONAL OKRS

N THE PREVIOUS CHAPTER WE LOOKED AT DIFFERENT approaches to finding and expressing the direction for your life: Mission, Purpose, Why, and Vision Statements, and the more concrete and time-bound Life Goals. We demonstrated that they are, in general, good for you, and we explained that our POKR Method is agnostic to which approach you choose for yourself.

But let's be honest: Who do you know who actually does any of that? Who has an inspiring Vision Statement, combined with some striking Life Goals, based on an expression of one's principles, purposes, and passion? We tried to count friends who do. The number was close to zero. We are not judging here: This is a complex topic, and few have the patience to apply the beautiful theory that we outlined in the previous chapter. We would usually rather just get going and execute on stuff, without over-thinking it. Hence, count us among those impatient folks.

So, if we start rather from scratch, what specifically do we need for Personal OKRs to work well? And might Personal OKRs even help us discover our purpose and mission in life? These are the questions we will answer in this chapter to provide you with a simplified path.

THE MISSION LAYER OF POKR EXPLAINED

Remember our POKR Burger from before? Our top bun is the "Mission" layer of the POKR Method. This describes the direction of travel, the overarching purpose for the Objectives we find important enough to focus our attention on thereafter.

Figure 11. Various Direction-Setting Concepts, with Principles, Purpose, and Passion as a Possible Foundation

As you know by now, we're open to different methods to achieve this. Here, though, we use "Mission" in its general dictionary sense, not as "Mission Statement," which is a lot more specific. We define "Mission" as:

a preestablished and self-imposed, strongly felt
goal, aim, ambition, calling, or purpose

or in simple terms:

an overarching sense of direction

You see what we're doing here, right? With one wave of the magic definition wand, we combined all these various directional approaches into one. Now, before all the esteemed life's purpose gurus either turn in their graves or shout at us, let's be clear: We're not taking anything away from the various approaches to finding one's meaning in life. Far from it. As we will discuss below, having clarity of purpose and direction is extremely useful for you.

However, it isn't important to nail your goal statement perfectly from the get-go; perfection is the enemy of progress, after all. Rather, it is important to have *one* or a combination of approaches chosen and reasonably followed to guide the next steps in the POKR Method.

Why then "Mission," and not some other word like *vision, direction, purpose,* or *North Star*?

We chose "Mission" because it strikes a balance between aspiration and practicality. While "vision" might sound too abstract, and "purpose" too philosophical, "Mission" is something everyone understands intuitively, from astronauts to entrepreneurs to weekend DIYers. It signals a commitment to action. Plus, we just really like the idiom of "Mission accomplished," which is typically used when you have successfully completed what you set out to do, which is what POKR is all about.

A PRACTICAL SHORTCUT: THE 5+1 APPROACH

To set meaningful Personal OKRs, you don't need to have a comprehensive life mission or an elaborate set of values. However, having a few foundational elements in place can make a big difference. Think of these as your personal compass; enough direction to set purposeful Personal OKRs without getting bogged down in endless introspections. Figure 12 illustrates what we have in mind:

Figure 12. The 5+1 Approach as the Mission Layer of POKR

Now here's what we recommend doing if you do not have a clear view of your life's purpose, why, or vision yet, as a mini self-discovery process (shown in Figure 13).

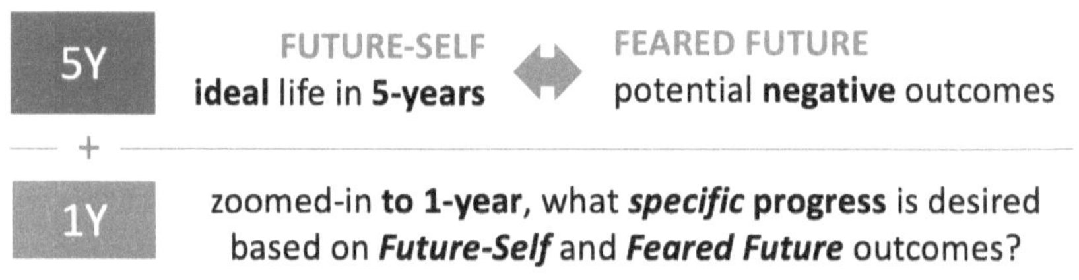

Figure 13. The 5+1 Approach in Detail

It takes a simple yet powerful set of steps to get through this. Here are the specifics, one step at a time:

5-Year Goal (5Y)

1. **Envision your Future-Self:** Imagine your ideal life in about 5 years' time. This is where you start to flesh out who you want to become and what you want to achieve. Call it "Future You," if you like, your projection for the best life you can realistically imagine. Think about what kind of person you want to be, where you'd like your career and health to be, the relationships you want to nurture, and even habits you want to adopt or let go of. This is going to be a bit raw but will be sharpened further down.

2. **Imagine a Feared Future:** Next, let's envision the opposite, where your worst-case outcomes, within reason, play out. This doesn't mean wallowing in gloom; it's about identifying what you'd most want to avoid. This step reinforces your commitment and can help to overcome fears that might hold you back.

3. **Reconcile Future-Self with Feared Future:** Now that you have a utopian and dystopian version of yourself, let's test the Future-Self version against the Feared one. You want to make sure that you did not forget elements in the positive picture, by using the negative one for comparison. The intent is to exit here with a validated Future-Self, that takes into consideration possible negative scenarios. It's a completeness check, if you will.

1-Year Goal (1Y)

1. **Distill a 1-Year Goal:** Finally, a 1-year time frame as a zoomed-in version needs to be crafted. Based on your refined Future-Self one-liner(s), what specific progress do you want to see a year from now? A bit closer than the 5-year direction but still daring enough to stretch you. Your 1-Year Goal should be clear enough to give you concrete Objectives and inspire a sense of excitement.

In the Appendix, you'll find a worksheet with questions to help you think through these steps. This is meant to be a quick-start guide, not an exhaustive set of life questions. Jotting down your answers, even if they're rough, will give you a solid foundation for creating aligned Personal OKRs and refining them over time.

LIFE'S COMPLEXITY

Before we go through the details, let's quickly bring back our five Life Categories. You might not be able to cover all five in a single year, but supposedly you will want to make progress on various aspects of your life toward your future you.

We'll need to keep these in mind as we go over the next section, to prevent a too-myopic view of the upcoming horizon (Figure 14).

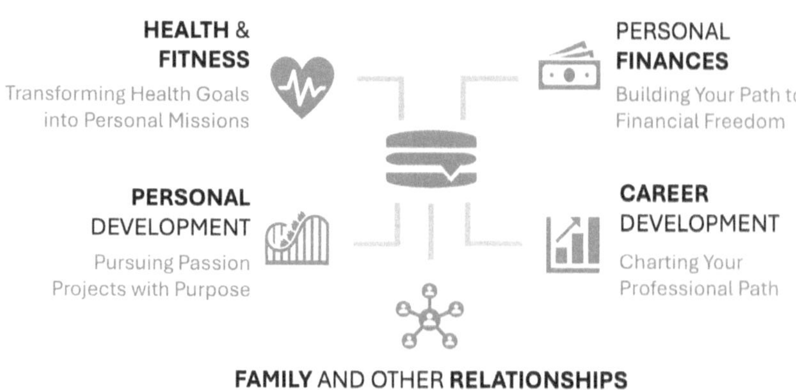

Figure 14. Life Categories as Dimensions of the POKR Burger

A WALKED-THROUGH EXAMPLE: RAHUL'S JOURNEY

Let's take a concrete example and run through these steps together, using a guinea pig to test-drive the 5+1 Approach.

Put yourself in Rahul's shoes for a moment. He is a 42-year-old software engineer who has been working at the same tech company for 8 years. While financially stable, he feels his life lacks balance and purpose. After reading about the 5+1 Approach, he decides to try this out.

Step 1: Envision Your Future-Self

Start by imagining where you'd like to be in 5 years. Push yourself to dream big, maybe even slightly beyond what feels achievable.

The process taps into the logic of future self-continuity, a concept in psychology that suggests the clearer and more detailed our image of the future, the more motivated we are to achieve it. Research supports that a vivid, aspirational future vision can increase our commitment to actions that bring us closer to that ideal.[1]

Rahul asked himself the following questions, and came up with some useful results across all Life Categories:

- **Family and Other Relationships**: What kind of relationships will I cultivate?
  Deeper connections with my immediate family and a small circle of friends who challenge and support my growth.

- **Health and Fitness**: What would my ideal health look like?
  A body that feels energetic and capable, free from the warning signs of diabetic health issues that run in my family. Prioritize consistent sleep, mindful eating, and regular movement, while abandoning late-night coding sessions, excessive caffeine intake, and using work to avoid family time.

- **Personal Finances**: How do I want my finances to develop?
  Maintaining financial security that gives me freedom of choice.

- **Personal Development**: Which item(s) on my bucket list will I have achieved?
  Completing a challenging mountain trek and publishing a book that shares my technical expertise. Also developing a new, practical, artisanal skill like woodworking.

- **Career Development**: Where do I want my career to go?
  Evolve beyond pure coding into a role with more impact and meaning.

As seen above, this often results in a rather lengthy set of paragraphs, and that's okay. Let's see if we can simplify that into a small set, or even a single one-liner. We don't want to lose the essence of your previous exercise but need ideally something that you can easily remember and execute on.

Here's how Rahul summarized it:

> [G] **In 5 years, I've transformed into a man who balances technical leadership with creative craftsmanship, who prioritizes health and family without sacrificing professional growth, who creates financial freedom through mindful choices, and who finds fulfillment in sharing knowledge with both his children and his community, embodying the integrated life I've always aspired to live.**

All five Life Categories added up, in one neat paragraph. Looks nice for sure. If you're struggling formulating it this eloquently (as Rahul did), there are useful AI tools out there that help you to come up with drafts. On our book website we have some suggestions for you.

Step 2: Imagine a Feared Future

Your Feared Future is an exercise in considering what could happen if you don't pursue your goals. The time horizon is the same 5 years as for the Future-Self exercise. Unlike a vague worst-case scenario, this is a version of a realistic but undesirable outcome, where key areas like health, finances, or relationships have taken a negative turn due to inaction or poor choices.

This exercise is rooted in a behavioral strategy known as "mental contrasting," where imagining both positive and negative outcomes can motivate action. By visualizing what you want to avoid, you reinforce the importance of your goals and gain a sense of urgency.[2]

For instance, if your goal is to maintain health and fitness, your Feared Future might include a scenario where stress and lack of exercise have led to health issues. Seeing this outcome can create a stronger commitment to prioritize wellness as a part of your Personal OKRs.

Rahul reflected on his Feared Future by asking himself:

- **Family and Other Relationships**: What might my relationships become without intervention?
  My children growing distant and viewing me merely as a provider rather than an engaged father, while my marriage could deteriorate into a relationship of convenience, lacking intimacy and connection.

- **Health and Fitness**: What could my health look like if I don't address the warning signs?
  Progressing from prediabetes to full diabetes, requiring daily medication, experiencing chronic fatigue, and perhaps facing serious complications that would impact my quality of life and longevity.

- **Personal Development**: What opportunities might I miss if I don't make time for personal growth?
  Might reach retirement age without ever exploring my creative interests, making a meaningful community impact, or developing a sense of purpose beyond work.

- **Career Development**: How might my career stagnate if I don't evolve?
  Becoming increasingly irrelevant in a rapidly changing industry, passed over for interesting projects, and potentially vulnerable to layoffs as companies prioritize those with updated skills.

Based on these reflections, Rahul articulated his Feared Future in a crisp paragraph:

In 5 years, I could find myself pigeonholed in the same technical role, while younger developers with newer skills surpass me. My children might be teen-agers who view me as a distant provider rather than an engaged father. My health could deteriorate to full diabetes requiring medication, with chronic fatigue limiting my activities. My marriage might exist in name only, with both of us living parallel lives under the same roof. My dreams of creating something tangible with my hands and giving back to the community could remain unfulfilled as I default to more screen time and passive entertainment.

This Feared Future served as a powerful motivator for him to make changes now rather than postpone action. What is more: From our own experience, it can sometimes be easier to envision the Feared Future than the Future-Self. As humans, we tend to put an emotional premium on a potential loss.

Actually, we tend to be twice as much impacted by the possibility of los-ing something than gaining it. It's called loss aversion.[3] You can use this to your advantage here: Don't just "dream" about your future, as most visioning exercises emphasize (your utopia). But dig deep(er) into your worries and fears (your personal dystopia).

Step 3: Reconcile Future-Self with Feared Future

Negative emotions about a potentially disadvantaged future will be a massive motivation to "turn the ship around," so to speak. Let's tap into that! However, we want you to embrace your future in a positive, pragmatic, and motivated way.

So, let's use the Feared Future projection to test if our Future-Self is comprehensive enough to serve as a Mission that can guide us.

Rahul takes his Future-Self, and uses the Feared Future to probe for any gaps:

FUTURE-SELF	FEARED FUTURE
I've transformed into a man who: Balances technical leadership with creative craftmanship. Prioritizes health and family without sacrificng professional growth. Creates financial freedom through mindful choices, and: Finds fulfillment in sharing knowledge with both his children and his community. Embodying the integrated life I've always inspired to live.	I could find myself pigeonholed in the same techincal role, while younger developers with newer skills surpass me. My children might be teenagers who view me as a distant providers rather than an engaged father. My health could deteriorate to full diabetes requiring medication, with chronic fatigue limiting my activites. My marriage might exist in name only, with both of us living parallel lives under the same roof. My dreams of creating something tanglible with my hands and giving back to the community could remain unfulfilled as I defauly to more screen time and passive entertainment.

Table 1. Reconcile Future-Self with Feared Future

While performing this cross-check, he notices that the prospect of a failing marriage wasn't well considered in his Future-Self. To correct that, he adds a corresponding statement: "...to elevate my marriage to a true partnership, honoring each other's individual needs and desires."

This refined version of his Future-Self is now a shining light that will help Rahul navigate the upcoming horizon with clear(er) priorities. A Mission worth living!

Step 4: Distill into 1-Year Goal(s)

A 5-Year Goal is great as a Mission but hard to execute on. Motivating, but not yet actionable. We need a shorter time frame that makes the long-term goal feel more accessible.

The 1-Year Goal is where you get more precise, striking a balance between ambition and realism. When we say 1-Year Goal, what we mean is a set of goals that you want to achieve in the next year on the way to your Future-Self.

Don't force yourself into a too-narrow view of your life, reduced to an overly simplistic one-liner motto. That's rarely how life works. You likely see this in your own work. Corporate vision and mission statements often try to be short and catchy. But they end up vague and almost meaningless, making them pretty useless. Let's not fall into that trap. It's okay to be a bit more elaborate when it comes to what matters most: your private life.

Your 1-Year Goal should have enough detail to fuel excitement and enough ambition to feel like a challenge. It bridges the gap between your long-term dreams and actionable steps, grounding your Personal OKRs in achievable milestones.

Rahul asked himself some key questions about his 1-Year Goals, based on the 5-Year Mission from above:

- **What specific outcomes across different areas of life would make me feel accomplished in one year?**
  He identified concrete achievements in each category: strengthened family bonds, improved health metrics, diversified income, expanded technical leadership, and achieved tangible creative outputs.

- **Which parts of my Future-Self can I realistically start working toward this year?**
  He recognized he could begin establishing the core habits and systems in all five areas: Creating family rituals, addressing his health proactively, building financial structures, developing leadership skills, and making space for creativity and community.

- **What actions would have the greatest leverage across multiple life areas?**
  He identified that improving his sleep and reducing work hours would benefit his health, family relationships, and mental space for passion projects simultaneously.

- **What skills do I need to develop first to enable my longer-term goals?**
  He recognized that leadership skills, woodworking fundamentals, and financial literacy were foundational capabilities he needed to build this year.

- **How will these 1-Year Goals help me avoid my Feared Future?**
  He understood that each goal directly addresses an element of his Feared Future: Family rituals prevent disconnection, health interventions target his prediabetes, career development keeps him relevant, and creative projects fulfill his need for meaning beyond work.

Based on these reflections, Rahul established these 1-Year Goals across all Life Categories:

Family and Other Relationships

Cultivate deeper connections with my children by spending intentional time with them. Nurture my relationship with my spouse to strengthen our bond. Rekindle meaningful friendships by reconnecting with old friends.

Health and Fitness

Improve my overall health through mindful eating and weekly exercise routine. Embrace outdoor wellness and build endurance along the way.

Personal Finances

Strengthen our financial future to optimize investments and build dedicated college funds. Create financial flexibility by developing a passive income stream. Gain peace of mind by putting a clear, accelerated mortgage reduction plan into action.

Personal Development

Explore creativity through woodworking. Begin the journey of authorship by drafting a technical book. Give back to the community by volunteering at the local community center.

Career Development

Elevate my leadership capabilities by completing a certification and paying it forward through mentoring. Expand my technical skills by learning a new programming language. Share my knowledge and insights via public forums.

And if you prefer the one-paragraph approach, this is how the above would sound, if summarized:

[G] **Strengthening family bonds through regular quality time, improving health through better habits and exercise, and**

enhancing financial stability with strategic planning and passive income. Professionally, aim at career growth through certification, mentorship, and public speaking, while also nurturing personal passions like woodworking, writing, and community volunteering.

Rahul's 1-Year Goal now provides clear direction for his quarterly Personal OKRs, while stretching him enough to make meaningful progress toward his longer-term Future-Self. They balance ambition with achievability, focusing on initiating key habits and systems that can accelerate his progress in subsequent years.

From Goals to Quarterly Objectives: Rahul's POKR Strategy

Looking at his comprehensive 1-Year Goal, Rahul recognized that attempting to tackle all of the goals simultaneously would be overwhelming and potentially counterproductive. This is where the power of POKR comes in, allowing him to break down his ambitious 1-Year Goals into focused quarterly Objectives with specific, measurable Key Results.

We will cover these in much more detail in the next part, but we want to demonstrate one key element here: prioritization and scheduling across the year in quarterly intervals.

Rahul decided to prioritize different aspects of his 1-Year Goal each quarter while making only minimum progress in other areas:

- **Q1 Focus:** Health Foundation and Family Rituals: Rahul prioritized health first because reversing his prediabetic condition was time-sensitive and would provide energy for other goals. Family rituals were paired with this because they required minimal efforts and would immediately improve his quality of life.

- **Q2 Focus**: Career Development and Financial Planning: With health improvements underway, Rahul could focus on career growth to secure his family's future, while also creating the financial architecture needed for his longer-term plans.

- **Q3 Focus**: Personal Passion Projects and Health Progression: This quarter built on health momentum while introducing creative fulfillment. A strategic pairing that helped Rahul connect with deeper purpose and prevent burnout from career-focused activities.

- **Q4 Focus**: Career Visibility and Financial Progress: By year-end, Rahul could leverage earlier work to establish his leadership presence externally and launch his passive income stream, creating dual momentum for year two.

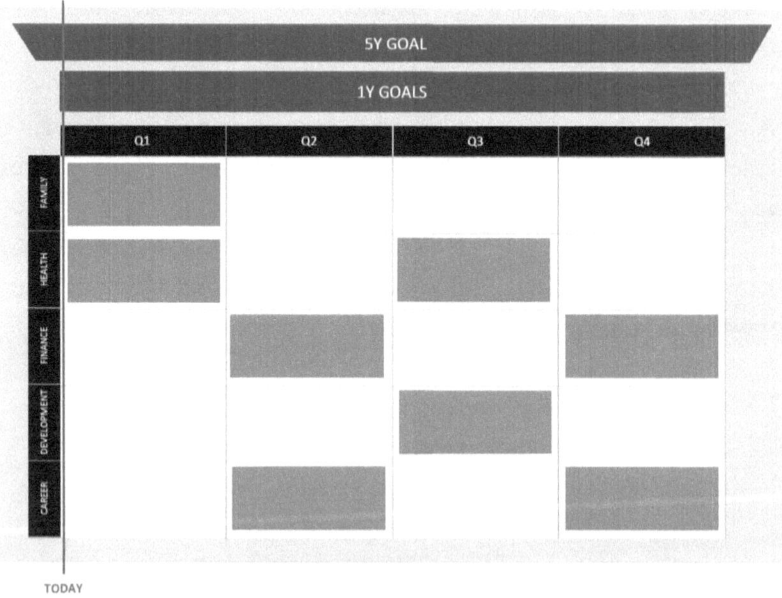

Figure 15. Personal OKR Canvas, Example

He uses a Personal OKR Canvas to visualize this earmarking, showing the focused areas across the entire year (Figure 15).

This quarterly approach allowed him to transform a vague dissatisfaction into a concrete plan, spanning all important areas of his life. In Part III of the book, we'll explore exactly how to translate these quarterly focus areas into specific Objectives and Key Results.

CAN PERSONAL OKRS HELP YOU FIND PURPOSE?

Consider this: What if you could run controlled experiments with your life's direction? Personal OKRs give you a way to discover your purpose. They help by providing a structure for acting and reflecting on your progress.

When you're unsure of your life's purpose, Personal OKRs become a sandbox for experimentation. Each quarter provides an opportunity to test what resonates, turning abstract ideas into concrete actions. For example, here's an exploratory OKR for one quarter:

[o] **Test impact of community service on personal fulfilment.**
[KR1] Volunteered at three different organizations
[KR2] Reflected on personal fulfilment levels using a questionnaire (e.g., 1–10 scale)
[KR3] Interviewed five long-term volunteers about their experience

By running with such Objectives for a short three-month period, you get a better feel for what kind of volunteering might suit you. That can inform the setting of future goals. Instead of guessing and shooting widely in the blue sky, running a set of such controlled experiments allows you to test the waters first. And experience shows that this can lead to increased clarity about life purpose and enhanced well-being.[4]

Think of it as sketching a mural: You add lines, adjust details, and over time, the vision sharpens. The key is approaching Personal OKRs as a learning tool, not just a productivity hack. Purpose isn't a destination; it's revealed through the journey of setting and pursuing meaningful Objectives.

WHAT'S NEXT?

Remember Sarah from the beginning of the previous chapter? Like many of us, she wondered if she needed a perfectly crafted life vision before she could make meaningful progress on her personal goals. Now we can see that while having these elements can enhance our journey, they aren't prerequisites for getting started. Sarah could begin with the 5+1 Approach we outlined, envisioning her Future-Self, acknowledging her Feared Future, and creating a 1-Year Goal, to start making progress on her aspirations.

As you move forward, you'll find that acting through well-crafted Objectives often reveals more about your purpose than endless contemplation ever could.

Speaking of well-crafted Objectives: In Chapter 6, we'll dive into exactly how to create them. You'll learn how to transform your aspirations, whether they come from a fully developed mission statement or from the three-step mission we just explored.

We'll learn how to turn them into clear, compelling Objectives that drive real progress. And we'll show you how to craft Objectives that are both inspiring and achievable, ensuring they light that fire of motivation while remaining grounded in reality.

KEY TAKEAWAYS

1. The POKR Method is agnostic about which direction-setting approach you use (Mission/Vision/Purpose/Why).

2. While Personal OKRs can be set without a fully defined Mission, having a sense of direction amplifies their impact. They can still be useful for short-term improvements while long-term clarity develops.

3. The 5+1 Approach offers a practical shortcut. Instead of overanalyzing purpose, individuals can focus on three guiding steps:
   a. Envisioning their Future-Self in 5 years.
   b. Identifying a Feared Future to avoid stagnation.
   c. Setting a 1-Year Goal that bridges long-term aspirations with immediate action.

4. Life is complex, so covering multiple categories is key to ensuring a holistic approach to one's journey, even if that means being a bit more elaborate on how to formulate the goals themselves.

5. The beauty of Personal OKRs is that they work both ways: They can be guided by a clear Mission if you have one, or they can help you discover your Mission through structured experimentation and reflection.

STRATEGY

"Things which matter
most must never be
at the mercy of things
which matter least."

—JOHANN WOLFGANG VON GOETHE

SIX

SETTING POWERFUL OBJECTIVES

F YOU'VE EVER SET A NEW YEAR'S RESOLUTION THAT FIZZLED out quickly, you know that setting targets isn't the hard part; sticking to them is. And you're not alone. Most New Year's resolutions fail by February at the latest! Let that sink in: Most resolutions have a half-life of one month, and often less.

One study found that 88% of participants failed to keep their resolutions, even though 52% were confident of success at the start.[1] That is not a great figure. Why would you even aim at something that has the success rate of the equivalent of flipping a coin? Many fail because we expect to make big changes practically overnight. That's not how sustainable changes are made, so it's important to break bigger goals into smaller steps and stay the course.

As the saying goes: How to eat an elephant? Bite by bite.[2] You otherwise get a serious stomachache. Step-changes sound great in theory. They attract us because they seem bold. However, they tend to fail more often than small, gradual changes do. Baby steps are usually a better course of action.

That's where Objectives come in. An Objective, as part of the Personal OKR approach, isn't just a target; it's a meaningful, time-bound commitment that lights a fire in you. Unlike vague resolutions, which turn out to be mere *wishful thinking*, Objectives are crafted to be inspiring and actionable, pushing you to stretch just enough beyond your current limits to grow. And that's where growth happens: just beyond the point of comfort, where it starts to sting.

Furthermore, who said you can only have a singular Objective? Life's complex, and there are multiple dimensions that we need to address at the same time (so much for keeping things simple, but bear with us; we have a solution for it). Hence, we need to cater to a multitude of categories, without losing sight of the overall big picture.

Figure 16. Strategy: Personal Objectives

This chapter will guide you through the art of setting Objectives that are more than just wishes. Figure 16 shows you the level of the POKR Method that we are addressing now.

You'll learn how to create qualitative targets that resonate on a personal level, embrace the power of *less is more* to avoid spreading yourself too thin, and refine your Objectives into clear, achievable targets.

By the end, you'll understand how to set Objectives that do more than just sit on paper: They drive you to act and get you closer to fulfilling your goals, as you have defined them, based on what we discussed in the previous chapter.

WHY YOUR OBJECTIVE MATTERS MORE THAN YOU THINK

An Objective should be more than just a "to-do" item on a list (too small) or 1-Year Goal (too grand). It's less about what you want to accomplish; it's primarily about *why* it matters to you. When an Objective resonates emotionally, it gives you a reason to push through obstacles, maintain focus, and stay committed even when motivation wanes (and it will).

Think of your Objective as the next milestone in your personal Mission. It should get you excited to get out of bed in the morning. For example, "improve fitness" is a typical target, but it's also uninspiring. A better Objective would be:

[o] **Run a half-marathon by the end of the year to prove to myself that I can accomplish anything I set my mind to.**

Notice the difference? The second Objective connects to a deeper purpose, turning a generic fitness target into something that feels urgent and personal.

Christina Wodtke, an advocate for using OKRs in personal life, learned this firsthand.[3] After burning out in the tech world and struggling with stomach and back issues, she didn't set an Objective to simply "preserving health." Instead, she investigated which activities were proving supportive for her to lead a sustainable, happy life. She realized that she "needed to teach, write and run."[4] It wasn't about following a diet or exercise plan; it was about redefining what health meant to her, and what Objectives she needed to pursue to achieve this.

This captures the essence of what we're aiming for: a clear, compelling direction that guides your efforts over a specific time frame.

WHAT DOES A "GOOD" OBJECTIVE LOOK LIKE?

An Objective should have two basic characteristics:

1. It should be qualitative.
2. It should be time-bound.

Here's what that means in practice.

Objectives Are Qualitative

You might be wondering why we emphasize qualitative properties for Objectives. After all, aren't specific, measurable targets better? Let's not jump the gun: While measurability is crucial for Key Results (which we'll cover in the next chapter), Objectives serve a different purpose.

Qualitative Objectives tap into your emotions and aspirations. They paint a vivid picture of the future you want to create, allowing you to connect with your targets, literally and figuratively, on a deeper level. This emotional resonance is a powerful motivator, driving you forward even when faced with obstacles.

Consider these two statements:

[o] **Increase my savings by 20% this year.**
[o] **Achieve financial freedom and security for my family.**

While the first is specific and measurable, the second speaks to deeper values and aspirations. It's more likely to inspire sustained effort and creative problem-solving. The first is more a cold KPI; the latter has an emotional ring to it.

The Objective is not about hitting a specific metric; that comes later with your Key Results. Instead, it should reflect a broader, more meaningful aspiration. It's about the "what" and "why," not yet the "how." For instance, "Become a more confident public speaker by July" is a stronger Objective than "Give three speeches," because it captures the essence of the change you want to make in yourself.

Objectives Are Time-Bound

Time-bound doesn't mean setting a far-off, indefinite time frame. Instead, create a sense of urgency by choosing a time frame that pushes you to act.

Quarterly Objectives (3-month targets) work well because they're long enough to achieve meaningful progress but short enough to maintain a sense of urgency. This time frame strikes a balance between ambition and practicality, allowing you to set challenging targets while staying grounded in a realistic timeline.

The power of this quarterly approach is also at the heart of Brian Moran's similar concept of the "12-week year."[5] When working with a 12-week horizon, you naturally feel more engaged and motivated, as each week becomes crucial to your success.

Breaking down larger, long-term aspirations into quarterly Objectives makes it easier to monitor progress and course-correct if needed, ensuring that you don't get too far off track. Moreover, the relatively short duration keeps motivation high, as the deadline feels tangible and reachable.

Another advantage of quarterly Objectives is that they create natural checkpoints for reflection and adjustment. At the end of each quarter, you can evaluate what worked and what didn't, and make informed changes for the next period. This iterative process helps foster a growth mindset, as you continuously learn from your efforts and apply those lessons moving forward.

The ability to quickly reassess and pivot keeps personal targets dynamic and aligned with changing circumstances or priorities, rather than being rigid commitments that lose relevance over time. You should, however, stick with your Objective during the quarter, and not change it mid-flight (unless in exceptional cases). We will cover this in much more detail in Chapter 10.

A handy comparison might be useful here: enterprises versus startups. The former are rigid in their goals setting (e.g., 5-year plans), compared to the latter that are willing to pivot quarterly. We want you to be a personified startup. *That's* the mindset we need to instill in you!

Most importantly, this approach naturally combats perfectionism (a natural tendency of us authors, so we've been told) by forcing a focus on progress rather than flawless execution. As the saying goes: *"Perfection is the enemy of progress."* So, a bit of messiness is okay; let's just contain it well. Setting Objectives with clear deadlines helps a lot: "Expand my knowledge in data science [by the end of Q1]", with Key Results such as "completed advanced analytics certification with score above 85%," will keep you focused and driven.

Monthly, interim targets can be used to set Key Results. To make a bigger target manageable, break it down into smaller milestones that serve as steppingstones. Let's call them "inchstones," shall we? If your Objective is "Launch a freelance writing business," an inchstone could be "built a portfolio website within the first month." Each inchstone should feel like a mini achievement on the path toward the bigger target. This can even be shorter than a month, if it is a sufficiently significant inchstone for your quarterly Objective.

For example, when we set out to write this book, our first step was to agree on a few basic things:

- Write out our book idea
- Set up a Trello Board
- Agree on book Objectives
- Come up with a first outline and table of contents
- Do a writers' agreement

Among others. We set a very ambitious target to get that done in the first 2 weeks and called it "Set up the process and tools for collaboration, finalizing all six steps [by Oct. 31]."

As our Objective for the quarter was to finish the first draft of the book including a first round of editing, we broke this down further into "Finish the first draft of the POKR book [by Nov. 30]" (first 2 months) and "do one round of editing on the first draft [by Dec. 31]."

Since Objectives are already time-bound by the quarter, we don't generally include a date in the definition of the Objective; they simply "inherit" the final date by the end of the quarter that they are earmarked to. For Key Results, we do include a deadline, though, as that can fall anywhere within the quarter.

LESS IS MORE: THE CASE FOR FEWER OBJECTIVES

It can be tempting to set multiple Objectives, thinking that the more targets you pursue, the more you'll achieve. After all, we all have a lot of intentions in all areas of life, be they financial, family or relationships, health, career, or personal projects. But in reality, the opposite is true. When it comes to Objectives, less is more.

By focusing on fewer, high-priority targets, you increase your chances of making meaningful progress. A scattered shotgun approach dilutes your efforts and leads to burnout, which is exactly what we want to avoid.

A good rule of thumb is to set no more than three Objectives at a time. We will discuss variations and exceptions to this later in this chapter on how to cover multiple different categories, but for now repeat after us: "*I shall not set more than three Objectives per quarter.*"

Or put differently: *Focus, focus, focus!*

For first-timers, we even recommend starting with one Objective only. This doesn't mean you're limiting your ambitions; rather, you're channeling your energy toward the targets that matter most. Consider Personal OKRs as a spotlight rather than a floodlight. They're there to illuminate what's truly important, not to cast a dim glow over everything.

When Wolfram first began using Personal OKRs during a gardening leave between jobs, his enthusiasm led to overambition. He embarked on too many ventures simultaneously, from setting up companies and starting several courses to learning a musical instrument and pursuing exercise targets, among others. The result: a fun-filled quarter, but ultimately, nothing was fully completed.

We will see later how you can integrate this focused area of your life with everything else. Life goes on while you build your dreams, so using Personal OKRs to focus on a small set of key areas while having a system to manage everything else is crucial to making this work in practice. If you were to go off focusing solely on your key projects and Objectives, while ignoring or severely limiting your attention for other aspects of your life, you would soon face the consequences (our wives are certain to remind us of our social and family commitments).

Aaron Aiken, a *Medium* author, illustrates this principle well. He had numerous ambitions, from starting a freelance business to improving his health. Instead of tackling everything at once, he decided to prioritize his Objectives: "Land a remote full-time job" and "Pay off student loan" in the first quarter of a new year. By narrowing his focus, he was able to make significant strides in both areas.[6]

A WORTHWHILE TARGET?
HOW TO REFINE YOUR OBJECTIVES

The process of setting an Objective starts with a broad idea but needs refining to become actionable. In Chapter 5, we discussed how to reflect on areas of your life that would have the most significant impact if improved, and position them within your values, life mission, and longer-term ambitions.

This, by definition, will mean that the goal is important for you, and potentially also for others. The most powerful Objectives resonate with your core values and long-term perspective for your life. They should feel meaningful and important to you, not just things you think you "should" do.

Here are some steps to help you craft Objectives that inspire action:

1. Be specific and ambitious, yet achievable.
2. Check for emotional resonance.
3. Be clear and concise.
4. Write it down.

Be Specific and Ambitious, Yet Achievable

Your Objectives should push you to grow without setting you up for failure. A good Objective should be challenging enough to stretch you beyond your comfort zone but not feel impossible. If you're confident that you can easily accomplish the target, it's too easy. If it feels utterly out of reach, it may be too ambitious.

At Google, Objectives are set such that 70% fulfilment is considered success, encouraging ambitious target setting.[7] As John Doerr, who introduced

OKRs to Google, put it, the sweet spot for an OKR grade is 60% to 70%; if someone consistently gets 100%, their OKRs aren't ambitious enough.[8]

What does that mean for you when you are defining the Objective? Obviously, it's framed as full achievement. You wouldn't say, "I want to do 70% of the garden shed build." Instead, ask yourself, how confident are you that you can achieve this Objective in the quarter, on a scale from 1 to 10. If it's a 1, the Objective is too easy. If it's a 10, it's too hard. Aim for an Objective that falls around a 6 or 7; challenging enough to require significant effort but not so daunting that it feels out of reach.

If you fail, it's a learning opportunity. Just reflect on what went wrong and adjust future Objectives and Key Results. Ask yourself:

- Does this target challenge me to grow or improve in a meaningful way?
- Does it push me out of my comfort zone into areas where I feel uncertain or even a bit afraid?
- What skills, knowledge, or strengths will I need to develop to achieve this target?

Michael Bungay Stanier, in his book *How to Begin*, calls this requirement for targets to be "daunting," by which he means stretching yourself beyond your comfort zone.[9] A worthy target should challenge you to grow, require you to learn new things, and push you into uncharted territory. It should feel a little scary, but in a good way; the kind of fear that signals you're about to do something transformative.

We found that, in practice, it helps to balance your set of Objectives between the truly boundary-moving ones that are daunting and inspiring, but where you truly don't know whether you will fully achieve them (and that would be okay, too), and ones that are "stretch" or new activities, but which are more realistic.

The main reason for this is motivation: If you set out to achieve three truly transformational and overly challenging targets at the same time, you're more likely to fail on all. Remember, this is about making measurable progress on targets that are important to you. You should feel good about your achievement at the end of the quarter, not completely demoralized.

Let's say you listened to us before and set only three Objectives (well done, by the way), one for each of the following areas of your personal life:

- A health-related Objective: "Fix my sleep issues to be more energetic each day."
- A relationship-focused Objective: "Capture my mom's life memories in a journal."
- A personal project you want to finish: "Launch a forwarding business to sell my first product on Amazon."

The first is a foundational Objective: you need that to get a lot of other things done better, faster, easier. While you can make good progress on this in a quarter, health is a longer journey, so this might evolve later. The second is time-bound and specific but should not be too daunting (depends on your relationship with your mother, of course). The third one might be more of a stretch if you haven't started a business on your own before.

Check for Emotional Resonance

Ask yourself if your Objective excites you. If it doesn't, rephrase it until it does. For example, "Get in shape" might not inspire you, but "Run a 5k to prove I'm capable of overcoming my limitations" might. The language you use matters because it frames how you approach the target.

M. B. Stanier calls this requirement for a target to be "thrilling."[10] It needs to be something you're genuinely passionate about, a target that energizes you and sparks curiosity or desire. This is the part of the target that connects to your intrinsic motivation. Ask yourself:

- Does this Objective make me feel alive and engaged?
- Is it something that excites my imagination or taps into something I care deeply about?
- Would pursuing this Objective bring joy, excitement, or personal fulfillment?

If an Objective doesn't feel thrilling, you're likely to lose interest or motivation over time. By selecting an Objective that excites you, you'll have the enthusiasm and energy to push through challenges and remain engaged even when the process gets difficult.

Be Clear and Concise

Your Objectives should be easy to understand and remember. Aim for simple, straightforward statements that capture the essence of what you want to achieve. Meaning: Keep it short.

Share your Objectives with a friend or family member. Can they easily understand what you're aiming for? If not, how can you make your Objectives clearer and more concise?

Instead of "I want to get back to writing when I'm not busy and maybe finish that book idea I've been thinking about for years," say "Complete the first draft of my novel."

Write It Down

Finally, putting your Objectives in writing turns them from abstract ideas into concrete commitments. When you write down your Objectives, you're more likely to act on them. Keep them visible, whether in a journal, a task management app, on a whiteboard, or pasted to your fridge, so they stay top of mind.

We will delve into the various options to capture and track your Objectives and Key Results in Part IV, Execution. Good practices are coming your way there.

ASPIRATIONAL VERSUS COMMITTED OBJECTIVES

For company OKRs you often find a separation between "aspirational Objectives" and "committed Objectives."[11] In the company OKR framework, committed Objectives refer to Objectives that an individual or team is fully dedicated to achieving. These Objectives are nonnegotiable, meaning they must be met regardless of circumstances. Put differently, they are binary in that they are either success or failure, they either get done or they don't. And the intention is that they better get done.

Unlike "aspirational Objectives," which are more about stretching beyond current capabilities, committed Objectives are typically grounded in a clear, attainable plan with specific resources allocated to ensure success. The success criteria for committed Objectives are usually set at 100% completion. Failing to achieve them can indicate a breakdown in planning, execution, or resource allocation, as they are expected to be achieved without exception.

In the personal context, committed Objectives can be used as well, though in our humble opinion they should be the exception rather than the rule. Here is why:

We all have commitments that must get done. No doubt about it. There are taxes to declare, doctor appointments to do, children's school obligations to fulfill, essential car maintenance, renewing important documents like passports or licenses, and so forth. Some of these have serious consequences if they don't get done and need serious attention. For that reason, some authors suggest a mix of targets, first defining committed targets and then aspirational ones. But that just takes us back to the original problem: We focus on the day-to-day stuff first and get nothing else done.

Let's go back to the ground rules above: Objectives need to be ambitious, meaningful, and aspirational (i.e., aligned with your Mission). And, as we've discussed, time-bound. They are must-dos more often than not.

Few people get their kicks from doing taxes; if you do, let us know; we've got some you can help with. Yet, we all agree that they need to get done. Many obligations that might be considered for committed Objectives are also not large enough to take significant time (i.e., not over the quarter). Remember the whole point about applying Personal OKRs in the first place is to organize ourselves as such that we make measurable progress on things that matter but tend to be crowded out by the urgent stuff.

There are, of course, genuine cases where these rules apply. For example, if you're getting married, planning your wedding is a committed Objective:

- It clearly aligns with your life's Mission (we assume).
- Most weddings are a big, ambitious undertaking (unless you are a cheapskate).
- And they are time-bound; there's typically a wedding day set, and you would want to start planning this a long time in advance (a quarter or more).

Essentially any big event in life (like a wedding, graduation events, important anniversaries, etc.) require a lot of planning to get to an acceptable level of quality. Other examples are:

Figure 17. Examples of Committed Objectives

These examples share key characteristics that make them suitable as committed Objectives:

- They require sustained effort over months.
- They have clear success criteria, and it's all or nothing (there is no 70% done dissertation).
- They need systematic planning and execution.
- They have significant consequences if not completed.
- They typically can't be postponed indefinitely.
- They should also generally be ambitious and meaningful.

So, what to do with the other commitments? Are we advocating not doing your taxes or saying goodbye to your doctors? No, of course not. Those will not be forgotten. We will still be planning and tracking them in your task management system. For details see Part IV on Execution. But we want to keep them out of the Personal OKRs. They are the necessary activities we need to do to keep things running, but they won't excite us to the level of our Personal Objectives and Key Results.

Let's take a closer look at our five Life Categories of Objectives to see what science and experiences tell us about how to set them well.

LIFE CATEGORIES COVER ALL YOUR BASES

Here's how you can set meaningful Objectives using the Personal OKR Method for the most important categories of your life: family, health, finances, career, and personal passion projects.

Figure 18 outlines the idea of the POKR Burger covering multiple dimensions.

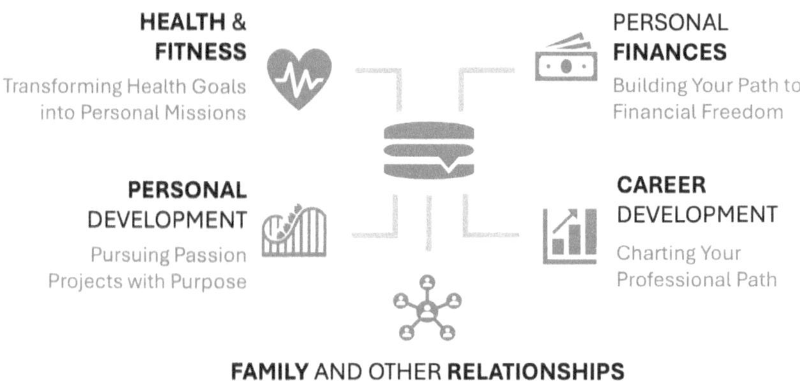

Figure 18. Life Categories as Dimensions of the POKR Burger

Family and Other Relationships: Investing in Your Social Capital

Let's be honest, talking about family and friends in terms of setting goals can be difficult. Setting Key Results, something measurable, for interactions with family and friends can easily feel cringy. And there is always a risk we're overly structuring our relationships. Meaning, we don't want you to track your love life in Excel (technically possible, deeply unsettling, and bound to raise eyebrows over dinner). So, let's be careful and considerate about this.

That said, improving relationships is key for your well-being, and setting goals to improve those is a worthy cause. A famous 80-year Harvard Study of Adult Development showed that the quality of our relationships is the single strongest predictor of life satisfaction and longevity.[12] When setting Objectives for family relationships, focus on creating meaningful connections rather than just spending more time together.

Successful relationships aren't built on grand gestures but on frequent, small, positive interactions.[13] The truth is, relationships are more like tending a garden than following a blueprint: They need regular attention and care, but also room to grow in unexpected and beautiful ways. This means setting Objectives that prioritize daily microconnections (daily rituals, like walks together) over sweeping targets. For instance, instead of "Spend more time with family," consider "Create daily opportunities for meaningful exchanges with each family member." This shifts the focus from quantity to quality of interaction.

Want to change your relationship with your teenage children? Want to become a trusted confidant and supporter of your children's dreams and challenges (as a Yearly Goal)? How about setting the following Objective for a quarter: "Deepen my connection with each of my children through shared one-on-one time and open conversations." This can lead to regular one-on-one time ("dad dates" or "mom dates") with each child, engaging in their interests, and creating safe spaces for open dialogue about their lives. We've tried that ourselves with our families and the results were promising.

Some more examples for inspiration:

[o] **Become a more engaged parent by consistently showing up for what matters to my kids.**

This works well with Key Results like "attended 100% of scheduled school or extracurricular events" and can be done within a quarter.

[o] **Build shared rituals with each of my kids to strengthen our bond through fun experiences.**

Supports Key Results like "launched a weekly shared activity [game night, reading time, art, sport]" or "documented five new things we tried together." Again, focus on establishing new routines and activities that bring you closer together.[14]

Once this behavioral change is established through the use of Personal OKRs, it is a new habit that sticks for the long term. We cover more on how POKR helps you here in Chapter 14.

Research indicates that when parents intentionally foster strong relationships with their teenagers, it leads to more meaningful interactions and strengthens the parent–teen bond.[15] Furthermore, creating low-pressure environments encourages adolescents to share important aspects of their lives, enhancing communication and trust within the family.[16]

There are three key principles for family Objectives:

1. **Quality over Quantity**: Focus on the quality of interactions rather than only track time spent together.

2. **Individual Connection**: One-on-one time with each family member leads to stronger bonds than group-only activities.

3. **Shared Growth**: Families who set Objectives around learning or experiencing new things together will experience higher levels of connection.

People with strong social networks live longer and report higher life satisfaction.[17] Consider Objectives like "Build a supportive community of friends who share my values and interests." This might involve joining clubs, organizing regular gatherings, or taking initiative in maintaining long-distance friendships. The key is to make relationship Objectives specific and aligned with your values rather than focusing on surface-level interactions.

Health and Fitness:

Transforming Vague Targets into Personal Missions

Many people start with broad Objectives like "Get healthy" or "Lose weight," but these lack the inspiration and clarity needed for sustained motivation. Individuals are more likely to maintain healthy behaviors over time when those behaviors are aligned with their personal values and identity, rather than focusing solely on outcomes like weight loss.[18]

For example, instead of "Lose weight," consider what that weight loss would enable in your life. Your Objective might become "Achieve a level of fitness that allows me to actively participate in my children's lives" or "Build the strength and endurance to pursue my passion for hiking mountain trails."

"Longevity is not about adding years to your life but adding life to your years," longevity expert Dr. Peter Attia often emphasizes. This profound perspective encapsulates his mission to optimize health span and develop evidence-based strategies to enhance the quality of his patients' lives.[19] This led him to define specific Objectives and supporting protocols for sleep quality, strength training, and cardiovascular fitness, turning an overall mission for better health into a comprehensive system for long-term well-being.[20]

Another good place to start for inspiration on health Objectives is Dr. Michelle Segar's research on sustainable fitness motivation.[21] She found that people who set Objectives around immediate rewards were more successful than those focusing on distant health outcomes. This insight helps in framing Objectives that connect to daily quality of life rather than just long-term health benefits. Place consistency first and sustain a physical movement habit, such as "Move daily to boost energy and mood." For example, focus on well-being and stress reduction habits.[22]

Consider the following examples of transforming vague health targets into meaningful Objectives.

Instead of "Exercise more":

[o] Develop strength and flexibility to play pain-free tennis with friends.

[o] Build cardiovascular fitness to confidently complete a 5k run with my running club.

Instead of "Eat better":

[o] Master healthy cooking to create enjoyable, nutritious meals that energize my day.

[o] Develop sustainable eating habits that support both my fitness targets and my social life.

Remember that health Objectives often intersect with other life areas. A well-crafted health Objective might support your career goals ("having energy for peak performance"), family targets ("being active with your children"), or personal passions ("staying fit for your favorite activities").

Personal Finances: Building Your Path to Financial Freedom

Financial Objectives should go beyond simple savings targets to address your broader life mission. People who connect their financial targets to specific life purposes are more likely to achieve them.[23] Instead of "Save more money," effective Objectives might be "Build financial independence to support my family's dreams and future security." This connects your financial targets to your deeper motivations.

Here are some core principles for effective financial Objectives:

1. **Align Goals with Personal Values**: Setting financial goals that resonate with your core values increases commitment and follow-through.[24] When your Objectives reflect what truly matters to you, be it family security, freedom to travel, launching that dream business, or community contribution, you're more likely to stay motivated and achieve them. If a goal doesn't spark any real excitement or purpose, you'll drop it faster than a boring Netflix series. When your heart is in it, saving and budgeting feel less like a chore and more like working toward a life you actually want.

2. **Make Good Habits the Default (Automate and Systemize)**: Automating savings and investments reduces reliance on willpower and helps maintain consistency. By setting up automatic transfers or deductions, you create a system that supports your financial goals with minimal ongoing effort. Financial Objectives can be around establishing new financial habits that will last beyond the quarter they are introduced. Nobel laureate Richard Thaler argued that successful financial Objectives need to account for human psychology, not just numbers.[25] He demonstrated how nudging, a term he coined, may help people exercise better self-control when saving for a pension, as well as in other contexts.

3. **Break Down Goals into Achievable Milestones**: Dividing long-term financial goals into smaller, manageable milestones makes them less daunting and more attainable. This approach allows for regular progress checks and adjustments, keeping you on

track toward your larger Objectives.[26] Big targets (like "paying off six-figure debt or amassing a huge down payment") can feel overwhelming, so break them into bite-sized chunks that you can actually achieve in the near term.[27] Each small win, whether it's saving your first $500 or paying off one credit card, is cause for a mini celebration (in a modest, goal-friendly way, of course).

4. **Adopt a Money-Savvy Identity (Be the "Saver" You Aspire to Be)**: Viewing yourself as someone who is financially responsible can positively influence your behavior. This identity-based motivation encourages actions that align with your self-perception, making it easier to stick to financial plans. Frame your Objective as part of your identity. Instead of thinking "I want to save money," tell yourself "I am a saver: I will reduce my credit card debt by 50% by year-end." It's a subtle mind hack that makes smart choices feel natural. A person who is "good with money" will instinctively skip the impulse buys. In fact, when saving becomes part of who you are, it stops being a decision each time and starts feeling like second nature. So, go ahead, give yourself a positive financial nickname (Frugal Friend? Budget Boss?) if it helps. It might feel silly, but viewing yourself as the kind of person who handles money wisely creates a self-fulfilling prophecy: You'll act in line with that money-savvy persona.

To give some examples for financial Objectives: here's Michael, a software developer, who set the 5-Year Goal of "Create multiple streams of passive income to achieve financial freedom." This was translated into a 1-Year Goal of "Lay the groundwork for three new streams of passive income" and several Objectives including purchasing a rental property, developing online courses, and starting a small side business, all while maintaining his primary career.

Another example might be "I am a saver: Develop a robust financial foundation that allows me to pursue my passion for travel." This could involve specific targets for debt reduction, emergency fund building, and investment growth, all aligned with the ultimate goal of having the freedom to explore the world.

Career Development: Charting Your Professional Path

In a career context, Objectives often focus on gaining new skills or reaching a professional milestone. Remember that we're talking about your own Objectives for your career, not individual or department-level OKRs you might have defined in your organization or job. Think about this category to either help you advance in your current profession or find a new one, with the current organization or not.

Again, it's important to be specific and inspirational. Instead of "Get a promotion" (nothing wrong with wanting this, of course), try "Develop expertise in data analytics to become a go-to person for my team." This Objective focuses on building a specific skillset that will make career advancement more likely. This is also borne out by science: Professionals who set structured career Objectives are more likely to achieve their desired career outcomes.[28] The key is focusing on development rather than just advancement.

Again, some guiding principles for effective career Objectives:

1. **Skill-Based Focus:** Professionals who set Objectives around specific skill development are more likely to advance than those focused only on position titles. Focusing on a job title is like skipping to the boss level in a video game without the necessary power-ups; it rarely ends well. When you make skill growth the star of your Objectives, the titles (and raises) tend to follow as a natural side effect. Objectives that focus on learning new skills could be formulated like "Master the fundamentals of SQL for

data-driven decision-making," "Strengthen my public speaking skills so I can lead client meetings and internal presentations with ease," or "Level up my storytelling skills to make my work more impactful and easier to champion."

2. **Network Development**: It's not just what you know but who you know—and who knows you. A huge portion of career opportunities come through networking; in fact, the majority of jobs are filled via personal and professional connections rather than cold applications.[29] Building relationships might feel like extra work (or even awkward for introverts), but it's career rocket fuel. Whether through finding mentors, attending industry meetups, or other activities, investing in your network means more doors will open when you're ready to walk through. Select Objectives that develop your network, such as "Reconnect with mentors, peers, and past colleagues to foster long-term career momentum," or "Build a stronger internal network to learn, collaborate, and grow beyond my current role."

3. **Learning Orientation**: Lifelong learning is the cheat code for a resilient, satisfying career. People who set continuous learning goals, always updating their knowledge or picking up new tricks, tend to earn more promotions and report higher job satisfaction.[30] Examples of Objectives for learning could include: "Deepen my understanding of emerging trends that are reshaping my industry" or "Turn learning into a weekly habit so it becomes part of how I grow professionally." The takeaway: No matter how senior you get, always keep the spirit of a student and never stop learning.[31]

Christina Wodtke, when transitioning from the tech world to a set of new roles, didn't just set the Objective of "Write a book." She framed it as "Model life as a professional author," which made the target more impactful and meaningful to her.[32]

Jonathan, whom we introduced in a previous chapter, set an Objective to become conversationally fluent in Spanish. Here's how he defined his Objective:

[O]   **Speak basic conversational Spanish to prepare for our South America family trip.**

He then set Key Results supporting this 3-months' target with monthly intervals (see Chapter 7 for specifics).

PERSONAL DEVELOPMENT: PURSUING PASSION PROJECTS WITH PURPOSE

If you have a passion project, the Objective could be more than just "Work on my novel" or "Build the man cave" (don't get us wrong: we recognize the importance of such endeavors). Instead of "Work on my novel," use "Complete the first draft of my novel to bring my creative vision to life." This Objective not only gives a deadline (the implicit end of the quarter for the Objective), but also ties the target to a personal purpose, making it more motivating.

Dr. Carol Dweck's research on "growth mindset" adds another dimension, showing that people who frame personal development Objectives as learning opportunities rather than performance targets achieve better results.[33] And that's a great way to think about this in general: We want you to exhibit a "growth mindset" in how you approach life's challenges, with POKR being here to help you to "operationalize" it.

If you plan to learn to play a musical instrument, an example of a performance-target framing would be "Master 10 classical piano pieces by the end of the year." We can rephrase this as a learning opportunity like this: "Develop my musical abilities through piano practice, to play at the school concert." This works better as an Objective, because this is linked to an aspirational goal. The "10 classical piano pieces" are much more suitable to include as a Key Result to measure whether we achieve our Objective.

Remember your outcomes from step one, the Mission and 5+1 Goals? How having a Mission or long-term plan is the foundation from which we build Personal OKRs? In our experience, personal development Objectives work best when they meet the following:

- **Connection to Larger Life Purpose**: Aligning goals with a broader sense of purpose enhances motivation and commitment. This alignment fosters a deeper connection to the goal and makes you more resilient in the face of challenges.

- **Inclusion of Specific Learning Components**: Goals that incorporate clear learning Objectives tend to be more effective. This specificity aids in tracking progress and maintaining focus.

- **Balance Between Challenge and Achievability**: As we discussed before, having stretch goals can be very energizing. High goals lead to greater effort than low goals.[34] Setting goals that are challenging yet attainable strikes a balance that optimizes performance. Overly ambitious goals can be discouraging, while too-easy goals may not provide sufficient motivation.

- **Incorporation of Regular Feedback Mechanisms**: Regular feedback is crucial for adjusting strategies and maintaining momentum toward goal achievement. It allows individuals to recognize progress and make necessary modifications.

Wash, Rinse, Repeat

Just as there are many roads leading to Rome, there are many ways to define an Objective. We encourage you to play around with the wording of your

Objectives until they meet the above requirements. You might not get this 100% right the first time, but rest assured you will get better with practice.

When Wolfram first started using Personal OKRs for getting into shape, he failed to be specific about the motivation. The target was to generally "get into shape" but it wasn't linked to a "why." While he made good progress (after all, the Personal OKRs helped him to get into a habit of reserving time for gym workouts, getting a personal trainer, and tracking miles run per month), this was more because of the Key Results doing their work, rather than an overarching inspiring reason for getting into shape.

In the next round, he changed this to "Run the Singapore Sundowner half-marathon in [Dec.] with Sebastian in under 2 hours." Never having done any long-distance runs before, and after having this target on the bucket list for many years, if not decades, this provided a clear, motivational target, which still was a stretch. This had the added benefit of making this a mutual Objective with somebody else, thus providing positive peer pressure and accountability. More on that important aspect of Personal OKRs in Chapter 8. And since you're asking, no, we didn't quite get to under 2 hours, but we did finish the run; did we mention that Objectives should be aspirational in nature?

How Long Does It Take to "Get Good" at This?

As with everything new or semicomplex, it might take a while for you to become comfortable with defining appropriate Objectives. In an enterprise context, firms usually take an entire year to become reasonably okay in defining them. For your Personal OKRs, it should be a bit faster given that you don't have to align them with levels above or below. That is, unless you consider your partner and/or family a stakeholder group to align with. Please don't go down that path.

Having patience is important in mastering Personal OKRs. Be okay with not "getting it" fully on the first round (first quarter); you'll get better with each cycle. It's better to have bad Personal OKRs to begin with than having no Personal OKRs at all. Quality will inevitably improve over time; just trust the process. Practice makes perfect.

What If I Can't "Complete" an Objective?

As you will see when we cover "Key Results" in Chapter 7 as well as in Chapter 8, it is perfectly possible, and actually likely, that you won't be able to complete an Objective in its entirety, that you "fail" on some. That's okay. Remember, Objectives are often "stretch by design," so not being able to complete some is part of the journey.

When we talk about the planning routines to define Objectives, you'll take into consideration your "success rate" from past periods, to judge what your new periods' Objectives should look like. Here, it is okay to decide to "roll over" Objectives from the past period, to essentially continue on, possibly with different Key Results.

So, don't beat yourself up if you didn't entirely succeed on an Objective. Take it as an opportunity to fine-tune it for the next round. The method is resilient enough to account for failure, so have trust in the process.

SETTING OBJECTIVES THAT INSPIRE ACTION

Let's be honest: We started this chapter talking about New Year's resolutions, and those statistics probably felt familiar. We've all been there: setting ambitious targets in January only to see them fade by spring. It's a common enough experience that it's become something of a cultural running joke. But it doesn't have to be our story.

Those sobering statistics weren't meant to discourage you. Instead, think of them as a wake-up call. They highlight why we needed a better approach in the first place. Traditional resolutions often fail, not because we lack motivation, but because we're using the wrong tools for the job.

Throughout this chapter, we've seen how Objectives with the POKR Method offer a different path.

As you move forward with setting your own Objectives, carry with you this essential contrast we established at the start: The difference between a resolution that fizzles and an Objective that inspires isn't luck or willpower, it's in the process itself. By crafting Objectives that are meaningful, time-bound, and stretched, you're not just setting targets; you're creating a roadmap for sustainable change and genuine progress.

WHAT'S NEXT?

The journey from intention to achievement starts with a well-crafted set of Objectives. By applying the principles we've explored, you're now equipped to set targets that don't just inspire action, they sustain it.

In the next chapter, we will turn to the second component of Personal OKR's, the Key Results that represent the measurable steps to achieve your Objectives. Let's take a look at the next level down!

KEY TAKEAWAYS

1. **Objectives Versus Resolutions**: Unlike vague resolutions, Objectives within Personal OKRs are meaningful, time-bound commitments that inspire action and drive progress.

2. **Make Objectives Qualitative and Time-Bound**: Focus on emotionally resonant targets that connect to your "why" and set quarterly deadlines to maintain urgency.

3. **Less Is More**: Limit yourself to three key Objectives per quarter to channel your energy effectively and avoid burnout.

4. **Balance Challenge with Achievability**: Set Objectives that stretch you beyond your comfort zone but remain within reach (aim for a 70% success rate).

5. **Aspirational over Committed**: Focus on targets that inspire growth rather than routine tasks, unless a commitment is large, meaningful, and time-bound.

6. **Quarterly Approach for Momentum**: Break long-term targets into quarterly Objectives with smaller milestones ("inchstones"), fostering steady progress and adaptability.

7. **Define OKRs Across Key Life Categories**: Personal OKRs should cover family, health, finances, career, and personal passion projects to ensure balanced growth and fulfillment.

8. **Meaningful Change Doesn't Happen Overnight**: it requires clear direction, careful pacing, and sustainable steps forward. It's like the difference between having a destination in mind and actually mapping out your route to get there.

SEVEN

CRAFTING IMPACTFUL KEY RESULTS

THE POWER OF MEASURABLE PROGRESS

MAGINE YOU'RE ON A ROAD TRIP TO A DESTINATION YOU'VE never visited before. You have a clear idea of where you want to go, which is your Objective. But how do you know if you're on the right track? How can you tell if you're making good time or if you need to adjust your route? This is where Key Results come in.

In the world of Personal OKRs, Key Results are the measurable signposts that tell you whether you're progressing toward your Objectives. They transform your inspiring, qualitative targets into concrete, quantifiable outcomes.

Real-life experiences show that people who track specific metrics related to their targets are significantly more likely to achieve them than those who don't.[1] It's not just about numbers. It's about clarity and staying motivated by seeing progress.

In this chapter, we will explore the main principles of creating Key Results. We will see how they differ from traditional SMART Goals. You will learn from real-world examples in various life areas. We will also highlight common pitfalls to avoid. Finally, you will gain practical techniques for setting Key Results that lead to meaningful progress.

Figure 19 outlines where we are now in the POKR Burger context.

Figure 19. POKR Burger Context: Strategy in Action!

WHAT ARE KEY RESULTS?

Key Results are the measurable, time-bound outcomes that define success. In other words, if you achieve (all of) your Key Results, you correspondingly achieve your Objective. They answer the question: "How will I know if I have succeeded?"

Each Key Result should be specific, measurable, and time-bound, providing clear indicators of progress. While Objectives paint the bigger picture, Key Results provide the detailed brushstrokes that bring that picture to life.

You might have heard the common saying "What gets measured gets managed." We would rather say, "What gets measured mindfully gets improved," and this insight lies at the heart of effective Key Results.[2] But not everything that matters can be measured, and not everything that can be measured matters. The art of selecting Key Results lies in identifying the right metrics that truly indicate progress toward your Objective.

CRAFTING EFFECTIVE KEY RESULTS

If Objectives are the "why" behind your Personal OKRs, then Key Results are the "how." The challenge lies in choosing Key Results that are not only meaningful but also actionable. It's easy to set lofty targets without a clear plan to measure success, but well-crafted Key Results help bridge the gap between intention and achievement.

There are a couple of deceptively simple ground rules for defining Key Results:

1. One person (you) is in charge and in control; that's the "personal" in Personal OKR.
2. It needs to be measurable; if it's not measurable, it's not a Key Result. A simple test: Do you have a number in there?
3. Your Key Results are aligned with their Objectives in terms of outcomes, time frame, and ambition level.
4. They are framed in past tense; that way, you describe an outcome.

Let's take a closer look at these now.

You're the Boss: Accountability and Ownership

Every Key Result should have one clear owner (yes, we are talking about *you*). This seemingly simple rule, derived from Andy Grove's original OKR framework at Intel, provides the foundation for all effective Key Results. But I hear you say, "These are my Personal OKRs; isn't it obvious that this is me in charge and accountable?"

Well, first, there are projects that you might work on together with others: friends, family, clubmates, etc. For example, you might be leading the project to renovate your football clubhouse in your local community. And while that is okay to have many people contributing to one Key Result, you need to have one person who is accountable per Key Result:

you (again). Otherwise, the adage applies that when everyone is responsible, no one is.

Second, if you select Key Results, you need to ensure that you have whatever is needed to achieve the results and measure the progress yourself. If you want to learn Spanish and one of your Key Results for the quarter is "Had 15 real-time conversations with native Spanish speakers, each lasting at least 15 min.," you need to have access to said native speakers and not sit in a wilderness hut without internet.

If your Objective is to "Renovate our local football clubhouse to create a welcoming functional space for club members and supporters," and Key Results include "Got the renovation plans approved by the local council by Dec. 1," you need to be the one invited to the council meeting, for example. Again, you might need inputs and help from other people, but you need to be able to get those for your success.

And if you aim to celebrate the new clubhouse by "Hosted a clubhouse reopening party with at least 50 attendees by Jun. 1," you should have access to the invitee and RSVP list to track this result on a timely basis.

Now, we don't want you to drop these external dependencies entirely: They eventually become Tasks underneath the Key Result, just not a Key Result themselves. Details on how we go about that Task level is spelled out in detail starting with Chapter 9.

To recap:

- The person responsible (you) should be able to track progress without depending on others.
- Measurements should be based on readily available or easily collected data.
- Progress tracking should be timely and regular.

- Dependencies are real and important, but they aren't a Key Result themselves but become Tasks underneath.

If It's Not Measurable, It's Not a Key Result

Each Key Result has one specific metric to measure and track progress against; several Key Results under one Objective can use, and even should use, different metrics. Effective Key Results often combine different types of measurements. They need to be SMART.[3]

Specifics on that approach are touched upon in the upcoming section, "SMART Goals versus Key Results," but here is what that means in practice, on different Key Result types:

Figure 20. Key Result Types, Quantitative Measures (Percentages, Numbers)

Progress can be quantifiable through percentage completion (0–100%) or specific numbers (miles run, number of times something is achieved or completed, weights lifted). Here are some examples of quantitative Key Results:

- [KR] Ran 50 miles by the end of the quarter
- [KR] Read 12 books this quarter

[KR] Saved $5,000 in an emergency fund by the end of the year

[KR] Reduced social media usage to 30 minutes per day by December

[KR] Lost 10 pounds by the end of the next 3 months

This is the preferred way of setting Key Results. If you can, use quantitative metrics, which you can track easily and in a timely fashion. Anything that is tracked with a smart watch or other device (sleep tracker, running apps) can easily be used as a Key Result, if it supports the Objective and you can influence it.

Qualitative Measures with Clear Criteria (Satisfaction Ratings, Competency Assessments)

These are trickier, because they require you to define somewhat measurable and objective criteria for qualitative outcomes, such as quality of engagements, degree of achievement, etc. That might work in a business environment, where there are things like "Net Promoter Scores" or "Employee Engagement Scores." But for personal use it can easily feel and look contrived and make an industry out of tracking your progress.

Here are some examples:

[KR] Wrote five blog posts that got at least 20 positive comments from readers as measured by engagement through comments

[KR] Improved the organization of my home office by setting up a filing system with fewer than 10 items on the desk

[KR] Created a morning routine that leaves me feeling energized at least four out of five weekdays, measured by personal satisfaction and energy levels at the end of each morning

[KR] Cooked 10 healthy dinners that my family rates as a 7/10 or higher in taste

[KR] Improved communication with my partner by having weekly check-ins, rated as productive by both partners

You see how this becomes more and more contrived or artificial? Next, we have our spouse fill out weekly net promoter scores for us on our performance: "Honey, last night's performance I rate a mere 3 out of 10…" Just kidding, of course. We all know it was clearly a 5.

Qualitative measures with clear, natural criteria for defining success can work, but you need to be careful.

Self-Evaluated Key Results

This is where you assign a percentage or score to your own progress or achievement (e.g., "I got 70% out of 100%"). These are a special case of qualitative Key Results, with clear criteria. Here's why:

Self-evaluated results involve subjective judgment, but they still require a clear framework or criteria for how you assess progress. For example, you might rate yourself on how well you followed a routine, how much effort you put into a passion project, or how satisfied you were with the outcome. This evaluation can be expressed as a percentage, score, or other metric.

Criteria for the rating could include factors like consistency, quality, effort, or impact, making it qualitative but still measurable in a subjective sense.

For example:

- [KR] Rated the quality of my daily workout routine on a scale of 1–100, aiming at 80%
- [KR] Self-rated my progress on learning a new language, aiming to score 70% in fluency

In these cases, while the measurement is subjective, the criteria for evaluation are clear, allowing the Key Result to be tracked in a meaningful way.

Binary Completion Metrics (***Yes/No Achievements***)

These are results that focus on either achieving or not achieving a particular outcome. As we discussed in the context of committed Objectives, this is generally not advisable. For Key Results this can work, provided you gave other types of Key Results for the Objective, too. Avoid only having binary completion Key Results for an Objective. Here are some examples of binary completion Key Results:

- [KR] Completed an online course on digital marketing by the end of the month. The course is completed or not
- [KR] Meditated every day for 30 consecutive days. Achieved if done every day without missing a single one
- [KR] Planned and booked a family vacation for the summer. Vacation is planned and all bookings are made
- [KR] Wrote and submitted my novel manuscript to a publisher by the end of the year. It is either submitted or not

These would also be used for the (rare, please) cases of committed Objectives, which typically require a full achievement overall.

Outcomes Versus Activities

No matter what approach and type of metrics you use, not all metrics are created equal. Ask yourself:

- Does this metric reflect meaningful progress?
- Is it something I can influence directly?
- Will tracking this metric drive the right behaviors?

Be cautious of metrics that can be easily gamed or manipulated. They should genuinely reflect progress. For example: Hours spent on a task, number of meetings attended, amount of content produced, any type of social media and email activities, can be easily gamed by yourself, knowingly or subconsciously. Key Results are about outcomes, and less about activities.

For example, a Key Result of "Spent 5 hours a week learning a new skill" can be gamed by simply logging more hours but spending that time inefficiently or without focus, resulting in minimal real learning. One could hit "Attended 10 online webinars this month" by scheduling or joining unnecessary meetings while doing stuff in parallel just to hit the metric, even if they don't add value to the overall Objective. Focusing on "number of blog posts written" or "number of likes received" on a post can easily lead to a shift to quantity over quality, resulting in short or low-value content that technically meets the metric but doesn't achieve the intended outcome.

But, of course, this will never happen to you, our dear reader, right? But it's quite natural since it's based on the human psyche. When people manipulate self-set targets, knowing they are "fooling only themselves," this behavior can be explained by cognitive biases and the tension between short-term gratification and long-term targets.[4]

When individuals manipulate their own metrics, they often engage in self-deception or rationalization. This involves convincing themselves that they've met the target when, deep down, they know they haven't truly achieved the intended outcome. Research on self-deception shows that people often deceive themselves to protect their self-esteem or avoid uncomfortable truths.[5] They may game their own metrics to avoid feelings of failure or guilt.[6]

This behavior is also often a form of procrastination. Rather than tackling the real, meaningful work, individuals find easier, more immediate ways to feel productive.[7] "Attended 10 webinars" sounds great until you realize half of them were on mute while you folded laundry. That's like entering a marathon, sitting in the stands, and still expecting a medal. Presence isn't performance.

When people set a target and then fail to meet it, they experience cognitive dissonance, the mental discomfort that comes from holding two conflicting beliefs (e.g., "I value fitness" versus "I didn't work out today"). To ease this discomfort, they may change how they view the metric or manipulate how they measure progress. They essentially convince themselves they are still on track.[8]

Another relevant concept is the Progress Principle, which states that people are happiest and most motivated when they feel like they're making progress toward meaningful metrics.[9] However, when that progress is slow or difficult to measure, people might resort to creating the illusion of progress (e.g., checking off easier tasks, inflating metrics) to maintain a sense of forward momentum.

Tracking hours spent on a task without checking the result is like bragging about how fast your hamster runs...on a wheel. Sure, it's impressive cardio, but are we actually getting anywhere? Measuring movement isn't the same as measuring progress.

Therefore, let's not fool ourselves thinking that we are immune to this kind of self-manipulation. Instead, let's think about what we can do to minimize this risk when setting our Key Results. This comes down to favoring Key Results expressed as outcomes over those expressed as activities. In other words, remember to focus on the results you want to achieve, not just the activities you'll undertake to get there.

Here are several personal Key Result examples that emphasize this difference:

LIFE CATEGORY	ACTIVITY-FOCUSED KEY RESULT	OUTCOME-FOCUSED KEY RESULTS
HEALTH & FITNESS	Went to the gym 4 times per week	Increased bench press weight by 10% in 8 weeks
	Ran for 30 minutes every morning	Completed a 5K run in under 25 minutes by the end of the month
	Took a yoga class twice a week	Increased flexibility and be able to touch my toes comfortably by the end of 3 months
PERSONAL FINANCES	Spent 1 hour each week managing my budget	Increase monthly savings by 15% over the next 3 months
	Researched investments for 2 hours every weekend	Invested $1,000 in a diversified portfolio with a projected return of 7%
CAREER DEVELOPMENT	Wrote for 30 minutes every day	Completed a 5,000-word draft chapter by the end of the month
	Attended 2 networking events per month	Built 3 new professional relationships that lead to actionable opportunities within the next 3 months
FAMILY & OTHER RELATIONSHIPS	Spent 30 minutes daily meditating	Reduced daily stress levels by 50% (self-assessed) over the next month
	Had a weekly date night with my partner	Strengthened our relationship by having open, meaningful conversations about future goals at least twice a month
	Helped my kids with homework for 1 hour every evening	Ensured my children improve their math grades by one grade by the end of the semester
	Spent more time with the family on weekends	Planned and executed a family camping trip where everyone participates in an activity they enjoy

LIFE CATEGORY	ACTIVITY-FOCUSED KEY RESULT	OUTCOME-FOCUSED KEY RESULTS
PERSONAL DEVELOPMENT	Spent 1 hour studying French every day	Held a 15-minute conversation in French with a native speaker by the end of the quarter
	Read 2 self-help books this month	Implemented 3 key strategies from self-help books (like: POKR)
	Painted for 1 hour every day	Completed 3 original paintings that I feel confident enough to submit to a local art exhibition by the end of the quarter
	Spent 2 hours practicing guitar weekly	Performed one song perfectly in front of friends of family by the end of the month

Table 2. Outcome Versus Activity-Focused Key Results, by Life Category

Does this mean all activity-focused Key Results are bad, and should not be used at all? No! Like everything in life, balance is key. We recommend a mix of activity and outcome-focused Key Results.

When we discuss the relationship between *"habit formation"* and Personal OKRs in Chapter 14, we will see that for certain Objectives you will want to establish new habits as part of the journey. For example, health metrics such as "Slept 7 to 8 hours per night," "Ate five servings of vegetables daily," and "spent 30 minutes of quality time with family each day" all help to meet a certain health Objective.

Creating habits relies on doing the same thing after a consistent trigger, like a time or action. When you add a reward, it becomes easier. Over time, this process turns into something you do automatically. That is almost exclusively an activity-focused target by definition. We'll cover the criteria for using Personal OKR for habit formation in Part IV. For now, just know that activity-based results have their own purpose. We just don't want to "only" use activity-based results, to reduce the risk of self-deception.

The Power of Lead and Lag Indicators

When creating Key Results, it's important to know the difference between lead and lag indicators. Lead indicators predict and affect future performance. Lag indicators show past performance. One looks back, the other forward.

Let's look at examples for health Objectives.

Lag indicator:

- [KR] Reduced body fat percentage from 32% to 25% by the end of March
- [KR] Improved 5k run time from 45 min. to 30 min.
- [KR] Achieved a resting heart rate below 65 bpm

Lead indicators:

- [KR] Increased weekly step count to 70,000 (average 10,000 steps/day)
- [KR] Exercised at least three times per week for 30 minutes each
- [KR] Followed a balanced diet with at least 80% home-cooked meals per week

Simply put, your Key Results should ideally include both flavors. Lead indicators give you early feedback, helping you adjust. Lag indicators show if you've reached your targets.

Aligning Key Results with Objectives

Key Results take the lofty, feel-good targets from your Objectives and bring them down to earth with measurable steps. They connect dreaming big with getting things done. They help you stay focused, so you won't just daydream through the quarter!

There are three elements you need to align:

Make Them Time-Bound

Align your Key Results with the time frame of your Objective. If your Objective is quarterly (as we propose), your Key Results should have completion dates *within* that quarter. While stretching capabilities is good, the timeline must remain realistic.

Time-bound Key Results are essential for maintaining focus and driving momentum toward achieving an Objective. Regular check-ins help maintain momentum and allow for course correction.

A common practice is to earmark the completion of a Key Result to the end of a month, so that you can review it as part of POKRs' standard routines. As we've seen in the examples above, it's as simple as mentioning when you want that Key Result to be completed:

> [KR] Reduced body fat percentage from 32% to 25% by the end
> of March

Limit Key Results per Objective

As with Objectives, less is more when it comes to Key Results. Aim for three to five Key Results per Objective. This forces you to focus on the most important indicators of success. If it's more, the Key Results are either too small (more akin to Tasks than results), or you are packing too many things into one Objective.

This is a great chance to see if your Objective can be reached in a quarter. If you find more than five Key Results for one Objective, consider breaking it up into two separate Objectives. You can assign Objective 1 to Quarter 1 and Objective 2 to Quarter 2.

So, there is nothing bad about a lot of creative output from our Key Result brainstorming. Just be mindful that they serve a purpose: fulfilling an Objective, which is typically allocated to a quarterly cycle.

OBJECTIVE	
Impactful personal productivity book published successfully!	
KEY RESULTS Q1 (original)	**KEY RESULTS Q2** (new)
1. Book outline completed (Oct 30) 2. Draft chapters finished with 90% of content (Nov 15) 3. Editing of 100% of chapters performed (Nov 30) 4. At least 1 publisher signed (Dec 15) 5. ~~Book distributed to at least 5 stores (Dec 20)~~ 6. ~~Launch part with 300+ guests performed (Dec 31)~~	1. Book distributed to at least 3 stores (Jan 31) 2. Launch party with 200+ guests performed (Mar 30)

Table 3. Spreading Key Results over Several Quarters

In the scenario above, someone was a little too ambitious (totally made-up example, of course). Too many Key Results in Q1 created a situation of too much pressure, with the inevitable spillover to Q2. Not the end of the world, but certainly preventable, by being a bit more realistic in the first place. Limiting your Key Results per Objectives is a good way to achieve that.

Embrace the Challenge

The level of stretch for several Key Results collectively contributes to the overall level of stretch for the Objective, but it's about balance. Here's how they relate:

Each Key Result adds a bit of challenge, but not all Key Results need to be moon shots. If every Key Result is highly ambitious, the Objective becomes more of a reach. Conversely, if all Key Results are easily attainable, the Objective will feel underwhelming and uninspiring.

The "stretchiness" of an Objective is determined by how ambitious the Key Results are on average. If you have three Key Results, one could be a bold stretch while others are more achievable, creating a balanced overall Objective. This prevents burnout while still driving ambition. Like the Objective, you'll want to give the respective Key Results a *"confidence factor"* (i.e., how likely you are going to achieve them). There are different ways to express that, but a good practice is a scale from 1 to 10. If you have no idea (yet), go with the midpoint (= 5). These you will later review on a regular basis.

The overall stretch of the Objective depends on how ambitious your Key Results are. They should challenge you but not overwhelm you. It's like putting together a workout: You want some heavy lifts, but not everything needs to be max reps!

Staying in the realm of sports:

- Moon Shot Key Result: Half-Marathon personal best improved by 20% (<1:45 hrs.)
- Challenging Key Result: Structured training plan adhered to (85+%)

SMART Goals Versus Key Results: Same Same, but Different

You might have heard of or even used SMART Goals before (Specific, Measurable, Achievable, Relevant, Time-Bound). While Key Results and SMART Goals share many common elements, they serve different purposes and operate in different ways.

The key distinction lies in their scope and ambition:

SMART Goals tend to be conservative and fully achievable, while Key Results in the Personal OKR concept are intentionally stretching. Remember Google's famous "70% completion is success" principle. Let's look at how the SMART criteria can be used and adapted to transform a vague metric into a clear, actionable Key Result. We essentially can use the concept to "stress test" the quality of our Key Results.[10]

1. **Specific.** A Key Result should be precise, leaving no room for ambiguity. Instead of "Improved fitness," specify "Ran 20 miles each month." The more specific your Key Results, the easier it is to track your progress and know exactly what needs to be done.

2. **Measurable.** The Key Result must include a quantifiable element. If you can't measure it, you can't manage it. For example, if your Objective is to "Become a more confident speaker," a measurable Key Result could be "Gave three presentations by the end of the quarter" or "Increased audience feedback score to 8 out of 10."

3. **Achievable.** While Key Results should push you to stretch, they also need to be within the realm of possibility. Setting targets that are too far out of reach can lead to frustration. Aim for a Key Result that challenges you but also feels attainable with effort. A good litmus test is whether you believe there is at least a 70+% chance of achieving it. It's therefore like the Objective level, where we also want to shoot for 70%.

4. **Relevant.** Each Key Result should directly contribute to the achievement of your Objective. If your Objective is to "Improve physical health," a relevant Key Result would be "Completed a daily 20-minute yoga practice," not "Read one health-related book a month." Make sure the outcomes you track directly influence your primary target.

5. **Time-Bound.** Key Results need deadlines. Time constraints create a sense of urgency and help you stay committed. Instead of "Increased productivity," try "Increased daily focused work sessions from 60 to 90 min. within the next 30 days."

In summary: If you haven't used SMART Goals before, don't worry; the rules described in this chapter will get you there. If you have used SMART Goals, you can use these principles to help define your Key Results, as long as you stay ambitious and don't play it safe.

We Told You So: Common Mistakes to Avoid

When defining Key Results for the first time, be mindful of these common mistakes:

MISTAKE	DESCRIPTION	HOW TO FIX THEM
ONLY 1 KEY RESULT PER OBJECTIVE	Indicates either unclear objective definition or too narrow scope	Revisit Objective for clarity and expand scope to allow 3–5 meaningful Key Results
TOO MANY KEY RESULTS (6+)	Suggest Objective is too broad, or Key Results are too granular	Break into multiple Objectives or combine related Key Results
TASK-BASED KEY RESULTS	Key results should ideally represent outcomes, not single actions; You're likely trying to meansure too many things. ✗ "Went to the gym three times per week"	Combine related Tasks into meaningful outcome measures ✓ "Increased strength by lifting 20% more weight across five key exercises"
SINGLE-WORD KEY RESULTS	Lacks specificity and clear measurement criteria ✗ "Learning"	Expand into complete, measureable statements ✓ "Completed 3 online courses on digital marketing by Dec. 31"

MISTAKE	DESCRIPTION	HOW TO FIX THEM
VAGUE DEFINITIONS	Cannot by clearly measure or verified ✗ "Improved Spanish speaking abilities"	Apply specific metrics and measurement criteria ✓ "Held three 30-minute conversations in Spanish without using translation aids"
CREATING INTERDEPENDENT KEY RESULTS	Key Result relies on external factors outside of your direct control. With interdependent Key Results, it's hard to measure success based on your own effort and output. ✗ "Got team approval on project plan"	Key Result should reflect actions and outcomes you can directly influence. By focusing on what you control, you take full accountability for meeting your Objectives. Interdependent Key Results make it clear whether you've hit the target based on your own work ✓ "Completed project plan, meeting all 12 required criteria"

Table 4. Key Results Dos and Don'ts

Adapt Key Results as Circumstances Change

Life is unpredictable, and sometimes even the best-laid plans require adjustment. The key to effective Key Results is flexibility, being willing to adapt without abandoning your goals.

1. *Revisiting Key Results During Regular Check-Ins*

As we will discuss in more detail in Part IV: Execution, you should schedule regular check-ins, whether weekly or monthly, to review your progress.

Use these sessions to evaluate whether your Key Results still make sense given your current situation. You might have to abandon a Key Result if it isn't possible to achieve it anymore. We cover the rules for pivoting in Chapter 10.

2. Using Key Results to Pivot Without Losing Momentum

If you find that external factors (like an unexpected work assignment or health issue) have disrupted your progress, use this as an opportunity to pivot. Adapt your Key Results to reflect the new reality while still working toward your Objective.

For instance, if an injury prevents you from running, shift your fitness Key Results from "Ran 10 miles a week" to "Swam 100 laps per week."

Be mindful that the new Key Results still must be in the spirit of the Objective above; otherwise you might have to give up on it. Again: Changes to Key Results are described in Chapter 10.

3. Learning from Missed Key Results to Refine Future Goals

Missing a Key Result isn't necessarily a failure; it's feedback. When a Key Result is missed, analyze why it happened and what can be learned. Was the target too ambitious, or did other priorities interfere?

Use these insights to adjust future Personal OKRs to be more realistic and aligned with your current abilities and commitments.

Breaking (Them) Down, Not *Breaking Bad*

Just as with the overall Objective, large Key Results can be daunting. Breaking them down into smaller achievements creates manageable steps. There are a couple of approaches you can try if you feel Key Results are too big.

Inchstone Method

Start by identifying the key events you'll need to hit along the way to achieving your Objective. Then break those down into even smaller, measurable steps: inchstones, if you will. Each inchstone acts as a Key Result. This helps you see real progress and gives you frequent chances to celebrate. Think of inchstones as little wins on your way to a bigger target. For example, here is a revenue-oriented Key Result under a freelancing Objective:

[KR] Secured three new clients for my consulting business

That's a nice output metric, but you could add lead indicators and setup steps:

[KR1] Reached out to at least 50 prospects via email or LinkedIn by week four
[KR2] Held 10+ discovery calls with qualified leads
[KR3] Submitted five tailored proposals based on client needs
[KR4] Closed three new deals with signed contracts and first payments received

Another example:

[KR] "Prepared portfolio and applied to 10 art residencies"

This sounds creative but is a productivity Hydra. Using the word "and" in Key Results indicates a need to split them up. For example:

[KR1] "Selected 10 high-fit residency programs and tracked deadlines"
[KR2] "Updated and curated digital portfolio by week three"
[KR3] "Wrote tailored artist statements for top five applications"
[KR4] "Submitted 10 applications by end of quarter"

Here's another one from the Personal Finance area:

[KR] "Organized all family finances and created long-term investment plan"

That's like saying "just fix my whole future." And clearly this will take several months to do. So, let's break this down further:

[KR1] "Consolidated and categorized all current financial accounts by week two"

[KR2] "Created monthly budget tracker and tracked spending for 30 days"

[KR3] "Researched and selected three investment options aligned with goals"

[KR4] "Scheduled meeting with financial advisor and finalized plan by end of quarter"

These inchstone Key Results keep the momentum going, reward visible progress, and help prevent stagnation.

To sum up, if a Key Result:

- Contains multiple verbs ("wrote and submitted," "built and tested"),
- Spans multiple months, or
- Requires coordination across different people (family, trainers, colleagues),

...it's probably too big and needs to be split into inchstones.

And always consider elevating (and rephrasing) Key Results to their own Objective, if they are sufficiently large and important.

Steppingstone Approach

Imagine the path to your Objective as a series of steppingstones. What's the first stone you need to step on? The second? Continue until you reach your target. Oftentimes, these steppingstone-based Key Results build on each other and might even have to be executed in sequence.

For instance, if your Objective is to start a successful side business:

[01] **Launch minimum viable product**
[KR1] Defined and prioritized top three customer problems based on initial interviews
[KR2] Validated business idea by surveying 100 potential customers by end of month one
[KR3] Created a minimum viable product (MVP) including test with 20 users by end of month three
[KR4] Proved MVP is not just a Google Form duct-taped to a spreadsheet, by getting at least one user to say, "this is actually useful!" without being bribed.

[02] **Build initial sales of my new product**
[KR1] Tested at least three customer acquisition channels with cost per lead under $30
[KR2] Built an email list of at least 300 potential customers with >30% open rate
[KR3] Generated first $1,000 in revenue by end of month five (month two of second quarter)
[KR4] Achieved 20% month-over-month growth for 3 consecutive months

If you paid attention, you would have noticed that this Objective needs to be split and distributed over two quarters.

Skill Breakdown Technique

If your Objective involves developing a complex skill, break it down into its component parts. Create Key Results for each crucial subskill. For example, if you're learning to play guitar:

[01] **Master the basics of playing the guitar (thrumming style)**
[KR1] Mastered 15 essential chord shapes by end of month two

[KR2] Learned to perform five songs from beginning to end by end of month three

[O2] **Create and perform my first simple song on the guitar**

[KR1] Improvised a solo over a 12-bar blues progression for two minutes by end of month five

[KR2] Composed an original song and performed it at a family night by end of month six

Run That Past Me Again: The Power of External Validation

Similar to Objectives, a simple but powerful test for your Key Results is to show them to someone else without additional explanation. Ask them to describe how they would determine if the Key Result has been achieved. If they can't do this easily, or their understanding differs from your intent, the Key Result needs refinement.

We cover some helpful techniques to formalize this in Chapter 8.

Example questions you can ask:

- How would you measure success for this Key Result?
- What evidence would show it's been achieved?
- What questions do you have about measuring progress?

If they can't easily answer these questions, your Key Results likely need refinement.

REAL-WORLD EXAMPLES: TRANSLATING OBJECTIVES INTO KEY RESULTS

Let's explore how to create meaningful Key Results across different Life Categories, building on the examples from Chapter 6.

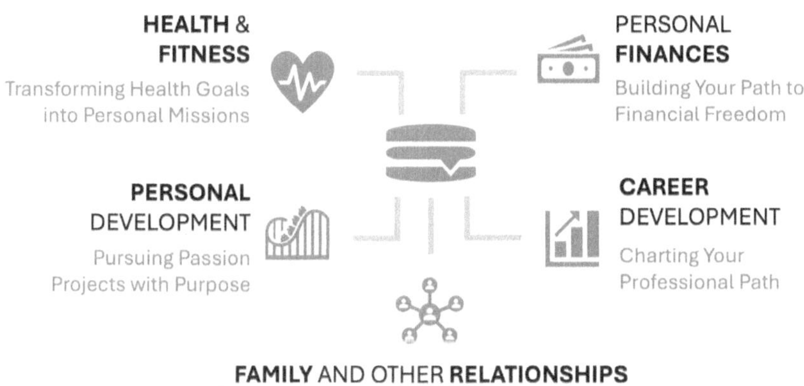

Figure 21. Life Categories as Dimensions of the POKR Burger

Health and Fitness

In Chapter 6, we saw Wolfram's evolution from a vague "get into shape" Objective to a more specific one, with his Key Results effectively breaking down this ambitious target:

[o]   **Run the Singapore Sundowner half-marathon in December with Sebastian in under 2 hours**

[KR1]   Completed 36 training runs (three per week) following the half-marathon training plan

[KR2]   Achieved progressive distances: 5k by month one, 10k by month two, 15k by month three

[KR3]   Maintained average pace under 6 min/km for all training runs over 10k

[KR4]   Completed 24 strength trainings (two per week) focusing on runner's muscle groups

Or consider this example from Ravi:

[O] Implement healthy habits to become a fitter version of myself

[KR1] Reduced body fat percentage from 20% to 18%

[KR2] Completed 48 workouts (four per week combining cardio plus strength training)

[KR3] Maintained a 500-calorie deficit on 80% of days

[KR4] Improved resting heart rate from 72 to 65 BPM

These Key Results cover various aspects of fitness: body composition, cardiovascular endurance, strength, and nutrition. They're specific, measurable, and time-bound within his 12-week time frame.

As Ravi moved ahead, he found tracking his daily calorie intake to be stressful and not helpful. As we discussed above, it's okay to make course corrections on Key Results, within reason. He didn't give up on his nutrition target. Instead, he shifted it. Now, he aims to eat whole, unprocessed foods for 80% of his meals. This change helped him stay focused on his health. He no longer had to worry about counting calories.

Personal Finances

Remember the four core principles for selecting successful personal-finance-related Objectives in Chapter 6:

1. Value alignment
2. Behavioral automation
3. Milestone-based progress
4. Money-savvy identity

We discussed how to set financial Objectives that gel with your broader goals. In this category, Objectives will therefore be related to attaining some degree of financial freedom or saving money for other endeavors and targets. Here are two examples of Personal OKRs in this space:

[01] **Building Emergency Savings: Build a rock-solid financial safety net for my family this quarter**
[KR1] Increased emergency fund from 1 month to 3 months of expenses ($9,000)
[KR2] Automated 15% of monthly income to dedicated emergency savings account

[02] **Improve my credit score, so that I can increase my chances to secure a mortgage for a new home**
[KR1] Paid off outstanding credit card debt by 25%
[KR2] Ensured all bills are paid on time over the next 3 months
[KR3] Reduced credit utilization ratio to below 30%

Before, we discussed Michael, a software developer. He established a 5-Year Goal: "Create multiple streams of passive income for financial freedom." This turned into a 1-Year Goal: "Lay the foundation for three new passive income streams." One key Objective is to purchase a rental property. If we take these Objectives and add Key Results, what might that look like?

[0] **Acquire a rental property that generates at least $500/ month in positive cash flow**
[KR1] Analyzed at least 15 potential rental properties, shortlisted the top three based on cash flow
[KR2] Secured mortgage preapproval with a competitive interest rate within the first month
[KR3] Submitted offers on at least two shortlisted properties within the quarter
[KR4] Finalized a purchase agreement with projected positive cash flow of $500+/month
[KR5] Ensured all legal and financial due diligence is completed before closing

This is also a nice example for a steppingstone approach to Key Results.

Career Development

Remember the possible Objective on skills upgrading?

[o] **Develop expertise in data analytics to become a go-to person for my team**

[KR1] Completed advanced analytics certification with score above 85%

[KR2] Built portfolio of three data science projects using real-world datasets

[KR3] Contributed to two open-source data science projects with accepted pull requests

[KR4] Published four technical blog posts about data science applications

[KR5] Led two internal workshops sharing data science insights with team

The Key Results were crafted to be both challenging and achievable. They allow tracking of learning progress and application of new skills in real-world scenarios.

Let's say you're transitioning from a traditional job to a freelance career. We'll set the Objective and Key Results correspondingly:

[o] **Start a freelance writing business**

[KR1] Launched a self-hosted blog with three published portfolio-quality posts by end of month one

[KR2] Published two or more original articles per week on Medium or LinkedIn for six consecutive weeks

[KR3] Pitched 10 freelance article ideas to editors or platforms aligned with niche

[KR4] Secured one paid writing commission or client contract by end of quarter

By tracking these Key Results, you'd be able to measure your progress and adjust along the way.

Personal Development

For Jonathan's language learning Objective from Chapter 6, effective Key Results might be:

> [O] **Speak basic conversational Spanish to prepare for our South America family trip**
> [KR1] Completed 90 Duolingo lessons (one per day, Jan.–Mar.)
> [KR2] Held 10 live practice conversations with native speakers (≥15 minutes each)
> [KR3] Watched five Spanish-language movies without subtitles
> [KR4] Passed entry-level Spanish test with >80% score by March 31

Jonathan's Key Results encompass various aspects of language learning: Structured study, real-world practice, immersion through media, and formal assessment. They provide a clear roadmap for achieving his fluency target.

As Jonathan pursued his Key Results, he realized he learned best through conversation practice. He modified his strategy for the next cycle. He raised his conversation target and lowered his structured study hours. This change let him focus on his most effective learning method while still tracking progress toward his Objective.

Family and Other Relationships

Recall the Objective on supporting your children's dreams? The following Key Results transformed this aspirational target into a more measurable outcome:

> [O] **Actively support one personal project my child chooses this quarter**
> [KR1] Helped define one project he's/she's excited about (e.g., building a Lego city, learning a dance, designing a game)

[KR2] Provided practical support for that project at least three times (e.g., research, logistics, materials, encouragement)

[KR3] Celebrated visible progress or completion of each project with a small ritual or shared activity (e.g., ice cream run, family demo night)

Notice how each Key Result contributes to the overall Objective while remaining independently measurable. And just to be clear: We are not saying that you have to model your entire family relationships via POKR. You still want to show up as the honest, open, and warm individual that you are. But using POKR to have clarity on what you want to achieve, and the pathway toward such target, can help turning an otherwise fluffy topic into something more tangible.

Mix and Match

It's also perfectly okay to mix and match Key Results from different Life Categories, if they support a particular Objective:

[O] **Reclaim my well-being and build a sustainable lifestyle**

[KR1] Worked 35–45 hours per week for 80% of weeks maintained

[KR2] Slept 7 or more hours for 85% of nights achieved

[KR3] Maintained three meaningful family dinners per week with no devices present

Since the Objective is one of work–life balance, the supporting Key Results come from work (work hours), health (sleep), and relationship (family dinners) perspectives. These Key Results transform a qualitative target into specific, measurable outcomes while maintaining flexibility for real-life variations.

WHAT'S NEXT?

The purpose of Key Results isn't just to measure; it's to drive meaningful progress toward your most important targets. When crafted thoughtfully and reviewed regularly, Key Results become powerful tools for personal transformation.

In Chapter 8, we look at the support from others you will need to stick to your Objectives and Key Results. Afterward, in an extensive Part IV, we'll explore how to integrate Personal OKRs into your daily routines, turning the POKR Method into a sustainable system for ongoing growth and achievement.

But first, let's see how we get you some help.

KEY TAKEAWAYS

1. **Key Results Measure Progress**: They are measurable, time-bound outcomes that define success for your Objective. If you achieve your Key Results, you achieve your Objective.

2. **Focus on Outcomes, Not Just Activities**: Key Results should track meaningful progress, using quantitative, qualitative (with clear criteria), or binary metrics while avoiding easily gamed or activity-based measures.

3. **You're in Charge**: Key Results must be within your control, with clear accountability and no external dependencies that could prevent progress tracking.

4. **Use Three to Five Key Results per Objective**: Keep Key Results focused and aligned with your Objective, ensuring they are time-bound and challenging yet achievable.

5. **Balance Lead and Lag Indicators**: Include both predictive (lead) and outcome-based (lag) measures for a complete view of progress and room for course correction.

6. **Leverage SMART Principles**: Ensure Key Results are Specific, Measurable, Achievable, Relevant, and Time-bound while maintaining a stretch mindset.

7. **Break Down Complex Targets**: Use techniques like inchstones and steppingstones to manage large or long-term Objectives and related Key Results (e.g., break into two Objectives over two quarters).

8. **Stay Flexible and Adjust**: Regularly review and adapt Key Results as circumstances change, using missed targets as opportunities for learning and refinement.

EIGHT

HOLDING YOURSELF ACCOUNTABLE

RICH ROLL'S EXTREME TRANSFORMATION

AT 40, RICH ROLL WAS A SUCCESSFUL ENTERTAINMENT lawyer. He struggled to climb a flight of stairs without getting out of breath. One night, after struggling up the stairs to his bedroom, he decided that things needed to change.

The day after his staircase revelation, Rich completely transformed his diet, laced up his running shoes, and dived back into swimming. Soon, ambition took over, and his journey toward participating in Ultraman started. Two years later, 50 pounds lighter, and fueled solely by plants, he astonished the triathlon and Ultraman communities. He became the first vegan to finish the 320-mile ultra-endurance event. He also placed in the top 10 male finishers with the second-fastest swim split.[1] Soon after, Rich was named one of the "25 Fittest Men in the World" by *Men's Fitness* magazine.[2]

While changing diet and having the right training program were key to success, he frequently talks about how "life transformation is a team sport." For him, investing in accountability was crucial. He found it by connecting with a community of like-minded people. "Going public with your goal breeds accountability. In turn, accountability breeds success," Roll writes in his bestselling book, *Finding Ultra*.[3]

WHY WE NEED ACCOUNTABILITY IN PERSONAL OKRs

In Chapter 6, we explored how to set meaningful Objectives, and in Chapter 7, we learned to define measurable Key Results. But even the best-crafted OKRs can fail without proper accountability. Here's where Personal OKRs face a unique challenge compared to their corporate counterparts.

In organizations, OKRs come with built-in accountability structures. Regular team meetings, performance reviews, and public dashboards create natural checkpoints for progress. When Google tracks their famous 70% target completion rate for OKRs, it's visible across teams. But what happens when you're tracking Personal OKRs without these institutional structures?

Without external support, we rely on our internal motivation to stay on track with our Personal OKRs. But motivation, as you might have experienced, is fickle. One moment, you're fired up to achieve your goals. The next, you find yourself distracted by a new Netflix series or scrolling through social media.

So, how do we fight this natural tendency to slack off? Spoiler alert: It's not about turning into a super human with perfect discipline (not everyone will be a Rich Roll). Instead, it's about building accountability systems with support from others.

Here's some striking research: People who write down their goals and share them with others tend to reach those goals more often. They also benefit from sending weekly updates on their progress. This is much better than just thinking about their goals.[4] Incorporating an Accountability Partner into your life boosts your chances of success. You'll be less inclined to deceive someone you hold in high regard. Therefore, when you commit to showing up this week, you're more likely to follow through.

Rich's example might be extreme (feel free to emulate his challenge, though). But, at the core are powerful ingredients that drive up your success rate when implementing POKR for your own life. In this chapter, we're going to show you how to do just that.

THE SCIENCE BEHIND ACCOUNTABILITY

Rich Roll's success stems from more than just luck or willpower. It connects to years of research on goals and accountability. The Zeigarnik Effect, discovered by psychologist Bluma Zeigarnik, shows that people finish tasks more often when they share them publicly. This is because the human brain tends to focus on unfinished business.[5] When people commit to someone else, they have a 65% chance of completing a goal. That chance jumps to 95% with specific accountability meetings with their partners.[6]

Why does this happen? One word: *commitment*. Sharing your goals with someone creates social pressure, according to psychologists. You're no longer accountable just to yourself but to another person. And humans, being the social creatures that we are, are far more likely to follow through on commitments when we know someone else is watching. Public commitments connect to our need for consistency between what we say and do.[7] When we share our goals, we tend to follow through. This helps us stay true to our self-image and past promises.

Think about it like this: Would you be more likely to hit your quarterly fitness Objective if you had to report your progress to a coach or friend every week? Of course! It's the same reason why fitness challenges or social media goals (e.g., running a 5k for charity) are so effective. By making your Personal OKRs visible and public, you add a layer of (largely positive) pressure that helps push you forward.

It's like having an internal nagging voice that sounds suspiciously like your mother, reminding you that you promised to clean your room, except now it's reminding you that you promised the entire internet you'd run a marathon.

Let's look at some of the key people who can help keep you on track.

WHO TO COUNT ON TO KEEP US ACCOUNTABLE

Accountability doesn't have to come from a single source. In fact, the more support you have, the better. When Rich Roll committed to his EPIC5 challenge, he quickly realized that just announcing his goal publicly wasn't enough. It required different types of accountabilities at different levels:

- Support of his family, especially his wife, Julie, helping him maintain his strict plant-based diet and training schedule.
- His coach, Chris, who devised a training regimen for something never attempted before.
- Hi friend and Ultraman training partner, Jason, who came up with the EPIC5 idea and challenged Rich to it during a visioning gathering with friends.

In addition, there is the role of the wider community he interacted with through his blog. "By making it social, daily tasks become fun, which in turn fosters the accountability for the success you seek," Roll explains.[8]

His experience reveals an important truth about accountability. Rather than searching for a single perfect partner, success often comes from creating a network of support. Each relationship serves a unique purpose in this network.

Now, you don't have to create a full team to support your Personal OKRs. Still, choosing a few key partners can make a difference! Figure 22 illustrates how different types of partners can enhance your success with Personal OKRs.

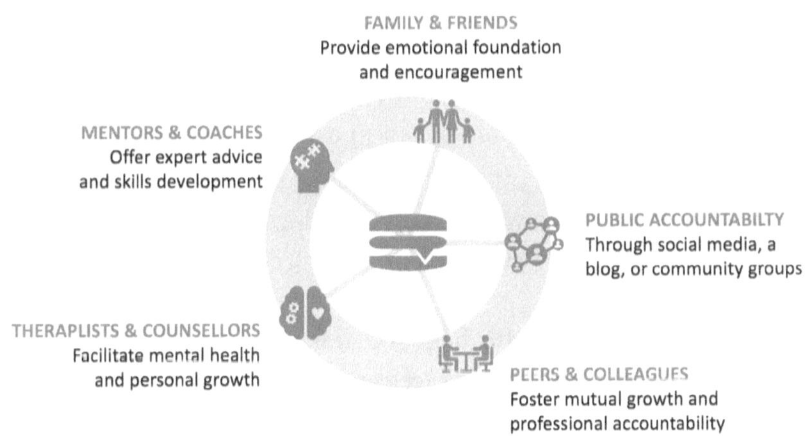

Figure 22. Whom to Count on to Keep Us Accountable

Family and Friends

Your closest relationships provide a foundation of daily accountability and support. These partners witness your daily habits, understand your deeper motivations, and have a genuine stake in your success. This can be a spouse, a close friend, a life partner, or other (extended) family members.

More than just observers, they often must adapt their own routines to accommodate your goals. A spouse who supports your early-morning writing sessions by handling breakfast for the kids isn't just holding you accountable; they're actively enabling your success.

Your family can be a powerful source of accountability, especially when your Personal OKRs directly impact them. For instance, if your goal is to improve work–life balance, telling your spouse or kids can motivate you to unplug after work. They will hold you accountable, often better than you do. It's a built-in accountability system that you can't uninstall, block, or put on "Do Not Disturb."

Michael Bungay Stanier, in his book *How to Begin*, introduces the idea of a "Spouse-ish" person: a trusted individual who's not necessarily your spouse but acts as your closest confidant in your personal or professional journey.[9] This person isn't afraid to call you out when you're slipping and is deeply invested in your success. Ideally, this is someone you trust implicitly, someone who won't sugarcoat things but will also celebrate your victories along the way. A good friend will do.

Family and friends can also help you test your Personal OKRs. For example, a friend might provide feedback on whether your Objectives are realistic or if your Key Results are measurable. They can also offer encouragement and new perspectives when you hit roadblocks.

However, these relationships need careful balance. Emotional closeness creates support, but it can make tough feedback harder to give. It's also important to keep accountability talks from overshadowing other parts of your relationship.

Peers and Colleagues

Peers traveling similar paths create a valuable form of accountability. They mix understanding with a healthy challenge. This group may include colleagues working on their OKRs, members of a professional network, or anyone pursuing similar goals.

Unlike family members, they can provide objective feedback from shared experience. They know the specific challenges you're facing because they're facing them too. This creates "horizontal accountability": mutual support between equals that can be particularly motivating.

Horizontal accountability sounds like a fancy yoga pose, but it's actually just the grown-up version of "you show me yours, I'll show you mine," except instead of comparing Pokémon cards, you're comparing progress reports and celebrating each other's small victories.

These relationships work best with regular structure. Meeting weekly or monthly, sharing specific progress metrics, and maintaining consistent commitment from all members helps keep momentum. The key is finding peers with similar levels of commitment and complementary experiences who can both support and challenge you.

If you have motivated peers who share the same goal, your Accountability Partner might be even more valuable: a true "success partner." Look for partners who are already pushing their limits and taking significant risks. By teaming up with them, you can push each other further than you could alone. A "success partner" is highly motivated and seeks someone to help propel them beyond their own capabilities.[10]

Roll's training partners offered what his family could not: hands-on experience and shared challenges. The same holds for yours truly. We both challenged ourselves to be better and push the boundaries, even if that meant some heated, but well-meaning, debates. Support and healthy competition in peer groups lead to better results. This is well documented in organizational behavior and psychology.[11] The key is finding peers who share your commitment level but bring diverse perspectives to the journey.

Mentors and Coaches

Mentors or professional coaches bring expertise and objectivity. They assist you in defining clear Objectives and Key Results. Plus, they offer valuable feedback on your progress.

A good mentor will ask tough questions: "How realistic is it that you will accomplish all these Objectives in this cycle?" or "Is this really the most important Objective right now?" or "Are your Key Results measurable enough?" Having someone with experience in your corner can significantly elevate your commitment level.

A mentor oftentimes *has been there, has done that*, and got the corresponding T-shirt. He or she might have executed the exact type of challenge in his/her past that you are trying to conquer now. Mentorship adds valuable experiences to your journey. It helps you bypass common mistakes that often happen when starting something new. Mentorship tends to come with advice and concrete suggestions on how to move forward, which also means that mentorship is rather context-sensitive; you might need to seek out different types of mentors for your various Objectives. Mentors are a bit like consultants, but the good kind.

A coach might have broader experience, but they bring empathy and patience. They create a safe space for you to find your own answers, regardless of the Objectives you have. That suggests you hold the answers in your conscious or subconscious mind. It's like a mirror, a trusted space. The coach supports you by asking thoughtful questions. This helps you discover those essential answers.

Unlike friends or family, they can share uncomfortable truths without emotional ties. Their distance from your daily life helps them see patterns clearly. They suggest changes based on solid frameworks, not personal opinions.

These relationships typically involve more formal structures: scheduled meetings, progress reports, and specific feedback protocols. While they might require a (modest) financial investment, research shows that professional mentors and coaches can accelerate progress significantly compared to going it alone.[12] If you consider the costs of mistakes, a good mentor or coach offers a pretty solid return on investment.[13]

If you've never had professional mentoring or coaching, we strongly suggest you try it. It is remarkable what a trusted, empathic copilot can do. As coaches ourselves, we might be a bit biased here, though.

Therapists and Counselors

Mentors and coaches focus on moving forward. However, our biggest obstacles to success can be psychological, not just tactical. The challenges we face now may have roots in our past. Former traumas can hold us back, affecting our progress toward a high-performing future.

Counselors can help spot and fix patterns that could sabotage your efforts. They provide tools for managing stress, maintaining motivation, and building resilience.

While not directly focused on your Personal OKRs, their support often proves crucial for sustaining long-term change. They can explain why certain patterns repeat. They can also help you find strategies to break through mental blocks. On the other hand, you can use Personal OKRs to apply strategies from your therapist. For instance, you can focus on building healthy habits like journaling, meditating, and exercising.

Think of it this way: A coach is like a GPS for your future. They help you navigate from where you are to where you want to go. A therapist is more like a skilled archaeologist, helping you dig up and understand the ancient ruins of your past that might be blocking your highway to success.

Public Accountability

Broader public commitment creates a wider accountability net. By sharing your personal OKRs and progress with a larger group, you create more accountability. You can use social media, a blog, or community groups for this. Your public declarations shape your identity, making it harder to quit when challenges come up.

This approach requires careful consideration. While public accountability can be powerful, it needs to be authentic and manageable. Consider starting with a smaller public group before expanding your circle. The key is to find the right balance between privacy and transparency, accountability and oversharing, as well as visibility and vulnerability.

The internet can be a powerful accountability tool when used correctly. A personal blog and one's social media followers can provide something akin to ambient accountability: a constant background awareness that people are watching and learning from your journey. It's like having 37 invisible gym teachers silently judging you from your Instagram story views.

So, think twice before posting your next great challenge on Instagram, LinkedIn, X, or whatever else your favorite doomscrolling network might be. We're not against this. We just want you to consider the potential downsides, too. The internet does not forget, after all.

It Takes a Village

The key lesson here is that different types of accountabilities serve different purposes in your Personal OKR journey. Family provides daily support and lifestyle integration. Peers offer practical advice and mutual motivation. Mentors and coaches bring objective assessment and technical expertise. Professional support ensures sustainable progress. And public accountability adds an extra layer of commitment through transparency.

When you start building your accountability system, focus on one or two key relationships. You can expand later based on your needs. Not every goal needs all types of accountabilities. The important part is matching the right support to your specific Objectives and Key Results.

PRACTICAL STRATEGIES TO BUILD ACCOUNTABILITY INTO YOUR OKRs

Now that you know who to ask for accountability, let's look at how to add it to your Personal OKRs:

Regular Check-Ins

Accountability only works if there's a system in place for tracking progress. This is where regular check-ins come into play. Set up weekly or biweekly meetings with your Accountability Partner or group to discuss where you're at with your Personal OKRs. Checking in regularly makes all the difference between goal setting and goal achieving.

During these check-ins, review your Key Results and adjust if necessary. Are you making progress? If not, what's holding you back? This ongoing review process ensures that you're always moving forward, even if it's just a small step.

We do not suggest creating any new events. Instead, use an existing routine: the *"End of Week: Celebration."* This is a great chance to discuss your weekly achievements with your Accountability Partner. Chapter 10 shows how this and other routines help you succeed.

No time for a real chat with your Accountability Partner(s)? No worries, we're all busy. End each week with an email to keep them in the loop. List your planned wins, actual results, and important misses in bullet points. Fire it off, ask for feedback, and don't stress if replies are sporadic; some input is better than none! We placed a simple template in the Appendix for your reference.

Feedback and Adjustment

Feedback is a gift indeed, especially when it's constructive. Once you begin your Personal OKRs, be sure to ask your Accountability Partners for feedback. Are your Key Results too ambitious? Are they clear enough? Feedback is key to refining your Personal OKRs. It allows you to adjust your goals, helping you avoid wasting time on misaligned Objectives.

The feedback loop also works as a motivation booster. When you know someone is tracking your progress, you'll want to make changes if things aren't working. You'll also celebrate when they are.

Testing Your Personal OKRs

Sometimes, the best accountability comes from pressure-testing your Personal OKRs. Share your Objectives with a mentor or colleague and ask, "Does this sound realistic? Do these Key Results align with my Objective?" Getting an outside perspective helps you avoid common mistakes. You can steer clear of vague goals and hard-to-measure results.

Testing also forces you to think through the feasibility of your Personal OKRs. Remember, OKRs are meant to be ambitious but achievable. Share your ideas early. This lets you improve them before you spend too much time and energy on something that may not be possible.

Public Declarations

Remember this: Sharing your goals and progress publicly is a commitment to your audience. Making your Personal OKRs public (through a blog, social media, family events, outings with friends, or a company newsletter) creates a sense of obligation. Once you share your plans with the world, people expect you to follow through. That's really the point.

You don't have to be an ultra-athlete with millions of followers to benefit from this approach. You can share your Personal OKRs with a few friends or in a private group. The important part is to keep others informed about your goals.

When one of your dear authors was embarking upon a full-marathon training, he shared that challenge with several coworkers, who, annoyingly, kept reminding him of his upcoming journey of pain. That created a virtuous feedback loop, to not give up easily or face humiliation. Similarly, we informed our friends and colleagues about our goal to write this book. This created expectations and raised the stakes for us. People asking us about our progress was a great motivator to keep going.

Managing Potential Challenges

Even the best-designed accountability systems face challenges. Understanding these challenges in advance helps prevent relationship breakdown and maintain momentum.

You Are (Always) Awesome!

One of the most common pitfalls? Too much positivity. When Accountability Partners, like close friends or family, act more like cheerleaders than enforcers, things can go off track. Instead of keeping you on track, they turn into enablers of "productive procrastination."

Imagine Tom, who set an Objective to "Become a compelling public speaker" with a Key Result to "Deliver a TED-style talk at the company all-hands meeting." His Accountability Partner and best friend, Susan, attends his practice sessions. But their conversations go something like this:

> Tom: "How was my presentation?"
> Susan: "Oh my gosh, you're so *brave* for doing this!"
> Tom: "But what about my actual delivery?"
> Susan: "So great! I'm just so *proud* of you for putting yourself out there!"

> Tom: "I knocked over the water pitcher and accidentally showed a
> slide of my cat."
> Sarah: "That just shows how *authentic* you are! Everyone loves cats!"

A week later, Tom delivers his talk. The audience feedback forms say to "meow less" and "face the audience, not the screen." When he asks Susan why she didn't point these out, she says, "I didn't want to discourage your *journey!*"

Excessive positivity, while well-intentioned, can prevent the honest feedback needed for genuine improvement. An effective Accountability Partner mixes encouragement with helpful criticism. They point out specific areas for improvement instead of only giving broad compliments.

One popular approach is the "radical candor" framework by Kim Scott, a former executive at Google and Apple.[14] This approach combines specific and sincere praise and kind and clear criticism. When establishing accountability relationships, explicitly discuss the importance of constructive feedback.

Too Many Cooks...

Another common challenge we will call "goal diffusion." This occurs when too many Accountability Partners dilute focus and create conflicting feedback. It's like trying to follow five different GPS systems at once, each one shouting a different route. The result? Confusion, frustration, and, often, inaction.

Consider someone setting a fitness-related Personal OKR: "Transform my physical health through consistent exercise and better nutrition." Your personal trainer recommends strength training five times a week. Meanwhile, your running club partner urges you to boost your weekly mileage. Your nutritionist stresses the importance of meal planning and tracking macros. At the same time, your spouse advocates for more rest days and intuitive eating. Everyone gives good advice, but unclear boundaries can lead to confusion and overwhelm. This can ultimately lead to inaction.

The lesson? While accountability is crucial, too many voices can dilute your clarity and commitment. It's best to select one or two trusted Accountability Partners. They should share your Objectives. This is more effective than relying on a committee of well-meaning but conflicting advisors.

Assign specific domains to each partner. For example, if you train for endurance sports, your running coach should focus on technique. The nutritionist should handle diet, while your spouse can support overall life balance. This approach avoids confusion from conflicting advice on similar issues. Assigning roles based on domain context is crucial.

WHAT'S NEXT?

We are now turning to the next layer in our POKR Method, the *Execution* layer, in Part IV. Let's look at ways to merge your Personal OKRs and support system with everything else in your life.

In this section of the book, we'll look at how POKR connects your Personal OKRs to your daily routine. It helps turn inspiration into everyday action. We'll look at ways to track progress, handle setbacks, and keep moving forward as you pursue your goals.

Let's start with Chapter 9.

KEY TAKEAWAYS

1. **Accountability Boosts Success**: Publicly committing to your goals helps you stay on track. When you have clear accountability, your chances of achieving results increase.

2. **Start an Accountability System Early**: Set clear, measurable goals. Define roles, like who gives feedback and who checks in. Schedule regular check-ins from the beginning of your accountability relationships.

3. **Use a Diverse Support Network**: Turn to family and friends for encouragement. Connect with peers for shared motivation. Find mentors or coaches for expert guidance. Use public platforms, like blogs or social media, to create extra accountability.

4. **Assign Clear Accountability Roles**: To avoid confusion, give each person clear support responsibilities. Don't let five people try to guide one decision.

5. **Check-Ins Build Momentum**: Weekly or biweekly check-ins, live or not, help you stay on track. They help you celebrate small wins and adjust when necessary. Use email updates if real-time isn't workable.

6. **Ask for Feedback**: Invite constructive input on your OKRs. Expect radical candor, not just cheerleading, especially from those closest to you.

7. **Test Your OKRs Before You Commit**: Share your Objectives and Key Results with someone. Ask them, "Is this realistic?" "Would you know if I succeeded?" If not, revise.

8. **Watch for Pitfalls**: Avoid feedback that is too supportive and doesn't include critique. Limit the number of opinions you consider. Ensure that accountability expectations are clear. All can derail your progress.

9. **Structure Beats Willpower**: Accountability is strongest when it's part of your routine. Connect it to your weekly reviews, end-of-week reflections, or family planning meetings.

PART IV

EXECUTION

"There is time enough for everything in the course of the day, if you do but one thing at once, but there is not time enough in the year, if you will do two things at a time."

—LORD CHESTERFIELD

NINE

EXECUTION MATTERS

SOMETHING IS MISSING

JONATHAN DID IT BY THE BOOK: HE HAD A GREAT 5-YEAR MIS-sion that served as his North Star. He set a proper 1-Year Goal across Life Categories he cared about. We remember his wish to spend more time with his kids, don't we? He broke all this down into a few Objectives and Key Results. Even getting a motorcycle license made the list.

Still, it didn't work. The daily madness of dealing with "stuff" kept infringing on his good intentions. Those promising Key Results were half-started and half-forgotten just two hours after he wrote them down. Who would have guessed that getting a motorcycle license means finding a driving school, registering there, and buying some essential gear before mounting a bike? What about all that non–Personal OKR madness that defines our daily life?

All the energy spent defining goals felt like pure overhead. It was just going through the motions. Wasted effort? Jonathan wondered what was different from his legacy "ideas notebook." Just fancier words and colorful images. What was he missing?

VISION WITHOUT EXECUTION IS HALLUCINATION

You may have seen this headline in different forms, often linked to Thomas Edison.[1] A strong Vision or Mission, shaped by Objectives and Key Results, is only half of the journey. It may even be less than that. Think about your Personal OKRs as a good (initial) plan that now needs to be matched by a great layer of effective execution. As Mike Tyson wisely said, "Everybody has a plan until they get hit".[2]

Here's a Gentle Reminder About the POKR Method

Figure 23. The POKR Burger with a Focus in This Part on Execution

The top bun represents the Mission, manifested by your goals. Your Personal OKRs are the central part, and the bottom bun stands for the Execution components.

In Part II, we covered the different ways to give you that all-important North Star. We suggested a simple 5+1 Goal approach for the Mission layer to keep it clear and practical. In Part III, we focused on the Strategy layer. You should still remember how to create strong Objectives with effective Key Results. Starting with this chapter, we're entering Part IV where we'll look at the lower bun of the POKR Burger, the one that Jonathan in our little story above didn't, literally, execute on. Getting this right is the difference between a gourmet burger and junk food. Figure 23 highlights that section.

DO I REALLY NEED TO *DO* "EXECUTION"?

Could you skip this entire Part IV of the book, if you want to keep it high level? Absolutely. Go for the junk food, if that's your thing. However, keep in mind that for Personal OKRs to work, you need to weave them into your daily routine. It's unlikely you'll succeed without focusing on time and task management. In our experience, businesses often fail with OKRs because they didn't consider the daily impact properly. It simply didn't "stick."

When we discuss critical success factors (a consultant's way of saying what's important), a solid integration from Mission to Execution is key. Remember from Chapter 1 that linking to your existing ways of working is a core promise of POKR!

A BUSY MARKETPLACE PROMISING "PRODUCTIVITY"

The market is packed with productivity tools, methods, and approaches, often known by a three-letter acronym: GTD (Getting Things Done), we're looking at you.[3] Each one promises to transform how you manage your time and tasks. Yet, many of us find these systems fall short. Why is that? Because productivity isn't the same for everyone. We all think, work, and perceive time differently. What works wonderfully for one person can feel awkward or ineffective for another.

This is why it's crucial to find a system that suits you. The ideal one should fit your personality, habits, and goals. This creates a natural flow instead of a forced one. The good news is that whatever method you choose, or even one you already use, can easily integrate with POKR.

But first, let's consider how our individual brain wiring affects our choice of productivity tools.

MOST TECHNIQUES ARE "BIASED"

Let's face it, most productivity systems come with built-in preferences. They assume we're all wired the same way: logical, structured, single-tasking go-getters. But we're not. Personality assessments like Myers–Briggs, DISC, and OCEAN show that our personalities vary widely.[4] Yet the productivity world tends to favor the "left brain" type: people who thrive on order, lists, and linear thinking.[5] That's why systems like GTD and time-blocking work great for some but feel like a straitjacket for others. While the left brain/right brain theory has been debunked by neuroscience,[6] the broader point still holds: our thinking preferences shape which tools feel intuitive and which feel like wearing someone else's shoes.[7]

Another big bias? Perception of time. Most productivity advice comes from cultures (think Germany, the US, Japan) where doing one thing at a time is the gold standard, known as monochronic time perception.[8] These tools promote time-blocking, batching, and focusing on one task until it's done. But not everyone works that way, especially creatives, leaders, and anyone juggling competing priorities. People from polychronic cultures (Latin America, Africa, the Middle East) often switch between tasks fluidly and value relationships over rigid schedules.[9] For them, rigid planning tools can feel not just awkward but downright counterproductive.

Finally, many tools lean toward convergent thinking: solving problems efficiently with one clear answer.[10] That's helpful when filing taxes or planning groceries, but not so great when your work thrives on innovation and open-ended exploration. If your best ideas come while shower-thinking or doodling on napkins, chances are a structured matrix won't capture your magic. Creative and divergent thinkers often find that traditional time management advice doesn't leave room for serendipity or flow. What they need isn't tighter control, it's more breathable space.

Figure 24 summarizes these divergent traits.

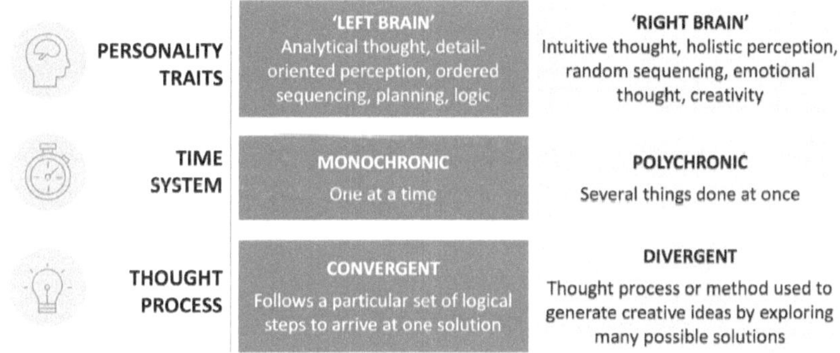

Figure 24. We Are All Wired Differently, Which in Turn Impacts Our Choice of and Effectiveness in Using Productivity Tools.

You see the problem, right?

To stereotype a bit: If you are a Western introvert with an analytical personality, time and task management techniques are your playground. If you differ from this mix, it may be more challenging. If you're creative, or in a polychronic environment, traditional methods can feel too rigid. They may restrict flexibility and nonlinear problem-solving. Also, they can limit your ability to respond to new opportunities.

What's the solution? If you don't naturally work in a left brain, monochronic, convergent way, you might benefit from:

- **Nonlinear productivity tools**: Mind maps, Kanban Boards, whiteboards
- **Time-blocking with flexibility**: Loose scheduling, buffer zones

- **Energy-based task management**: Working in cycles, not rigid slots
- **Polychronic-friendly techniques**: Context-based work, thematic scheduling
- **Divergent-friendly systems**: Creative time buffers, incubation periods

Just remember that there is no right or wrong here, no better or worse. Just personal preferences. It's also not black or white: Every individual will be somewhere on a scale for these dimensions. Gender, cultural factors, etc. all play a role. We're sharing these dimensions to show that you need to find the time and task management methods that work for you.

But independently of your preferences, POKR will be able to support you. Many popular time and task management techniques attempt to address execution challenges. We don't want to leave you to navigate this alone. Just like with the top bun, we'll share our practical perspective without imposing anything. If you already use time and task management techniques that work for you, let's integrate them!

At its core, execution deals with two questions:

1. **Task**: *What* work I do. This means defining, prioritizing, executing, and visualizing it.

2. **Time**: *When* I do the work. This involves cadence, events, calendarizing actions, and routines.

These two are obviously closely linked, so we'll be jumping between them a bit. For example, the visual Kanban system integrates both views in a process view, and your humble to-do list is typically for a specific time block, mostly a day.

TASKS: WE LOVE *SIMPLE*

Regardless of how your brain functions, we must outline the "work" needed to finish a Key Result and the Objective. Let's simplify this:

Figure 25. Mini-Hierarchy

We call the Execution layer a collection of "Tasks." These are the actual "work" activities needed to achieve a Key Result. Think of it as a simple "Key Result → Task" hierarchy, or a 1:n cardinality for the math enthusiasts here. Figure 25 shows this mini-hierarchy.

A "Task" is the lowest level in our POKR Method. Ideally, each Task should be achievable within a day or small increments of a day. That's 8 hours for a normal human. If a Task needs more than a day, it's probably a collection of Tasks itself. This approach pushes you to think in small, manageable pieces of work. It breaks down a Key Result into elements that can be executed rapidly.

This also helps you estimate the work needed for a Key Result. It gives you a nice dopamine boost when you complete a Task. Finishing a Task and feeling proud of it is rewarding. It's the little things that make life worthwhile.

It probably does sound a bit time-consuming to do this, and it might indeed be. But as Dale Carnegie supposedly said, "An hour of planning can save you 10 hours of doing." The advantages clearly outweigh the effort to put it in place. Give it a go. After a cycle or two, it will become second nature. The first one is going to be rocky, but that's true for anything new.

How many Tasks are a good volume per Key Result? That depends on the complexity of the Key Result, but you probably want to land at a maximum of seven Tasks. Anything beyond is leading to a cognitive overload, and we don't want that.

The link between Tasks and Personal OKRs is the backbone of an effective goal execution. Linking Tasks to Key Results enables effective prioritization, time allocation, and better progress tracking. Without defined Tasks, how else would you achieve this?

A general caveat when we deep-dive into the Execution components:

We generally focus on Tasks linked to Personal OKRs, not on non-OKR work. Some of the techniques we outline may also work for non-Personal OKRs. So, feel free to use them there, too. We discuss non-OKR touchpoints in various sections. Chapter 12 shows how to use GTD and Kanban Boards for non–Personal OKR Tasks. However, we will mostly avoid that topic. It's too broad for a clear, prescriptive stance.

So, let's begin with simplicity. You can then "evolve" in your Personal OKR journey, starting with the basics.

Tasks Definition: The KISS Minimum

As a minimum, you'll need a simple list of Tasks under each Key Result. Without this, execution isn't possible, leading to the issues we mentioned earlier. Other components, such as prioritization techniques, calendar integration, and the Kanban Board, represent advanced practices. They are optional in that sense.

There are various ways we can deal effectively with the Task layer beneath Key Results. Some are rather basic whereas others might require a bit more explanation. "Keep It Simple, Stupid" (KISS) falls clearly in the former category.

In KISS, every Task is equally important.[11] A Task is something that must be done to achieve the Key Result. No need to focus too much on priorities or importance.

To get the Key Result done, brainstorm the activities you need. List them and link each one to the Key Result. Every Task has equal weight in contributing to the Key Result. This should take you no longer than 10 minutes for each Key Result. You already put a lot of effort into creating great Objectives and strong Key Results. So, why wear yourself out by overthinking Tasks? This method is for you if you want to finish the job quickly.

Let's see how KISS could apply to a past example. Recall Jonathan's language learning Objective from Chapter 6. Let's see how a mini-hierarchy of Objective → Key Results → Tasks looks:

[O] **Speak basic conversational Spanish to prepare for our South America trip**

[KR] Completed 100 hours of Spanish study using apps, textbooks, online courses

[T] *Download a primary language-learning app (Duolingo, Babbel, etc.)*

[T] *Enroll in an online Spanish course (Coursera, Udemy, a structured B1 course)*

[T] *Use spaced repetition flash cards (e.g., Anki, Quizlet) for vocabulary building*

[T] *Practice grammar exercises from a textbook or website (e.g., SpanishDict)*

[KR] Had 30 real-time conversations with native Spanish speakers, each lasting at least 15 minutes

[T] *Find language exchange partners on apps like Tandem, HelloTalk, or Italki*

[T] *Join a local or virtual Spanish conversation group (Meetup, Facebook groups)*

[T] *Schedule at least two conversation sessions per week with native speakers*

[T] *Practice grammar exercises from a textbook or website (e.g., SpanishDict)*

[T] *Prepare topic lists with useful phrases before each conversation*

[T] *Incorporate new vocabulary from conversations into a routine*

[KR] Watched 50 hours of Spanish-language content (movies, TV, YouTube videos) with subtitles

[T] *Create a watchlist of Spanish-language movies, series, and YouTube channels*

[T] *Use Spanish subtitles instead of English to improve comprehension*

[T] *Listen to Spanish podcasts (Duolingo Spanish Podcast, Coffee Break Spanish)*

[KR] Scored 80% or higher on a B1 level Spanish proficiency test

[T] *Take an initial online placement test to assess current level*

[T] *Register for a recognized B1 Spanish test (e.g., DELE, SIELE)*

[T] *Use mock exams to familiarize with test format*

WHAT'S AHEAD: STRUCTURE OF PART IV ON EXECUTION

To go deeper on time and task management, we divide this topic into related subsections that build on one another. Figure 26 also shows that these form the core components of the Execution layer of POKR:

Figure 26. Execution Level of POKR Has Some Good Practices That We Offer You to Choose From. No Obligations Though.

We will cover these components in the separate chapters that follow:

1. Chapter 10: **Cadence** Makes Productivity Sustainable (Over Time)
2. Chapter 11: **To-Do** Lists: **Organize** Tasks Basics
3. Chapter 12: **Calendar** Integration
4. Chapter 13: **Kanban Boards**: Visualize Task **Flow**
5. Chapter 14: **Habit Formation** with POKR: A Match Made in **Productivity Heaven**

And as promised, we aren't forcing any of the above on you. You might have actually used some of these techniques already before today. Perfect! The idea is that you can continue to do so, just under the POKR umbrella.

In fact, most of what follows here is optional. If you have a particular time and task management system in place that works for you, maybe only consider the chapters that relate to how to integrate Personal OKRs into that. For example, if you are using a personal Kanban Board for task management, skip over to Chapter 13 to learn how to manage your Personal OKRs in that system. If you are using to-do lists instead, check out Chapters 11 and 12.

If you are still looking for help in choosing approaches or considering changing what you do, read on. Whatever you do, we do recommend you read the chapters on cadences and habit formation, as they are key components to getting POKR right.

In the remainder of this chapter, we quickly run through the content of Chapters 10 through 14, to help orient you. You can then decide where to deep-dive in, later.

STANDARD ROUTINES ARE YOUR BEST FRIEND

OKRs stand out from other strategy frameworks because they require standard routines as a cadence. That's a fancy way of saying that we need to perform certain actions that just happen to take place in reoccurring time intervals: for example, weekly.

This is a key POKR component. We got inspiration from the OKR concept used in businesses, first. Then, we combined ideas from Lean, quality, Agile, and the startup world. The result is a pragmatic set of standard routines!

The intention is to focus only on the relevant questions, at the relevant time (i.e., you don't need to worry about your yearly goals when you are reviewing your weekly progress). Neither do you want to think about the next quarterly POKR cycle when you plan the current one. *Reducing your cognitive load* is the technical way of expressing that concept.[12] It's a repeating theme that will be with us several times.

POKR routines take place on a yearly, quarterly, monthly, weekly, and if you really want, daily level. An example for the yearly routine cascade is visualized in Figure 27.

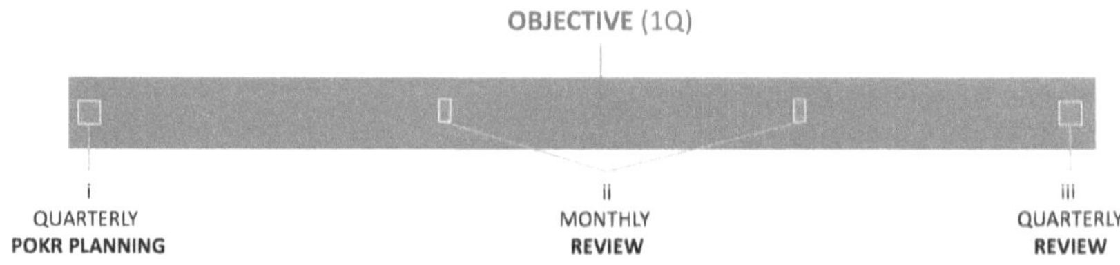

Figure 27. Quarterly Routine Example of POKR

But let's be honest: It takes some discipline to pull this off successfully. Funnily enough, the fact that these routines are standardized, and occur at clearly defined time intervals, helps dramatically to create a rhythm where the right action takes place at the right time. Hence, also the name, "cadence."

"Left brain" individuals will love this right away. You likely organize your life this way already. "Right brain" types may find it harder to grasp at first. However, the prescriptive nature of POKR routines will help them, too.

Having a standard routine etched on your calendar sparks self-accountability. Chapter 10 provides specific details on the suggested routines that will help you get going and stay on track with your Personal OKRs.

TO-DO LISTS: THE BASICS OF ORGANIZING TASKS

TASK	STATUS
A	✓
B	✗
C	✓

Figure 28. To-Do List

A collection of Tasks defined with the KISS approach forms a list. A simple list, that is. A list of Tasks, or: a To-Do List. And these are popular. Very! Most people have a love-hate relationship with them though. But they can be very powerful, if used appropriately.

Not every Task is equally important. This book is full of wisdom like this. We know. While a KISS-based To-Do List might be a good start, experience shows that they quickly become a problem, simply because they are so one-dimensional: They lack depth and nuance.

To improve this, we need to introduce some gray areas. This is where prioritization methods come in. There are several, such as MoSCoW, ABCDE, and the well-known Eisenhower Matrix. Each method helps you assign a priority to a Task. Once you do that, you'll know where to start.

We give you the rundown on what makes To-Do Lists so useful, and how POKR boosts their benefits while reducing drawbacks. We cover specifics on that in Chapter 11.

CALENDAR INTEGRATION AND TIME TRACKING

JAN	FEB	MAR

Figure 29. Calendar Integration

Prioritizing Tasks is a great way to focus on the right actions first. But how do we ensure we complete work on time? This is where proper time management is important. It has two key aspects:

First, put your work on the calendar. When Tasks are visible in a place you check often, they are more likely to get done. This is better than simply letting them sit on a busy To-Do List. The goal is to link Tasks from your To-Do List to your calendar. This helps reveal any scheduling conflicts. "Calendar Integration" is one of the most effective ways to get things done.

Second, once you've been through a quarterly cycle, how well did you do? How good was your assessment of the complexity of a Task, its priority, and its placement on the timeline? What can you learn from one cycle to the next, to get better? "Time Tracking" is where we discuss this.

Both will be covered in Chapter 12.

KANBAN BOARDS: VISUALIZE TASK FLOW

If a dry bullet list of Tasks is not your thing, if you're a more visual type of person, then Kanban Boards could be your approach of choice. The goal is to organize work on a board with columns and swim lanes and visualize this in a way that you can always see and with which you can interact with what you need to work on. This helps you focus on the most important Tasks first. In simple terms, work flows from left to right on the board.

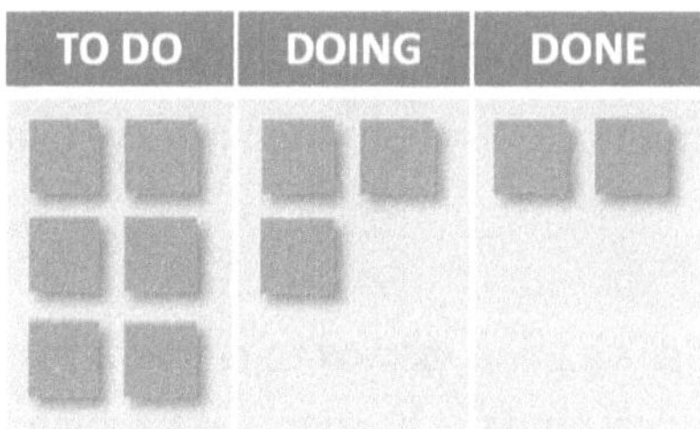

Figure 30. A Standard Kanban Board

The simplest version of a Kanban Board looks like Figure 30.

POKR uses the Kanban method to help you focus on what needs your attention now. This is useful even when many Objectives and Key Results are in progress.

We provide a great way to track your Personal OKRs and other important areas of your life. Chapter 13 explains how POKR uses Kanban techniques. It combines Personal OKRs and other Tasks into one clear view.

HABIT FORMATION WITH POKR:
A MATCH MADE IN PRODUCTIVITY HEAVEN!

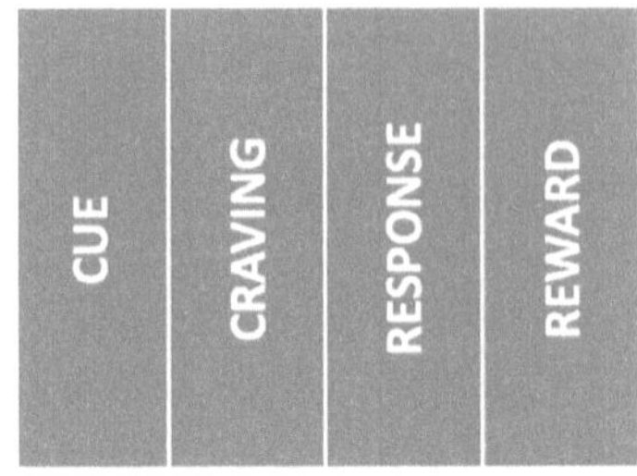

Figure 31. A Habit-Forming Process

Want to quit smoking? Want to start a fitness routine? Need a better sleep schedule? These targets fall into the "new habit forming" category. Forming a new habit can be tough. We've all been there. Many popular books have been written about it, and countless TED Talks cover the topic.[13] Let's not forget the self-help industry (yes, life coaches, you try to help, too).

What's often missing is a good *method* to *establish* that desired habit. It's not that we don't understand the barriers for forming and sustaining new habits, or that there's no process for it (cue-craving-response-reward for the *Atomic Habits* fans out there). But we might simply lack the required *scaffolding* to effectively *execute* on it.

So, what practical, all-in-one method can help us? You guessed it. POKR is made to help you set and achieve effective Objectives. Forming new habits is one type of Objective. Plus, developing a habit fits perfectly into a quarterly Personal OKR cycle. It also needs regular check-ins to keep them going. POKR provides all this right from the start.

So, POKR is the method to formulate, establish, and sustain new habits. Why would you want to do that separately via a different pathway? If it's important, and new habits usually are, it is meant to be part of a Personal OKR anyway.

Chapter 14 tells you all the details on how that will work.

WHAT'S NEXT?

Next, we are going to cover the importance of proper standard routines in detail in Chapter 10 to provide a pragmatic *time* scaffolding.

This is a really important, "crunchy" part of the book with lots of exciting details to munch on!

KEY TAKEAWAYS

1. **Execution Is the Missing Piece**: Even with clear Personal OKRs, poor execution leads to failure. Targets need to be actively integrated into daily life through structured action.

2. **Time and Task Management Are Essential**: Successful execution relies on managing both when to work on targets (time) and what to work on (Tasks). Without these, Personal OKRs remain ideas rather than results.

3. **One-Size Productivity Systems Don't Fit All**: Traditional time/task management techniques often favor structured, "left brain," monochronic thinkers. Adapt systems that fit your personality, work style, and cultural preferences.

4. **Break Down Key Results into Smaller, Manageable Tasks**: Ideally, completable in a day, these Tasks provide clarity, prevent overwhelm, and create motivation.

5. **Use Routines and Task Prioritization to Stay on Track**: Standard weekly, monthly, and quarterly routines ensure consistency.

6. **The Execution Framework Offers Flexible Approaches**: This includes simple To-Do Lists, task prioritization techniques, calendar integration, Kanban Boards, and habit formation methods. Use what works for your personal style.

CADENCE MAKES PRODUCTIVITY SUSTAINABLE

THE ROAD TO SUCCESS REQUIRES A GOOD RHYTHM!

ONE OF THE AUTHORS' STRATEGY PROFESSORS USED TO say that "the road to success is paved with the roadkill of good intentions".[1] It did stick with me, Prof. Gupta. See? I did pay attention in class!

We've journeyed far in shaping a meaningful life Mission. We detailed effective Objectives and Key Results. We also explored how to connect these targets to your day-to-day reality.

Having done just that, Natasha felt great about her POKR implementation: Having an awesome 5-Year Goal in place, the 1-Year version has been established too, and she came up with a set of stretchy yet inspiring Objectives and Key Results for the first quarter, not forgetting that the

Key Results she wants to focus on have a nice list of Tasks underneath them. She's pumped to see her life take a structured turn for the better!

That feeling wasn't long-lived, though: By the middle of the second month, most of her Tasks were still incomplete, and some were simply not updated. The Key Result parents (read: Objective) were in different states of desolation, most simply outdated, too. And let's not even look at the Objectives; they were aspirational in the beginning but turned into an impossible mountain to climb. The quarter was halfway gone already, but her Objectives still looked innocently blank. The 5-Year and 1-Year Goals that got her going started to feel abstract and out of reach. What again was the difference to her yearly New Year's resolution situation, she wondered?

None of the Mission and Strategy pieces, and we are serious here, *none* of them matter if you don't wrap a rhythm of routines around them. The OKR framework is one of the few goal-setting frameworks out there that has clear expectations of "cadences." This means you need to plan and check your Personal OKRs often. It helps you stay focused on the right actions and allows you to learn from mistakes.

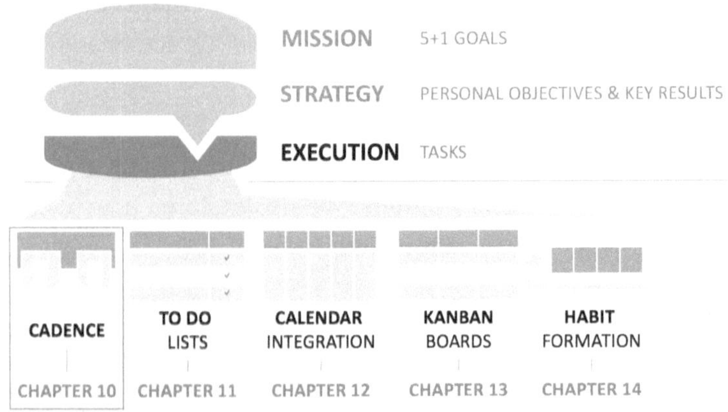

Figure 32. Execution Layer of POKR with Its Components

Figure 32 outlines where we are in the POKR Execution context. You remember from Chapter 9 that we really support adding Personal OKRs to daily routines. So, let's attack that problem and establish a sustainable rhythm to plan, refine, and review our Personal OKRs.

A SET OF ROUTINES

Even though the theory of Personal OKRs is relatively simple, there is still a minimum complexity that you must master. But as you have learned by now, not everything has to happen at the same time; let's recall the elephant that we didn't want to eat in one piece.

We can create a nicely scheduled set of routines that serve as timeboxes in which targeted action must take place. A snug corset, if you will. It makes you face the music often, but it does so efficiently, so it won't feel too heavy. Reducing the cognitive load is the aim here, distributing it over the timeline instead of looking at it "in bulk." A "breathable" corset it is.

Something we can borrow from the startup world: regularly inspecting and adapting. This drives the agile mindset we're often asked to show. The ability to "pivot" on short notice can only occur if we create opportunities to reflect and course-correct, if needed.

And for all the English majors out there: We use "routine," "event," and "cadence" as synonyms. They all refer to a set, recurring item in your diary.

OKR CYCLE = *ONE* QUARTER

Before we dive into the specifics of the recommended routines, let's briefly agree on what a Personal OKR "cycle" is. Considering that we ask you to inspect and adapt regularly, it is important to know when a cycle "resets."

Many ideas exist, but we have strong opinions on what makes sense. You didn't read this book to dive into an academic debate about several conflicting views, did you?

A Personal OKR cycle is quarterly. Full stop. Why? A quarter is a solid time frame to achieve progress on a midsize personal goal. A month would be too short, half a year or a year way too large (New Year's resolution coming back here?).

So, our simplified planning horizons are shown in Figure 33.

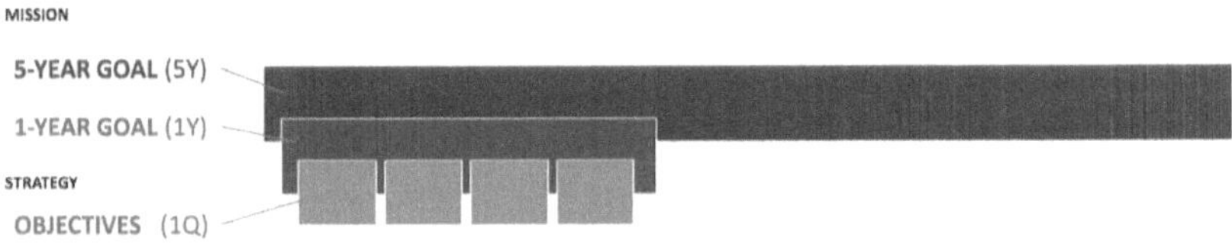

Figure 33. Simplified Planning Horizons

Some people advocate for a monthly OKR cycle, but we believe that approach is unnecessarily painful: It will require quite frequent plannings and reviews. It furthermore makes your Objectives (unnecessarily) smallish and only gives you a month to make significant progress on targets. Try to learn a foreign language in a month. Or prep for an endurance event. Or get your finances sorted. Maybe it's just us, but there's a difference between ambition and delusion.

Quarterly reflections also help us step back and see the big picture. They let us recalibrate our priorities. It's the sweet spot. Hence, we strongly advocate for a quarterly cycle, *but* with added Monthly Reviews. That way you get the best out of both worlds, kind of. Feel free to go for a monthly Personal OKR cycle, though, if you are okay with the mentioned downsides.

Figure 34 summarizes this; a year hence consists of four quarterly Personal OKR cycles:

Figure 34. Goals Vis-à-vis Objectives

Here's a simple list of the eight standard POKR routines. You can also find a table view in the Appendix for a quick overview of all:

YEARLY	Goal Setting, Review
QUARTERLY	POKR Planning, Review
MONTHLY	Review
WEEKLY	Commitment, Celebration
DAILY	Check-Ins (Optional)

We advocate for a fixed schedule here: i.e., you must schedule these for an entire year in advance. The advantage is that you don't have to *think* about your routines anymore after that. They are already in your calendar, planned ahead of time. For more on this, check Chapter 12 about the importance of timeboxing and calendar integration. A consistent rhythm clearly beats sporadic intensity.[2]

But of course, when "life" happens, feel free to push them out of the way for a day or two. Even the best discipline is faced at times with insurmountable obstacles. Yes, our kids' soccer practice at times overwrote the best-schedule planning routine, too. Don't sweat it.

You might think that eight events feel a bit excessive. Actually, they aren't. They're spaced out across the year, and each one has a specific purpose. If you add up all the events for the year, you'll find you spend less time on POKR routines than binge-watching just one season of your favorite TV series. Plus, you'll get your life back in order. Not a bad ROI, we'd think.

Thankfully, they all tend to follow a rather similar pattern. You have a routine at the beginning as well as at the end of a period, plus some interim check-ins in between, when appropriate:

- At the beginning we *plan* what we want to do.
- In between we *check* if we are on track.
- At the end we do a final *review* and *learn* our lessons for the next cycle.

The science behind this comes from the lean and quality movement. It's known as the Plan-Do-Check-Act cycle, or PDCA: you plan the work, execute it, check in if it worked out fine, and (counter-)act if it didn't.[3]

But let's dive into each of these routines to understand the mechanics better. We'll take a zoom-in approach here, starting with yearly ones, before going down to quarterly, monthly, weekly, and the optional daily one.

This is obviously not how you actually "live" them when implementing POKR: You can't first execute the entire year before going to quarter, etc. Would make for a strange journey. So, we'd recommend you read through the entire section, first, to get an understanding of how these routines work and how they are nicely integrated with each other. Then, you'd come back to them when you want to act on them.

Sound like a plan?

Yearly: All About Goals!

Probably the most potent routines happen at the beginning and end of the year. They are all related to your goals and help you calibrate the year toward the right focus, plus look back at your achievements, including learning for the next year. Figure 35 shows the cross-section of a year.

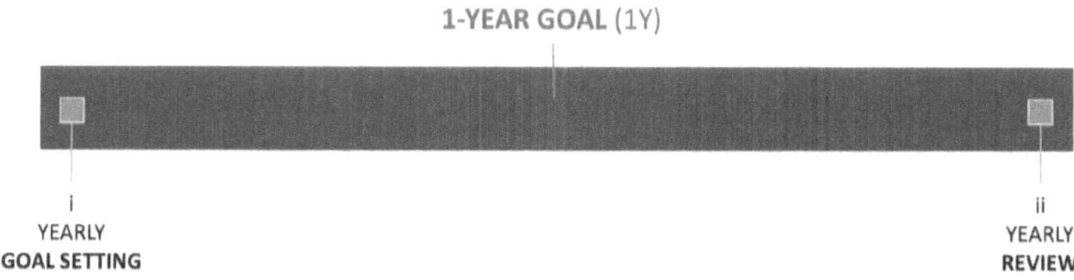

Figure 35. Yearly Routines

i. Yearly Goal Setting

The first "installment" of our dual events happens early every year. It helps us set our goals in the beginning. It's a maximum 2-hour event that occurs in the first week or thereabouts. Think of this routine as replacing your New Year's resolution musings. So maybe do the goal-setting routine on January 2, to have a recovery day in between?

At a minimum you'd need your 5-Year Goal as input, which tends to still be valid given that it has a 5-year horizon. As an output, you'll craft a single-line goal, which can guide you in the year that lies ahead. As a 1-Year Goal example, let's take Rahul's from Chapter 5:

> [G] **Strengthen family bonds through regular quality time, improve health through better habits and exercise, and enhance financial stability with strategic planning and passive income. Professionally, aim at career growth through certification, mentorship, and public speaking, while also nurturing personal passions like woodworking, writing, and community volunteering.**

It's best not to plan in isolation. Instead, involve a trusted friend or two. If this is your second yearly run or more, remember to include lessons from past cycles. Check out the Yearly Review event that follows for help with this.

Plus: Probably wise to share the outcomes with close family members. Print it out and hang it onto the fridge maybe? They need to understand your priorities clearly. Sometimes, they benefit from certain activities, and at other times, they must grasp the trade-off decisions you've made. We cover this in Chapter 15 as well.

The POKR Canvas (Figure 9) is a good way to bring it all together onto a single page, to remind you about your life's Mission and how to get closer to it across the year. A simple template is in the Appendix.

ii. Yearly Review

Now, let's pretend that the year is over (it passed fast, didn't it?). A lot of great action lies behind you. Congratulations! Let's see how you were doing. This routine has a dual purpose: *What* did I achieve, and *how* did I get here?

We spend a bit more time on this here: The intent and logic is very similar on the quarterly level, too. So, we keep it a bit more compact in those sections.

What Did I Achieve?

As with the other Monthly and Quarterly Review routines (see the respective sections that follow), you want to check on your progress in this maximum 1-hour routine, but here across the whole year, not just a month or quarter. The focus is on how you performed toward your goal(s).

Because your Personal Objectives and Key Results are already nicely updated from the Quarterly Reviews, you want to scan for overall results and reflect on outcomes, efforts, and growth achieved. Some sample questions you may ask yourself:

- What new Objectives and Key Results did I create "on the go" instead of preplanning them?
- Did the Objectives still matter by year-end? Why or why not?
- What Objectives truly moved the needle toward my goal(s)?
- Was I ambitious enough to drive intended growth?
- How true was I to my Mission?
- Where did I fall short on my ambition? Why?
- How balanced where the Objectives across my Life Categories?

Rahul, for instance, notices that his goal around "community volunteering" was not well represented beyond the first quarter. What looked important at the beginning of the year didn't get enough attention afterward. He made a note to do a more balanced job for the next year, or possibly question if this part of the goal was really important to him.

Theoretically, there's a lot of statistical "voodoo" one could imagine as part of a Review: Quarterly percentage of achievement, goal contributions based on Life Categories, etc. Your POKR Canvas can be a great foundation for some data analytics. Couldn't we create averages now per quarter, plot quarter-by-quarter changes, and maybe have a trend line across the year? Probably, but you'd mix apples with oranges and throw in some expired raisins. An odd fruit salad is the result. How can we take a finance Objective and average that with two relationship Objectives, for instance? The resulting "score" would be rather meaningless.

Let's keep this simple: What was your Objectives achievement across the year, did you hit your stretch target threshold (70%+), and what does that say about your goals? So, go easy on this and use the POKR Canvas to simply show your percentage result per Objective, maybe color-code it a bit (green: above threshold, red: below threshold), and focus on judging if that got you closer to fulfilling your Mission. And if not, consider what to do differently next year.

For those who still want advanced traffic light visuals and percentage-magic, we have some ideas on our website for you.

How Did I Get Here?

Where the Review looked at the outcomes in terms of achievement, we also want to look at the way you got here. This is called a Retrospective (from retro = backward looking).

You want to treat this as a judgment-free space to think back, along the lines of: what I need to stop doing, what I should start, and let's continue things that work well.

There are several popular Retrospective formats out there, but let's KISS this: Just add some bullet-pointed items to bring into your next yearly planning cycle. A simple "start," "stop," "continue" format is available in the Appendix.

You can, by the way, use the same tracker for all Retrospectives, whether quarterly or yearly. This keeps learning at the forefront every time.

Rahul, for instance, noticed that it took him considerable efforts to "brief" his life partner on his targets for the year, once he had them defined. For next year, he'll simply involve her in the journey right away ("start doing"). Furthermore, he notices that he deliberately stuck to the quarterly timeboxes, even though that sometimes meant "failing" on Key Results ("continue doing"). We are obviously big fans of Rahul's!

You might think to yourself: [*insert favorite son of god*], *this is so overengineered*. Why would I not simply stick to reviewing my past achievements and move on? We forgive you for thinking that way.

The power of incremental change only works well if we make conscious time to learn lessons on *how* we went about things. The last thing you want to do is be on autopilot with something that doesn't work for you. So, use Retrospectives as an opportunity to tweak your own way of working for the better, to experiment.

That's why we have it on all levels of the method. A continuous improvement approach is at the heart of POKR!

It's smart to hold Q4's Quarterly Review and Yearly Review back-to-back. This keeps their unique purposes intact (looking at a single quarterly result versus an overall yearly goal achievement) but also keeps your diary tidy.

Quarterly: POKR, Here We Come!

Here we are at the core of what POKR represents: the quarterly setting of Personal Objectives and Key Results! A quarterly cycle allows enough time to make real progress without feeling overwhelmed.

Similar to the yearly timebox, the quarterly one includes key routines: It begins with *planning* and concludes with a Review. Plus, there's a Monthly Review that fits in between. Figure 36 showcases that.

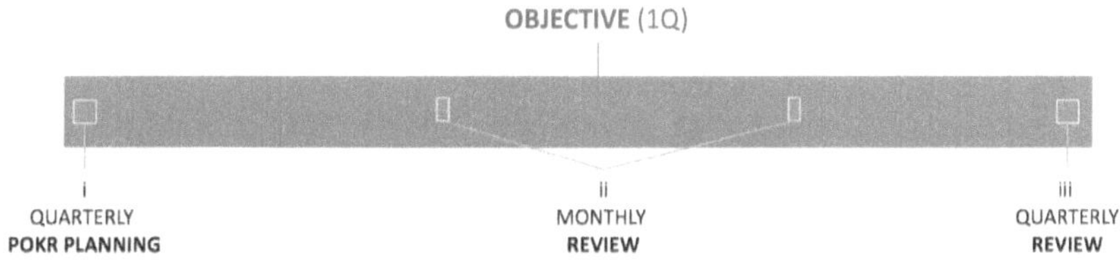

Figure 36. Quarterly Routines

i. Quarterly POKR Planning

This is the meaty piece of POKR! Personal OKRs are defined here, focusing on the upcoming quarter that has just started. Perform this maximum 1-hour routine right at the beginning of the new quarter, ideally in its first day(s). You're already familiar with the practical advice on how to formulate effective Personal OKRs.

If you completed previous cycles, you'll have insights and reflections from the most recent one. Let's factor those into the definition of your new cycle's Personal OKRs! For instance, you might have failed on some Objectives (happens to the best of us…), but you really don't want to give up on them. That's okay; it's fair to "roll over" (partial) Objectives or Key Results from one cycle to the other, if you deem them important enough.

Just make sure you consider the learnings from the past cycle in the refinement of Personal OKRs for the new one. What made you "fail" selective Objectives or Key Results? What would you want to do differently this time around to drive up the chances for success?

We acknowledge that sometimes Objectives form a "chain," whereas it might take multiple quarters to get you to a serious outcome. Writing this book, for instance, was a set of connected Objectives that needed to fall into place to bring you this beautiful result! Each individual Objective, though, was in itself contained in a three-month timebox. We would never violate our own rules, would we?

Key Results may sometimes lack clarity, which creates ambiguity. At other times, they can be unrealistically tough. Dial them up or down for the new cycle.

As an outcome of this routine, you want to have defined Personal OKRs for some categories, but not necessarily all. Remember: better to have a small number of powerful targets that you nail rather than too many that set you up for failure.

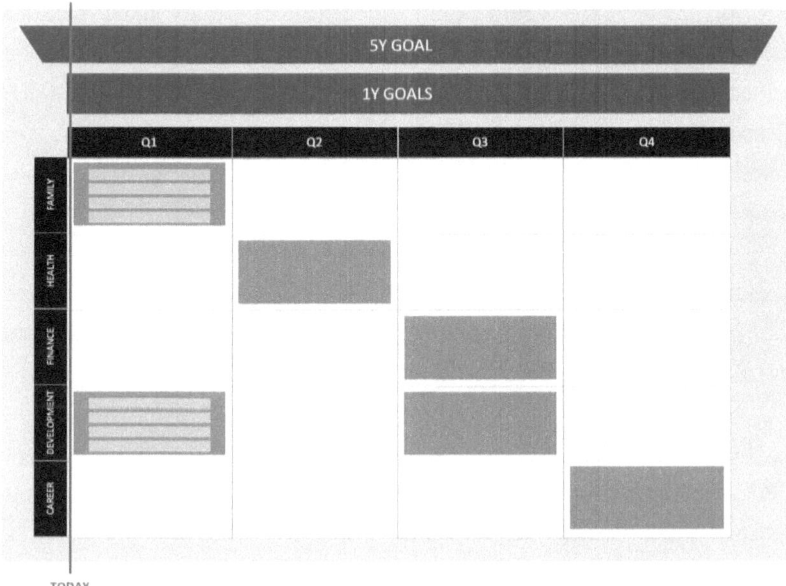

Figure 37. POKR Canvas, Example

Figure 37 is a reminder of Jonathan's planning approach from Chapter 2. His choice was to focus on just two Personal OKRs for the Quarterly Planning at the start of Q1. Therefore, some Life Category swim lanes will remain empty. That's perfectly fine; you won't have (to have) a Personal OKR in every quarter for every category.

As a general guidance, one to two Personal OKRs for a quarter are cool. If you can't stop yourself from defining multiple Personal OKRs per category and have filled all swim lanes, maybe you're biting off too much. Please remember: focus, focus, focus.

Especially when you start a new year, you have an empty POKR Canvas ahead of you. It can be tempting to try to fill the whole grid with Objectives. Please resist that! The strength of an inspect and adapt philosophy lies in taking it one step, cycle, or quarter at a time. Learn lessons each time before moving on to the next cycle. So, focus on the quarter at hand.

But you knew there would be an exception! There are likely personal milestones this year that are already set (an upcoming wedding, major relocation, etc.). You might want to use these for your Personal OKRs already: Add them to your POKR Canvas early in the year. Let's call them "Candidate OKRs." Thanks to Marty Cagan for this idea![4] The limitation: No Key Results, please, yet. Only Objectives.

"Candidate OKRs" are drafty in nature and will need to be refined. Reword them, define Key Results underneath, etc. when you hit that corresponding quarter as part of your planning routine.

At the end of this event, you commit yourself to the defined Personal OKRs! To signify that step, you'll want to give the respective Key Results a "Confidence Factor," i.e., how likely you are to achieve them. There are different ways to express that, but good practice is a scale from 1 to 10. If you have no idea (yet), go with the midpoint (= 5). And as you remember from Chapter 6, a 70% or 0.7 achievement is the target for an Objective. So, not all Key Results will have to come through to fulfill an Objective.

And then: Off you go. Make the magic happen!

ii. Monthly Review

A quarter is a great timebox to make meaningful progress, but it is a bit too long to simply find out at the end of 3 months that you missed a critical Key Result. That would be a shame, especially if there is still room to course-correct!

This monthly routine is maximum 30 minutes long. It allows you to take stock on where you are with your Key Results for this quarter, if you made the right progress, or if you must double down on some. It's an opportunity to inspect and adapt halfway through.

The steps are the usual ones, for Objectives of the current quarter:

1. Scan their Key Results and judge the progress across the respective Tasks lists.

2. If a Key Result is done: Congratulations, mark it as "complete." Also update the Objective with an improved progress (i.e., if now two out of three Key Results are done, the Objective is moved from 33% to 66% "complete").

3. If a Key Result is not done (yet): (Re)look at the confidence factor (scale 1–10) and dial that up or down with your newfound insights. You might also want to review any deadline that is assigned, if it is still realistic or if you want to shift it out (but within the quarterly cycle, please). And just for clarity: A half-done Key Result will not contribute to your Objective percentagewise. No partial credits, sorry.

4. Finally, scan the Objectives and see if your confidence in them has changed after the above adjustments (i.e., is it now more or less likely that you'll achieve them?). Tweak your confidence factor (1–10), similar to what you just did on the Key Results level.

Considering that a quarter has consistently 3 months (awesome how predictable things are at times), you'll do two Monthly Reviews. The third month is covered by the Quarterly Review itself.

It might be tempting to change some *in-flight* Personal OKRs as part of the Review. Please don't do that. Take them as they are. You will get a chance to learn your lessons at the end of the cycle. Then, you can choose a different path for the next cycle(s). If you would (be allowed) to change Personal OKRs midway through a cycle you'd deprive yourself of the possible learning that comes out of it.

Let's face the music. It may sound disharmonic, but it's better than creating a "moving target." Sure, that might look prettier, but it no longer reflects reality. Stay the course for the cycle and adjust only beyond as part of your next cycles' planning routine. A bit of pain is part of the journey!

Valid exceptions and nuances to in-flight changes are described a bit further down in this chapter.

iii. Quarterly Review

The quarter is over. Time to look at *what* you achieved, and *how* you got here. Like in the Monthly Review, update your Key Results and the Objectives above them.

But it is also an opportunity to assess your journey. You can figure out what to continue doing and what you need to adjust. It's about observing lessons of the past period. Use the Retrospective idea that we outlined in the Yearly Review already.

This event is identical to the yearly cousin, just the horizon of what we look at is different (here: the past quarter). And that's it! Thirty minutes of well-invested time.

Remember, this is a "rearview mirror" approach. We look back at your quarterly performance. The "way forward" is done in the next Quarterly Planning session.

Weekly: Commitment and Celebration!

We are getting a bit more granular now. Nothing beats a well-structured week, and the embedding of POKR key events will help you make execution so much smoother.

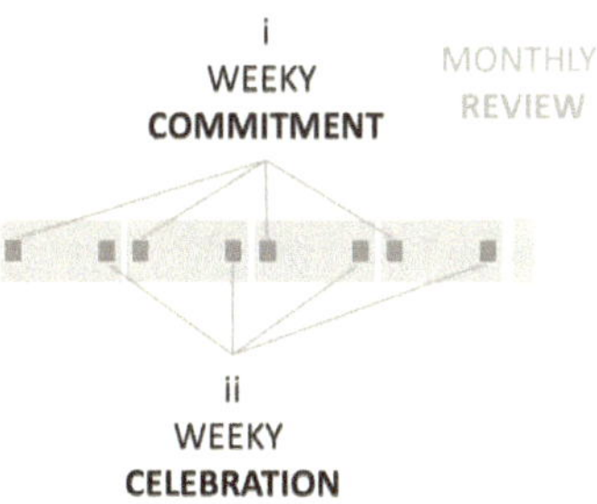

Figure 38. Weekly Routines

Weekly routines are pivotal for calibrating Tasks and keeping them aligned to their Key Results (also discussed in Chapter 11).

Furthermore, regular weekly reviews help to maintain focus and to adapt to changes in priorities.

As per the yearly and quarterly timeboxes, the week also has a key event at the beginning and the end, with some check-ins in between. Figure 38 shows how that would look conceptually for a typical week. Let's start, literally, at the beginning:

i. Start of Week: Weekly Commitment

On the weekly timeboxes we deal primarily with the Task level below Key Results, to make your Personal OKRs actionable. Breaking down Key Results into smaller, time-bound Tasks makes them clearer and easier to achieve.

The Weekly Commitment is a maximum 30-minute planning routine at heart, with Sundays being often a good time to schedule these. Such temporal landmarks (a great term, isn't it?) are shown to improve target activation and set you up properly for the coming week.[5] As productivity expert Michael Hyatt said, "What gets scheduled gets done."[6] You express the intentions for the week by:

1. *Looking at Personal OKRs for this quarter* (choose those you think you want to focus on this week).
2. Defining Tasks per Key Results for this week.
3. Considering spillover Tasks from the previous week(s). This probably requires a bit of refinement.
4. Add them to your To-Do Lists and/or visualize them in your calendar, or put them onto your Kanban Board (see Chapters 12 and 13 respectively for specifics).

As with any other routine, try to stick to the intended time focus, which here is "this week." Don't worry about the weeks thereafter; you'll deal with that in next week's Weekly Commitment event. You see, managing your cognitive load continues to remain really important to us.

By the end of this routine, you'll commit to completing the Tasks you just defined or refined, even if some carried over from before. To show your commitment, check your conviction. Update your confidence factors on the Key Results. Adjust them up or down based on how you feel you're doing now.

ii. End of Week: Weekly Celebration

How did the week go? All Tasks that were planned executed flawlessly? Probably not, but it's good to make time to look at this. This is a Review-type routine, where you check progress on your Tasks that are tied to Key Results. Weekly check-ins are deemed optimal for maintaining good, forward momentum. Run this for 30 minutes maximum, at the end of the week (maybe an early Saturday morning).

If you do Daily Check-Ins (see the next section), then you'll already have updated your Tasks with progress information (fancy talk for: is the task done or not?). If you don't do the optional Daily Check-Ins, now's the time to update the Tasks.

Besides updating them, now is also the time to celebrate what you have achieved in the past week. It might not be much, but baby steps add up! And establishing the celebration of small wins as part of your routine cascade will lead to a better commitment over time. Make it a habit of rewarding yourself. (For us, it's cake. Definitely cake. Maybe a glass of single malt. Yes, there is possibly that.)

Practically speaking, you can do the Weekly Commitment and the Weekly Celebration one after the other. In a corporate context, we typically set the Commitment for Monday morning and the Celebration for Friday afternoon. However, since we're focusing on Personal OKRs, it's probably more suited for the weekend. See what makes the best sense for you.

A bonus output of this routine is a quick summary of what you've achieved and sending that to your Accountability Partner(s). Why not bring your Accountability Partner into this routine, and jointly walk through what you have achieved in the past week?

A simple template for that is in the Appendix.

Daily Check-In (Optional)

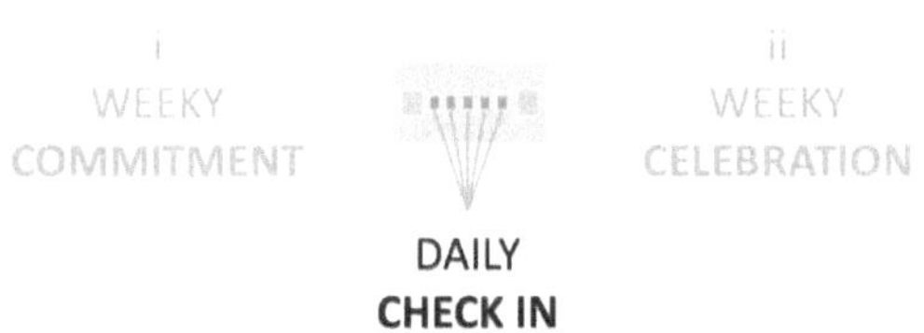

Figure 39. Daily Routines

Wedged between the weekly twin events of Commitment and Celebration, we offer a daily routine that can help you stay on top of things:

The POKR version of the corporate "daily scrum" or "stand-up meeting." It is an optional routine. This can help you, especially at first, to strengthen some POKR techniques.

"Optional" because it might feel too much effort after a while, and it could become counterproductive (you already look at this weekly). But for those of us who want and need a gentle reminder of the priorities of our life, see it as a warm-up for the day. It's a maximum 15-minute routine, usually done at the beginning of the day.

Unfinished Tasks use up mental resources.[7] They stay in our minds until we review and plan them again. So, cleaning up your calendar/To-Do List daily might, literally, provide peace of mind. You likely faced roadblocks yesterday that stopped you from finishing your plans. Review these now, fresh, before any other action can help create a more realistic "plan" for the day. So, feel free to move Tasks around as a consequence. No need to wait for the weekly planning routine.

The Progress Principle says it well: "The best way to boost emotions, motivation, and perceptions at work is to make progress in meaningful Tasks."[8]

MID-FLIGHT CHANGES: OKAY, WITHIN LIMITS

You might wonder if you could change your active, in-flight Personal OKRs. These are the ones you're currently working on this quarter, and you want to adjust them. And we've thought about that ourselves, in the corporate and private space equally. It's a question that requires a set of simple rules. Without them, anything would be possible all the time, and that is not going to work in your favor. To quote Winston from *John Wick*: "Rules. Without them we'd live with the animals."[9]

POKR as a method is here to protect you from yourself: We don't want to create a moving target, do we? And let's remind ourselves of expectations:

A 70% fulfillment rate is great, across all Objectives, all categories, all quarters. A single Objective that you "fail" on is nothing to be concerned about. What counts is that you get close(r) in the pursuit of realizing your life's Mission. And you never really "fail." You learn, to get better over time. Every "failure" is an opportunity to learn.

Your POKR Canvas should represent the most accurate information, at that point in time. If the circumstances change from one point forward, so should your POKR Canvas.

Some rules are helpful, but exceptions are needed. With the following table, we think we have struck a good balance. In that spirit, let's take it one level at a time, starting at the bottom of the POKR Burger:

LEVEL	ADD	CHANGE	REMOVE
TASK	✓ Anything goes (within the spirit of the Key Result parent and the current POKR cycle)		
KEY RESULTS	✗ No	✗ No	✗ No (you might abandon them though)
OBJECTIVES	✓ Yes (if capacity/ time left in the current cycle)	✗ No	~ Maybe (if physically impossible to complete them)
SINGLE-WORD KEY RESULTS	Not applicable	~ Maybe (if dramatic changes in circumstances)	Not applicable

Table 5. Change of POKR Elements Mid-Flight

Tasks

The good news: On this level, go to town. *Add, remove, change.* It's totally up to you. Well, always within the spirit of the Key Results that they are assigned to, of course. The Execution layer of POKR is intentionally flexible, because that's where the rubber hits the road. You need flexibility here. A Task is suddenly obsolete? Remove it. Two new ones fall from the sky? Add them. It takes you longer to complete an activity? Change the deadline.

One caveat though: You are still operating within the same POKR cycle; i.e., don't spill into the next one. That would require the Quarterly Planning routine to kick in.

Key Results

The guidance here is simple: *Stay with them.* Don't come up with new ones; don't remove any. You might "fail" on some but succeed on others. In the aggregate, you are likely still coming out above the 70% that would typically constitute a success for an Objective.

It's okay to abandon singular Key Results, as in: not putting any energy into them anymore. But keep them under the Objective; don't remove them. It's probably a good learning opportunity for a Retrospective.

Would you add new Key Results? That's pretty unlikely. If you did well in Quarterly Planning, new Key Results popping up out of nowhere would be strange. Keep these as candidates for the next cycle if they are important.

Objectives

Similarly, as for Key Results, you'd want to keep executing your Objectives. They were apparently important during your last Quarterly Planning, which can't be that far in the past (maximum 3 months, right?). Unless it is *physically impossible* to accomplish them anymore, and such circumstances can happen, of course. Life is unpredictable, in spite of what POKR might suggest at times.

You wanted to run a marathon but broke your ankle? We hear excuses. Just walk it off! Kidding. Here you need to pivot; replace the Objective with something that makes sense for the remainder of the quarter, if there is still time left. Switch to an upper-body strength session in the gym instead? Or less physically taxing activities like going for a meditation retreat? Alternatively, you indeed just declare that Objective "failed." It's okay. You have a good reason for it.

Connected to the above, is it okay to create additional new Objectives for a quarter that is mid-flight? It might seem strange that that happens. However, you may find that the other Objectives are completed faster than expected. So, go ahead and hold a mini–Quarterly Planning session to create new Personal OKRs for the rest of the quarter.

Just be careful not to overload yourself with too much ambition now. And if a new "half" Objective is not really meaningful for a running quarter, maybe it is better to park it for the next?

Mission: 5+1 Goals

Typically, you would look at your Mission (5-Year or 1-Year Goal) as part of the Yearly Planning routine, pretty much at the beginning of a new year. But if circumstances hit that are impactful enough, it might be necessary to tweak them, even midyear. It's rare, but there are curveballs that life throws at us (positive and negative) that might warrant such a step.

Losing a job that requires you to relook at your *finance* swim lane? Suddenly and unplanned, getting married opens up an entirely new category for *family and relationship*? You likely have good reasons to recalibrate your Personal OKRs. Start by reviewing your Mission (5+1 Goals). Also, check the Objectives for this quarter.

WHAT ABOUT NOT HAVING CADENCES, AT ALL?

This whole subject might feel a bit "micromanaging" at times. Where is the fun, creativity, room for experimentation?

There are indeed some who argue that this type of rigid adherence to cadences may stifle creativity and flexibility. Critics argue that placing too much emphasis on routines can create tunnel vision. These critiques have some truth to them, but a structured cadence keeps you moving forward. It also helps you handle life's unexpected moments. Adjusting during reviews helps avoid stagnation. It also encourages longer-term engagement with your Personal OKRs.

Yes, but is it still okay to not have cadences at all? We don't think that would be a wise choice. What might drive you to abandon the cadence approach? Is it because it is hard to establish them in the first place? Well, don't. As we've alluded to multiple times, good things take time. And particularly something that you might not have done before can feel "stifling" to begin with. Getting into good habits requires patience; maturity does not develop overnight.

We help you with predefined templates, calendar invites, etc. to ease the administrative burden. See the Appendix for further information. No need to build these things yourself from scratch. You're welcome.

Trust the process and stay with it at least for one cycle, or better, for two (quarterly) cycles. If it still doesn't feel "right," make it a point in your Review to better understand what is not working for you.

Some examples of what might cause that follows.

COMMON PITFALLS

There are two very "popular" extremes on how not to go about these routine cascades:

Overdoing It

Too much of the same isn't good for anything (cake, anyone?). Having too many routines can feel stifling. This leads to micromanaging and takes focus away from strategic targets. This will create unnecessary stress and complexity. The right balance is needed here.

We think our cascade hits the sweet spot. Each routine targets the right time frame: yearly, quarterly, monthly, weekly, or even daily. This approach guides you from Mission (goals) via Strategy (Personal OKRs) to specific Execution details (Tasks). Plus: some are optional, so feel free to tailor it to your liking.

And we talk about approximately 30 minutes per week, and roughly 1 hour per quarter. It's not too much to ask.

Underdoing It

Case in point: too few inspections (i.e., irregular Reviews). That defeats the inspect and adapt intention, which is a super-powerful feedback loop, creating a virtuous cycle that you don't want to miss out on.

You might end up misaligning your goals, risking that there's a lot of "action," but it is "blind" in nature, a lack of alignment.

Alternatively, you run out of momentum altogether. Or don't know where you are in terms of progress. Our outlined routines create the right level of attention, at the appropriate time. Discipline needs time to develop. Be patient with yourself.

WHAT'S NEXT?

Now that we have set up the basics of time management, let's shift focus. We'll explore practical tools and techniques for managing and visualizing Personal OKRs: Chapter 11 explores popular task management methods supported by POKR, after which we talk about timeboxing and calendar integration in Chapter 12.

KEY TAKEAWAYS

1. Cadences are essential for a good rhythm. Without them, any change effort may fail. Routines show how you work every day.

2. From now on, standard routines are the backbone of execution at all levels of the POKR Method.

3. Each routine is practical, is timeboxed, has a clear purpose, and includes defined inputs and outputs. See the specifics in the Appendix.

4. Routines occur at the beginning, the middle, and the end of a period; let it be a week, month, quarter, or year.

5. The time commitment is short. It's 30 minutes to 1 hour per week. This may change if you join optional events, like daily check-ins.

6. All POKR routines rely on proven science from Lean, Agile, and startup fields. These methods show effective and efficient ways to achieve breakthrough performance.

7. "Getting started" matters more than "perfection." Learning what works for you in each cycle is key.

8. Changes to Personal OKRs and Tasks are inevitable, but we need to follow a set of simple rules.

ELEVEN

TO-DO LISTS
The Basics of Organizing Tasks

WHEN GOOD INTENTIONS MEET BAD SYSTEMS

ANIKA STARED AT HER TO-DO LIST WITH A MIX OF FRUSTRA-tion and amusement. At the top sat "Learn Italian, 30 minutes," a key Task for her quarterly Personal OKR. Below it were 23 "urgent" items, from responding to emails to booking a dentist appointment. Three days later, the Italian practice remained unchecked while the dentist appointment was done.

"Maybe I should learn to say, 'I need a root canal' in Italian," she said, grabbing her third espresso of the morning. "Ho bisogno di un canale radicolare," if anyone's curious. Her language-learning app chirped another reminder, which she dismissed with a familiar swipe.

The irony wasn't lost on her. Six months ago, she'd set an ambi-tious Personal OKR to "Achieve B1 Italian proficiency" for her dream archaeology program in Rome. She broke the target into weekly goals. She downloaded top apps and found an Italian conversation partner. Yet here she was, watching her carefully crafted plan disappear under an avalanche of "urgent" Tasks.

Anika's story might sound familiar. Many people struggle to juggle long-term goals and urgent daily Tasks. They often give priority to what feels urgent right now. Urgency of the Task, cognitive fatigue resulting from too many items on the To-Do List, and individual skills (or lack thereof) play a role.[1] We create beautiful plans and ambitious Personal OKRs, only to watch them get buried under the endless stream of daily demands. But what if there was a way to make your lists of "stuff" work for your Personal OKRs, rather than against them?

In this chapter we look at To-Do Lists and how to tweak them for POKR success.

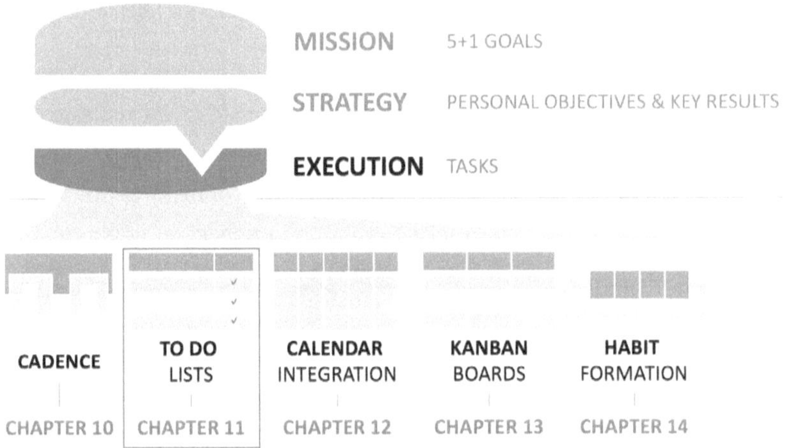

Figure 40. Execution Layer of POKR with Its Components

TO·DO LISTS: WHY WE LOVE (AND HATE) THEM

To-Do Lists are everywhere. Many people use them to organize their day.[2] A very simple version is shown in Figure 41: A Task is either done or not. A simple, unidimensional list of "stuff" that needs to somehow get done.

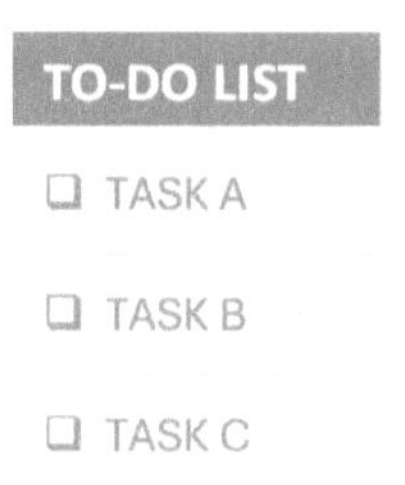

Figure 41. Simple To-Do List

Because most people use some form of To-Do List today, we want to illustrate how it is not a roadblock to use POKR. The opposite actually; we like to turbocharge your existing ones! If you are an avid user of To-Do Lists today, you'll probably see a lot of your Tasks moving over under Personal OKRs, where they get a lot more focus and attention.

But let's start with the basics. The popularity of To-Do Lists stems from their psychological and practical benefits. Writing down Tasks clears your mind, boosts focus, and helps you finish them. No matter the format, scribbled on sticky notes or organized in apps, every To-Do List has key functions, supported by science:

- **Cognitive Off-Loading**: Writing Tasks down literally frees up mental bandwidth. The Zeigarnik Effect shows that unfinished Tasks take up our mental energy. They stay on our minds until we have a clear plan to finish them.[3]

- **Anxiety Reduction**: People with structured To-Do Lists report that writing Tasks down has a calming effect.[4] Writing a To-Do

List before bed can even help individuals fall asleep faster by reducing worry about incomplete future Tasks.[5]

- **Progress Tracking:** To-Do Lists can boost motivation by providing a clear visual representation of progress. Checking off completed Tasks can give a sense of accomplishment and encourage continued effort, by giving us a little spike of dopamine.[6]

These strengths are amplified when To-Do Lists are used in service of higher-level targets, like Personal OKRs.

THE PROBLEM WITH TO-DO LISTS

Critics often argue that To-Do Lists are far from perfect productivity tools, and they are not wrong.[7] One common criticism is that Tasks of different complexities get mixed together. It's tough to compare simple Tasks, like "Take out the trash," with complex ones, like "Develop the quarterly marketing strategy." Mixing minor errands with big projects can confuse our priorities and overwhelm us.

Another challenge is the paradox of choice: When a To-Do List grows too long, it can lead to decision fatigue.[8] Instead of feeling motivated by clear next steps, you may find yourself paralyzed by too many options. Also, our brains can only handle about seven options before we're overwhelmed.[9] Making decisions is easier when you have fewer choices. A long To-Do List can make you feel like a deer in headlights or lead to epic procrastination, like spending an hour on email instead of actually getting things done.

To-Do Lists by themselves don't force you to do the things that are important, but which you don't really want to do. They don't have built-in "commitment devices." These tools help you commit to actions you might resist but know are beneficial for you.[10] Those need to be brought in through different mechanisms. Scheduling time with somebody to work on a Task together is one such commitment.

Finally, To-Do Lists often lack context. They don't show how urgent or important Tasks are, or if they depend on other Tasks. This overlooks the details needed for effective prioritization. For example, how long will each Task take? Do you have the time to do it that day?

Not all these problems can be solved by better To-Do List design. But some can. First, we will see how POKR helps with complexity, decision fatigue, and context for related Tasks. Then, we will explore general ways to improve your To-Do Lists, like better prioritization. For those challenges that can't be addressed that easily, we have a solution too, namely through timeboxing by calendarizing Tasks, which we will cover in Chapter 12.

Well-designed To-Do Lists can be very useful. So, we won't go as far as some detractors who advise abandoning them entirely.[11] They are simple to use, capture Tasks quickly, visualize the workload, and give us the psychological satisfaction of checking off completed Tasks.[12]

To-Do Lists offer flexibility for people with changing schedules or creatives who prefer not to have set times. They can adapt to sudden changes. Also, mixing short and long Tasks lets users blend quick wins with longer activities. This helps maintain momentum all day.

As we said before, everybody is different.

POKR-POWERED TO-DO LISTING

Lucky for us, the POKR Method addresses some of the issues with To-Do Lists directly.

1. **Simplifying Complexity**: By tying Tasks to clear Key Results, Personal OKRs create a natural filter, focusing on high-impact actions. For example, Personal OKR Tasks like "run 10 miles this week" are intrinsically tied to a larger purpose (e.g., the "marathon" as an Objective, via a Key Result "in-between").

2. **Reducing Decision Fatigue**: With Personal OKRs, the question "What should I do first?" is answered by alignment to Objectives, which are timeboxed to a single quarter.

3. **Adding Context**: Linking Tasks to Personal OKRs helps put them in context with larger targets. This way, you're less likely to focus on low-priority items. Use clear action verbs and add important details like deadlines and context info. This helps you decide when to focus on what. Key Results (with their Tasks) are defined by the desired outcomes.

Figure 42 outlines how that works practically. Tasks are organized underneath a Key Result, in a KISS version.

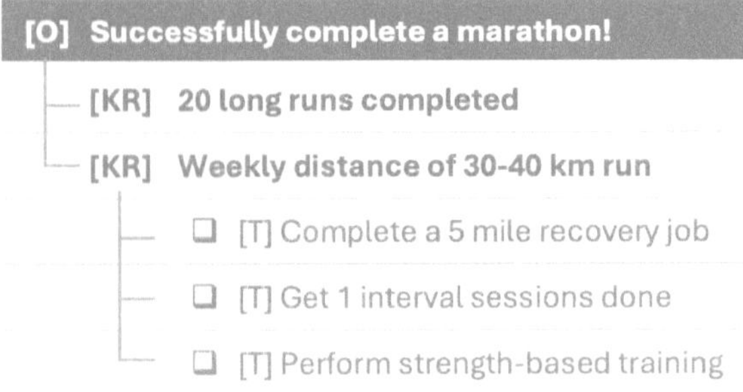

Figure 42. To-Dos as Tasks with POKR

But here's the challenge: How do we ensure Tasks linked to our Personal OKRs don't get buried beneath everyday urgencies?

The beauty of Personal OKRs lies in their focus; they identify what truly matters. A good To-Do List, then, should function as the tactical execution plan for those Objectives.

If your Objective is indeed to run a marathon, your Key Results might be "Do 20 long runs" or "Achieve 30 miles every week." A To-Do List keeps weekly runs in focus, whether it's a 5-mile recovery jog or an interval session.

It also helps manage other non-OKR Tasks, like scheduling dentist appointments, even if they aren't as enjoyable. Figure 43 shows this concept: Personal OKR Tasks share space with non-OKR ones. However, the POKR Tasks should get more attention. We don't separate POKR Tasks from their Key Result parents, as that would be harsh. Instead, we enable listing both, while keeping the strong POKR parent–child link intact. Think about it as different windows into the same backyard.

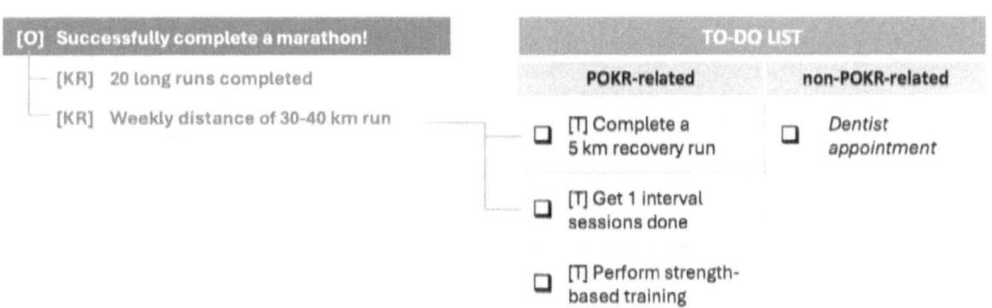

Figure 43. To-Do Lists of Tasks of OKRs and Non-OKRs

Time management experts often recommend using multiple To-Do Lists. You can create lists for current Tasks, future Tasks, or even tiny Tasks.[13] In this example, we basically keep a separate list specifically for our Personal OKRs.

As we learned before, a core principle guides us: Keep it short and simple. For that reason, we advocate to not have more than seven Tasks for a particular Key Result. That way, we significantly improve the odds that a Task actually gets done.

Next, let's see how to execute POKR To-Do Lists with maximum efficiency.

MAKE TO-DO LISTS GREAT, AGAIN!

Think of your To-Do List as a garden and your Personal OKRs as the prized roses you're growing. Like a skilled gardener tending to roses, your Personal OKR Tasks require special care. Don't let them get lost in daily chores.

Making the Important Urgent (Enough)

In task management, a common challenge is preventing urgent but less important Tasks from crowding out important but nonurgent ones. Personal OKRs will mostly be the latter. Although they have inherent prioritization, it is still necessary to ensure their completion within the designated time frame.

In the following table, we list some of the most common, research-backed ways to prioritize Tasks. For the two most common, we'll also explore how to use these methods with POKR Tasks. The idea is to apply these techniques to the To-Do Lists that you have established already, underneath the Key Results. It's not mandatory to prioritize them but it can help tremendously to focus on the right actions.

In the interest of space, we only focus on two main approaches and only at a high level. Check our blog and book website for more details. We also offer tools and templates that blend these methods for everyday use.

The most popular techniques and methods are:

TECHNIQUE	DESCRIPTION
EISENHOWER MATRIX (AKA COVEY MATRIX)	The classic urgent-important framework, validated through research and practice
MOSCOW METHOD	Categorizes Tasks into: Must Have, Should Have, Could Have, and Won't Have
ABCDE METHOD	Uses five levels of prioritization from "Must Do" to "Unnecessary" Tasks
POSEC METHOD	Prescribes a specific order: Prioritize, Organize, Streamline, Economize, and Contribute
IVY LEE METHOD	Listing six Tasks each day in order of importance
PARETO METHOD	Separate the vital from the trivial: The famous 80/20 rule
ACTION PRIORITY MATRIX	Categorizes Tasks based on their impact and effort

Table 6. Task Prioritization Techniques

For readers interested in the other approaches listed above, such as the ABCDE Method[14], POSEC[15], Ivy Lee[16], Pareto Principle[17], and the Action Priority Matrix[18], see the references provided for a deeper dive into their origins and applications.

Eisenhower Matrix

The classic: Named after US World War II general and later president Dwight D. Eisenhower, who had a clever way to sort Tasks. He said, "I have two kinds of problems: the urgent and the important. The urgent are not important, and the important are never urgent."[19]

This idea became known as the Eisenhower Matrix, especially after Stephen Covey highlighted it in *The 7 Habits of Highly Effective People.*[20] This popular method categorizes Tasks by urgency and importance, hence is one of the gold-standard Task prioritization techniques:[21]

Covey built on the Eisenhower Matrix, by adding time allocation tips for each quadrant.

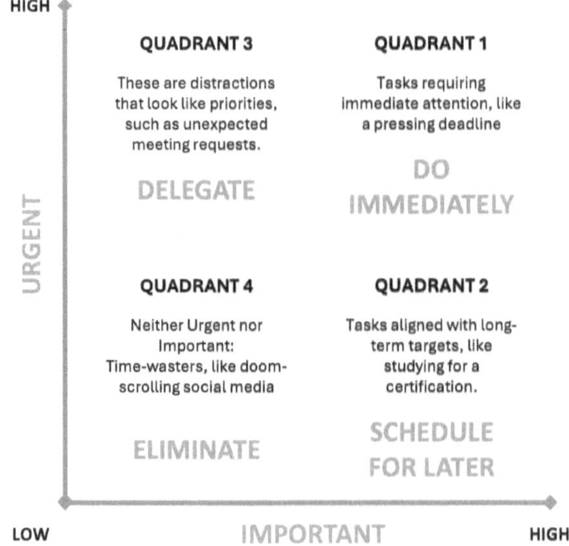

Figure 44. The Eisenhower Matrix

Most Personal OKR–related Tasks fall into Quadrant 2: important but not immediately pressing. For example, a Key Result for preparing a marathon could be "Run 80 miles this month." While each weekly training session isn't urgent, it's critical to achieving your Objective. To ensure these Tasks get attention:

- **Schedule Them in Advance**: Set aside time on your calendar for Personal OKR Tasks. Treat these as important appointments. (See *Calendar Integration* in Chapter 12 for more).

- **Create Inchstones**: Tie deadlines to smaller milestones within your Key Results to create urgency. For example, "Complete long run of 15 miles by mid-month."

Using the Eisenhower Matrix underneath Key Results can help to instill some "gray scale" to Tasks. Compare that to the KISS model, where every Task is equally important and it's up to you to decide every day which one to focus on and which not to. The Eisenhower Matrix approach gives you a bit more guidance on what to focus on first, second, third.

If you must drop some, at least you know quickly which ones: the less-important ones, and those that are not urgent or not important. (Why would you even list these in the first place, though?)

The MoSCoW Method

MoSCoW stands for Must, Should, Could, and Won't.[22] This method started in software development, but it works well for personal Task management, too.

Tasks are prioritized into four categories:

- **Must Have**: Critical Tasks that absolutely need completion.
- **Should Have**: Important but not essential.
- **Could Have**: Nice-to-have Tasks if time permits.
- **Won't Have**: Tasks deliberately excluded from the current cycle.

[O] Successfully complete a marathon!	MoSCoW
[KR] 20 long runs completed	
[KR] Weekly distance of 30-40 km run	
☐ [T] Complete a 5 mile recovery job	Must Do
☐ [T] Research cross-training methods	Should Do

Figure 45. MoSCoW in Action

Personal OKR Tasks typically fall under "Must Have" or "Should Have." If your Objective is to train for a marathon, "Run 20 miles this week" is a "Must Have."

On the other hand, "Research cross-training methods" is a "Should Have," as shown in Figure 45.

The risk with MoSCoW is that POKR Tasks get categorized mostly as "Should" rather than "Must," leading to delayed implementation. Two effective countermeasures to counteract this are:

- Designate specific POKR Tasks as "Must" items each week
- Regular review and recategorization of Tasks

MoSCoW as well as ABCDE are ways to give your Tasks a very quick priority, without overanalyzing them. A gut-feel judgment if you will. Speed is the objective here, not accuracy.

As mentioned, there are other popular methods for task prioritization out there. But whichever is used, the main point for us is to prioritize POKR Tasks throughout the day. These techniques can be useful, especially when they are integrated into our tools we use for the To-Do List. This applies to digital apps or even reminders in a paper planner.

Moving Forward with Smaller Tasks

Combining POKR with To-Do Lists has a big benefit: It shows clear progress. This visible ticking-off of Tasks gives a helpful psychological boost. The single most powerful motivator in knowledge work is the sense of progress, even if it is small. This is where thoughtful Task design becomes crucial.

Elena discovered this principle when she shifted from vague Tasks like "Work on novel" to specific, trackable items: "Write 1,500 words of

Chapter 3." Every evening, she saw her progress. She checked off daily Tasks and moved closer to her quarterly Personal OKR of finishing her first draft. "It's like building a wall," she explains. "Each day's words are another brick, and I can literally watch my novel taking shape."

Large Tasks that take a significant amount of time can seem daunting. There often isn't a clear time slot to complete them all at once. To address this, divide the Task into smaller parts and approach them one by one. You might even try the "do one thing" method to stay focused: Use your To-Do List as a reference, not a working tool. Write each task on a Post-it note, place it where you can see it, hide the full list, and focus. After completing the Task, cross it off your list, and repeat.[23]

Keep Multiple Lists for Different Areas of Your Life

Keeping separate lists can make it easier to prioritize Tasks. Tech-savvy users can pick digital apps. These apps let you flag important items, set reminders, and get deadline alerts while keeping separate lists. If you prefer traditional methods, using different pages in a notebook works well too.

There are different ways to do that.

- Some split Task lists into "Current" and "Future" Tasks.[24]
- Others use "Next Actions" and "Someday/Maybe" lists, as seen in the Getting Things Done method.[25]
- Another separates lists for non-time-sensitive important Tasks, for Tasks you need to do today, and for long-overdue Tasks you're unlikely to complete.[26]

Our To-Do Lists often overflow with pressing Tasks that demand immediate attention, essential responsibilities we fear losing track of due to the absence of a deadline, and simple items we include just for the satisfaction of crossing them off.

We like the principle a lot: Our POKR-related Tasks should ideally be on a separate list from all the rest.

But if you use a split like the examples above, you need to ensure that POKR-related Tasks are consistently added to the right lists (not the "unlikely to complete" one, please). And ideally POKR-related Tasks are then separated from the other Tasks within that list.

From Weekly Focus to Daily Action: Making the Bridge Work

Ever wrapped up your Sunday planning session like a productivity wizard, only to find yourself adrift by Wednesday? Been there. That's why bridging your weekly OKR-based planning (in the weekly Commitment and Review sessions) with your daily to-do execution is where the real magic happens.

Let's start with structure. Your weekly To-Do List should clearly separate:

- **POKR-related Tasks**: Organized by Objective, with each Task tagged to the Key Result it supports.

- **Everything else**: Non-POKR items that still matter but don't trace back to your current quarterly focus. Maybe use categories to structure the other Tasks a bit more.

Start by rolling over any unfinished Tasks from the previous week (yes, the ones you ghosted). Then prioritize, using the tools we described above. This is the moment to triage your list into the essential, the strategic, and the "can totally wait." Or any one of the methods described.

Now comes the secret sauce: Spread your POKR Tasks intentionally across the week. Don't stack them all on Friday like a sad productivity avalanche. Distribute them based on real-time availability and urgency. Then, for each day:

- Pull in that day's Tasks from the weekly plan.
- Mark POKR Tasks clearly: top of the list, bolded, starred, Ivy Lee'd, whatever works.
- Big or time-sensitive items go directly on your calendar (especially ones involving others or needing more than 30 minutes). We cover more on that in Chapter 12.

Yes, new Tasks will emerge during the week. Old ones will linger. But if your daily lists are grounded in a thoughtful weekly plan, you'll spend more time progressing and less time reacting.

Here's how Wolfram does it. I use a simple two-pager each week. One-page lists Tasks related to my two or three active Personal OKRs, broken down by Objective and tagged to the Key Result each Task serves. The flip side holds the rest. My non-POKR Tasks, grouped by evolving categories:

- Family
- Finances
- People to meet or message
- General maintenance/miscellaneous

These categories aren't fixed. I adjust them as life requires, but "Family" and "Finances" are always there. From this base, I sketch out daily Task lists for the week. I make sure each day includes top-priority POKR Tasks, and I schedule the big ones directly into my calendar. The ritual takes 15 to 20 minutes on Sunday and keeps my week (mostly) sane.

Handling the Unexpected

Even the best-designed system needs to handle interruptions and unexpected events. Anika's language learning journey offers valuable insights here. When an urgent work project threatened to derail her Italian studies, she didn't abandon her Personal OKR Tasks entirely. Instead, she applied what we call the "minimum viable progress" rule.

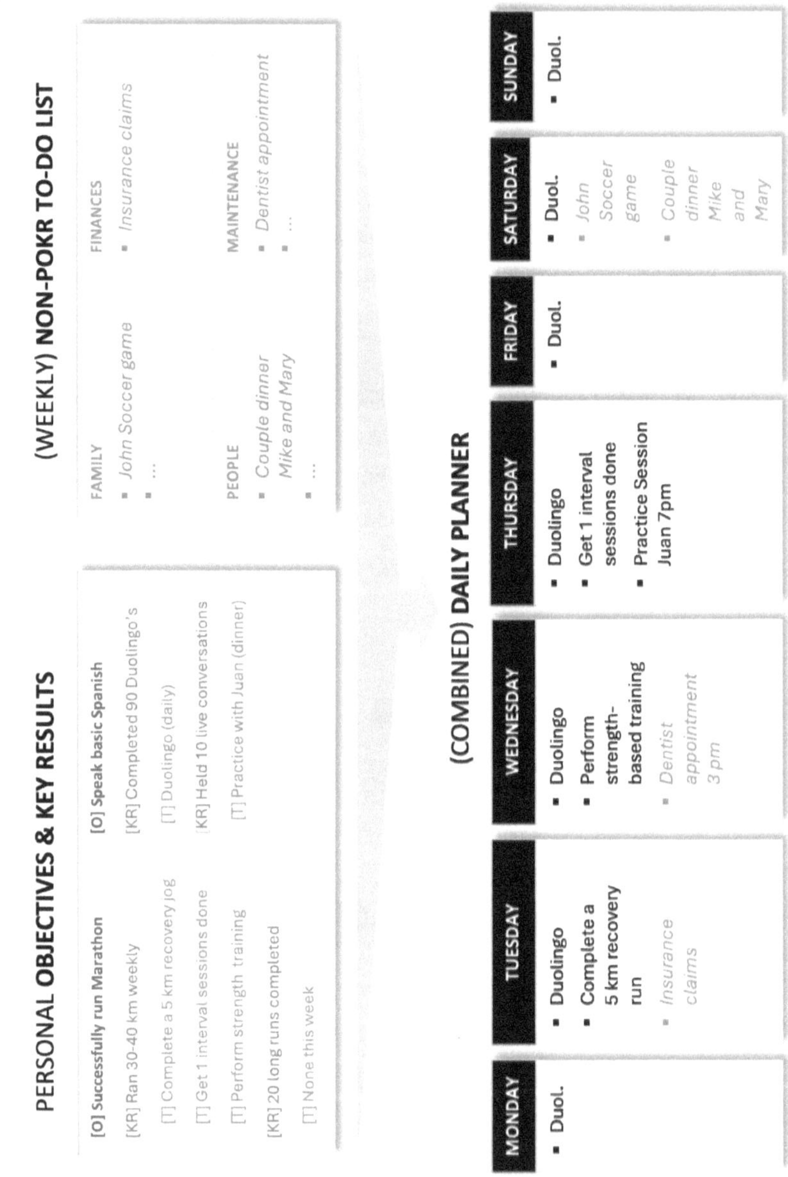

PERSONAL **OBJECTIVES & KEY RESULTS**

[O] Successfully run Marathon

[KR] Ran 30-40 km weekly

  [T] Complete a 5 km recovery jog

  [T] Get 1 interval sessions done

  [T] Perform strength training

[KR] 20 long runs completed

  [T] None this week

[O] Speak basic Spanish

[KR] Completed 90 Duolingo's

  [T] Duolingo (daily)

[KR] Held 10 live conversations

  [T] Practice with Juan (dinner)

(WEEKLY) **NON-POKR TO-DO LIST**

FAMILY
- *John Soccer game*
- *...*

FINANCES
- *Insurance claims*

PEOPLE
- *Couple dinner Mike and Mary*
- *...*

MAINTENANCE
- *Dentist appointment*
- *...*

(COMBINED) **DAILY PLANNER**

MONDAY	TUESDAY	WEDNESDAY	THURSDAY	FRIDAY	SATURDAY	SUNDAY
• Duol.	• Duolingo • Complete a 5 km recovery run • *Insurance claims*	• Duolingo • Perform strength-based training • *Dentist appointment 3 pm*	• Duolingo • Get 1 interval sessions done • Practice Session Juan 7pm	• Duol.	• Duol. • *John Soccer game* • *Couple dinner Mike and Mary*	• Duol.

Figure 46. OKRs and Non-POKRs into a Combined Daily Planner

"I knew I couldn't maintain my usual hour of study," she recalls, "but I committed to at least 10 minutes of Italian audio during my commute." This method kept her connected to her Personal OKR in a small way. It helped her stay focused during a difficult time. When the work crisis passed, she could ramp back up without feeling like she was starting over.

The Art of Task Visibility

Important but nonurgent Tasks often get lost in the daily rush. This is a common challenge. Tasks need to be both visible and actionable to get done. But how does this work in practice? This can be a calendar display showing the Tasks for the week, a daily planner for the daily Tasks that is always at hand, or a digital app on your phone.

Anika, our Italian language learner from earlier, set up a "language learning zone" on her desk. This space kept her Italian materials, progress tracker, and daily Tasks in view. "It's like having a constant gentle reminder of my commitment," she explains. "When I see my language materials every morning, starting my practice session feels like a natural first step."

Calendar Integration (Chapter 12) and certainly Kanban Boards (which we dedicate Chapter 13 to) are maybe the most sophisticated way of visualizing your Tasks.

The Role of Habits and Routines

A strong way to make sure Personal OKR Tasks get done is to tie them to existing routines. Anika linked her Italian practice to her morning coffee routine. "I don't even think about it anymore," she says. "Coffee and Italian are just part of how I start my day."

James Clear refers to this as habit stacking.[27] It helps make steady progress on Personal OKR Tasks. We will talk more about how Personal OKRs can help develop good habits in Chapter 14.

THE TECHNOLOGY QUESTION: APPS, ANYONE?

In our digital age, the question of whether to use paper or digital tools for Task management inevitably arises. The research here is fascinating: Writing by hand enhances memory and conceptual understanding, much better than typing on a keyboard.[28] That's one reason why dinosaurs like Wolfram still prefer paper-based To-Do Lists. However, digital tools offer obvious advantages in searchability and ability to sync across devices.

Features like workflow integration, smart scheduling, and reminders aren't just bells and whistles. They're meant to fix typical task management problems: forgetting what to do, getting overwhelmed, or giving up. If you've ever abandoned a system because it made your life harder, not easier, you're not alone.

Here are some points to look out for when choosing and testing tools for yourself:

- Use tools that align with your existing habits and systems. If using the tool feels like a chore, adoption drops. A key reason is friction. If the system doesn't fit with other platforms and routines, like email, calendars, or messaging apps, it often gets abandoned when life gets busy.[29] The best tools don't just help you manage Tasks; they stop you from managing the system itself. In short, the winners are tools that disappear into your routine but still catch you before you trip.

- Presenting Tasks in a clear visual structure helps users prioritize at a glance and reduces overlooked duties. We humans are visual creatures. We process information faster and remember it better when it's organized visually rather than in monotonous text. Many productivity apps employ visual cues like bold fonts, highlights, or drag-and-drop ordering to signal priority levels and Task status.[30]

- Modern digital Task tools now offer more than just static lists. They include "smart" Task routing. This means they have intelligent features that help users choose when and how to handle Tasks. This includes automated scheduling, priority recommendations, and context-aware Task suggestions. For example, if a user has a 30-minute gap, the system might suggest a quick Task that fits that time window, or if the user arrives at a certain location (say the library), the app could bring up Tasks relevant to that context (like "return books"). Humans often struggle with planning. We procrastinate, take on too many Tasks, or forget to set aside time for important but nonurgent items. Smart scheduling algorithms help address these issues. They use data and AI to optimize Task allocation. The goal is to prevent the classic scenario where a user keeps pushing incomplete Tasks from day to day until a backlog of 50-plus overdue Tasks snowballs. When that happens, the Task list has long ceased to be effective.

- Smart reminders can turn good intentions into action, but only when used wisely. They should support your focus, not replace it. Most digital Task tools come with some flavor of reminder: pop-ups, push notifications, emails. All designed to jog your memory when a deadline sneaks up or a task gets buried. The logic is simple: Reminders act as external memory aids. In practice, it's more complicated. Yes, they help with forgetfulness and last-minute procrastination. But lean on them too much, and you risk weakening your own initiative. A study on student study habits shows how this can backfire.[31] When students got daily app reminders to study, they did study more, on those days. But over time, they became less likely to study on their own. No ping, no action. In contrast, the group with no reminders built more consistent routines. The takeaway: Short-term nudges work, but they can train your brain to wait for a push instead of acting on its own. It's a classic case of borrowed willpower. Helpful in a pinch, but risky as a habit.

Focus on these core principles, not particular app gimmicks. This way, you can pick an app that truly enhances productivity and helps you achieve your targets. The key is finding the minimum effective dose of technology. More features do not always lead to better results.

Elena found her sweet spot with a hybrid approach. She maintains her daily writing Tasks and word count in a paper journal, creating that vital physical connection to her work. But she uses a digital tool for tracking her overall Personal OKR progress and managing her publishing Tasks. "Writing my daily targets makes me stick to them," she says. "Digital tracking shows me how I'm doing overall."

Wolfram tried many types of To-Do Lists, both paper and electronic. He said, "But I usually end up back with my tried-and-true piece of paper. Nothing beats the sense of accomplishment I get from crossing off a Task on a paper list."

You can find a list of tech solutions and apps on our website. There we also provide easy templates for simpler Task management approaches, including daily planners that are paper based.

HOW TO EMBED GETTING THINGS DONE (GTD)

Getting Things Done (GTD), David Allen's productivity method, isn't just a relic of the early 2000s.[32] It still holds up because it solves a timeless problem: mental clutter. The core idea is deceptively simple. Capture every commitment, Task, and random thought into an external system. Your brain stops playing the role of a leaky filing cabinet and can focus on actual work instead of remembering what you're supposed to do next. Think of it less as a To-Do List fetish and more as cognitive offloading for adults who don't want to forget their anniversary or miss a client deadline.

Few systems have had GTD's staying power. The process has five key steps: Capture, Clarify, Organize, Reflect, and Engage. These steps help users manage Tasks and clarify next actions. We won't go into detail about David Allen's book, but we will connect its elements to POKR. If you use GTD, you may want to know how to integrate its five-step system with POKR. We focus on the Task level of GTD here. Table 7 shows the mapping between GTD and POKR.

GTD STEPS			POKR COMPONENT
1	CAPTURE	everything you need to	Task Brainstorming
2	CLARIFY	what each Task involves	Task Brainstorming
3	ORGANIZE	tasks by category and priority	Task Prioritization Techniques
4	RELFECT	regularly to review your list	POKR Cadences
5	ENGAGE	and act	POKR Cadences

Table 7. GTD Meets POKR

A common critique of the GTD method is its lack of focus on connecting daily Tasks to higher-level goals. GTD presents the "Horizons of Focus" model, which spans from immediate actions to long-term Life Goals. Yet, many users feel the system stresses short-term task management more than aligning these Tasks with broader Objectives. This can create an efficient task management system that lacks strategic direction. So, productivity may improve but may not lead to significant progress. That's exactly what Personal OKRs provide: that link to goals. And as we have discussed before, goals provide mission, focus, and motivation.

Also, at the method's core, Allen preaches *task universalism*, meaning that when you get down to concrete actions, all work is created equal.[33] Having read our book so far, it should not surprise you to hear that we disagree with that as well. Just because you complete many Tasks doesn't mean you're focusing on the "right" ones (like your Personal OKRs). So, we do need a set of prioritization techniques (see "Making the Important Urgent (Enough)") and a clear link to your goals to make this work.

A more detailed mapping of GTD with POKR, and other popular frameworks for that matter, can be found on our website.

THE ART OF INTEGRATION: MAKING IT ALL WORK TOGETHER

The real strength of using POKR with To-Do Lists is not just in the tools. It's about how they come together to form a clear system for success. Like a well-conducted orchestra, each element plays its part in creating something greater than the sum of its parts.

Consider the journeys of our three achievers:

Elena completed her novel draft ahead of schedule, producing 64,000 words in just under 3 months. The key wasn't writing faster; it was having a system that ensured she showed up at her desk every morning, ready to write. "The combination of clear quarterly Objectives, Key Results, and daily Tasks made the impossible feel manageable," she reflects. "Each day's Task list was like a steppingstone toward my larger goal."

Sebastian not only completed his marathon but achieved his target time of 5.5 hours. His success came from the seamless integration of his training plan with daily task management. "Having my Personal OKR broken down into daily training Tasks made it real," he explains. "It wasn't just a dream anymore; it was simply what I did each day."

Anika achieved her B1 proficiency in Italian and was accepted into her dream archaeology program in Rome. Her success came from breaking a big language learning Objective into small daily Tasks. "The POKR Method gave me the big picture," she says, "while my daily Task list kept me moving forward one conversation, one grammar lesson at a time."

The good news is that everything we've discussed can also apply to non-POKR Tasks and general To-Do Lists. We encourage you to recycle these concepts wherever you see them fitting. We just don't want to explore the non–Personal OKR space too much here, though. That would go beyond the boundaries of this book. (We need to keep room for a V2.0, don't we?)

WHAT'S NEXT?

We have a good-quality To-Do List of Tasks, neatly prioritized, and ready to be executed. Nice! But how do we know *when* to work on them? And what if our judgments have been off a bit? Not to worry; there are, of course, good practices available.

We'll share ideas about "timeboxing" and "time tracking" in Chapter 12.

KEY TAKEAWAYS

1. **To-Do Lists Aren't the Enemy; Bad Ones Are**: To-Do Lists can boost focus, reduce anxiety, and deliver that sweet dopamine hit when you check something off. But when they become cluttered, undifferentiated dumping grounds, they bury your long-term goals under short-term noise.

2. **POKR Transforms To-Do Lists into Strategic Tools**: By anchoring each Task to a Key Result and Objective, your To-Do List becomes more than a reminder; it becomes a roadmap. POKR helps you focus on what matters, reduce decision fatigue, and see each Task in the context of your larger ambition.

3. **Start with Weekly Planning; Deliver Daily Action**: The secret sauce? A weekly planning ritual that separates POKR and non-POKR Tasks, distributes POKR Tasks across your week, and tees up each day with intention. This "weekly-to-daily" bridge is where Strategy meets Execution, and where most plans live or die.

4. **Prioritize like a Pro (Not a Procrastinator)**: Use research-backed methods (Eisenhower Matrix, MoSCoW, Ivy Lee, and others) to sort your Tasks. Personal OKR Tasks often land in the "Important but Not Urgent" zone, so make them urgent enough: timebox them, schedule inchstones, and move them to the top of your daily plan.

5. **Visibility, Simplicity, and Small Wins Fuel Progress**: Make your POKR Tasks visible via calendar, planner, digital board, or sticky notes and keep them actionable. Break

down daunting projects into small, momentum-building wins. Habits like "review daily over coffee" or "one key Task before lunch" can sustain your Personal OKRs even during life's curveballs.

6. It's possible to integrate popular productivity frameworks, such as GTD, with POKR logic. We can map them together quite easily.

TWELVE

CALENDAR INTEGRATION

GIVE IT TIME!

You can't touch the same water twice.[1] In a river, that is, which you step into. Okay, too abstract? Fair enough. We'll talk *time* next. It tends to flow in only one direction (skipping over the details of quantum mechanics here a bit).

Coming from the previous chapter, you have defined your actions appropriately in shape of Tasks. Let's place them on the timeline! Nothing beats having them front and center in a way that literally defines your day.

As usual, we are not going to force anything onto you. If you prefer to keep your Tasks as simple To-Do Lists, that's totally fine. Visualizing them with a bit more depth can be very powerful, though.

Let's talk *timely* execution!

Figure 47 shows where we are in the overall context.

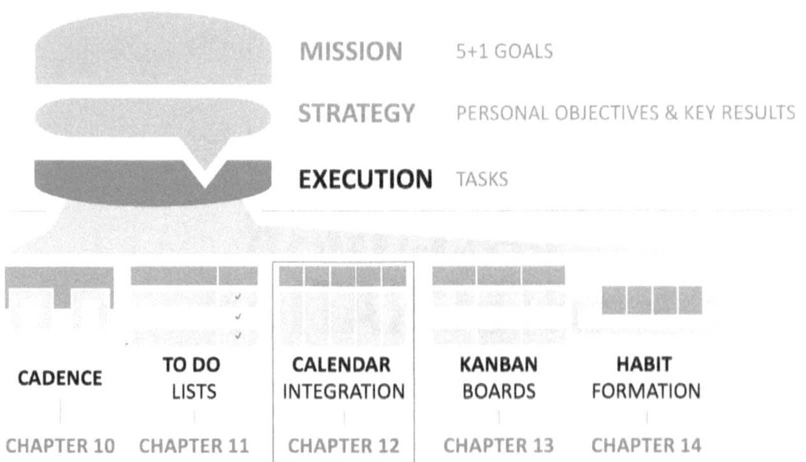

Figure 47: Execution Layer of POKR with Its Components

TIMEBOXING VIA CALENDAR INTEGRATION

The basic idea here is to schedule blocks of time for specific Tasks on your calendar. That means taking your Tasks off your To-Do List, estimating how much time each of them will consume, and transferring them into your diary. That structures your day and minimizes distractions.

Timeboxing is a term originally taken from Agile project management. It has been noted as one of the most useful productivity methods.[2] Recall our discussion about the shortcomings of To-Do Lists in the previous chapter? Choosing when to tackle each item can help with the paradox of choice. It also considers the diverse nature of Tasks, provides context for deadlines, and aids in managing other commitments. This approach can serve as a commitment device, helping you complete Tasks more efficiently.[3]

Timeboxing is therefore one of the most effective productivity hacks because it shifts the focus from trying to "get everything done" to managing your time with intention. Rather than letting Tasks expand indefinitely or constantly rewriting an ever-growing To-Do List, time-boxing gives each Task a reserved spot on your calendar.[4]

Having something visually manifested has proven to give you a higher chance of success. It's part of what's called "visual management."[5] So, placing Tasks from your Key Results onto a calendar can drive up your Task completion significantly. This simple shift has several game-changing benefits:

1. **It forces prioritization**: If everything can't fit on the calendar, then not everything can be a priority. Timeboxing forces tough (and necessary) choices.

2. **It limits perfectionism**: Knowing you only have 90 minutes to draft an article makes it easier to start without trying to write Pulitzer-winning prose.

3. **It transforms your calendar into a commitment device**: You're not just "trying to get things done"; you've got an appointment with yourself, or somebody else, to do them.

4. **It tames procrastination**: Instead of dreading a giant vague Task, you only need to "work on it for the next 45 minutes," which lowers the mental barrier to get started.

5. **It helps you measure reality**: Once you start timeboxing, you get a more realistic sense of how long things actually take, and how many Tasks you can handle in a day.

As some advocates put it, "Your calendar is your best To-Do List," because it combines time awareness with task management.[6] It requires you to decide which Task goes onto what day, though, and how long the Task will (roughly) take.

Practically speaking, we'd recommend a simple approach:

- Plan the placement of Tasks at the beginning of your week (as an output of your "Start of Week: Commitment" routine).

- Don't go beyond the current week; your planning accuracy beyond the current week will be rather "unsharp," and might be wasteful (a lot can change in the course of a single week).

For determining Task duration, here are some good practices:

- Take a best-guess estimate on how long the Task will take (we talk about "time tracking" in the next section). Thanks to our inability to be accurate here, be generous (probably double it). If you have trouble making up your mind, there are two easy alternatives:
  - Go for big blocks (half-day/4 hrs.) or,
  - simply block an entire, full day (works well if the volume of Tasks is compact, or the Task is juicy by nature: good for weekends).

POKR is for your private life. If you are a busy professional, your calendar might be already pretty loaded to begin with. But if something is really important, and Personal OKRs are by definition important, you'd want to use the early mornings, evenings, and weekends for placing related Tasks. Even with a nine-to-five day there is plenty of room to move you closer to your important targets.

Don't get too worked up if you can't complete a Task where you placed it. It was the best guess after all. Simply move it to another place on your calendar, if it must shift, or extend it, if you've started it already.

Figure 48 outlines that idea conceptionally: an already busy calendar, now infused with POKR Tasks at slots that feel appropriate.

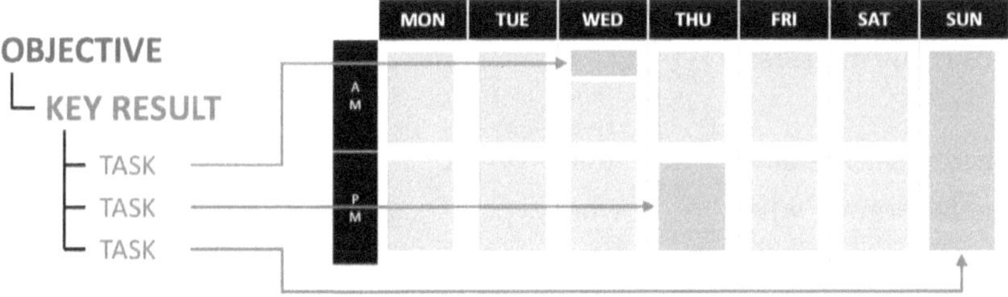

Figure 48: Task Placement on Calendar

Sebastian's journey gives us useful tips for applying what we've discussed. Training for a marathon isn't easy. You need various running blocks and some strength training to succeed. Honestly, for a first-time marathon runner, just "arriving" is the best strategy. The training volume is going up week by week, so some variability is required.

Initially, Seb tried to prepare for his training by using a simple To-Do List of Tasks for each Key Result. But that failed, for a variety of reasons:

- Flat lists don't really give you a "spatial" impression of flow (hence the flatness), with a limited dopamine hit when accomplishing one.

- Training time is significant, and it competes with other activities. This is hard to see if it's not in the same place as other commitments. Time is often our main constraint, so visualizing possible conflicts is important.

- There were no real "reminders" on when something was supposed to happen. It was always a manual, daily decision to make, resulting in missed trainings to "stack up" by end of the week.

This all led to frustration and a lack of preparedness. The breakthrough only came when Seb added the trainings to his calendar. *Every, single, day* there was one. (Okay, there were gaps for recovery. When you get older, this really matters.)

That not only gave him a sense of proper flow but also appropriate reminders for when to do what type of exercise. Conflicts with other commitments showed up right away, and could be dealt with immediately (oh, the sacrifices we make for good health).

Calendar integration and To-Do Lists are nicely going hand in hand, by the way: the Task on the list is simply scheduled on the calendar. You can think about this in a three-step mini process:

1. Define Tasks underneath Key Results.
2. Make lists of all Tasks to form a To-Do List.
3. Place Tasks from your To-Do List on the calendar (including non-POKR ones, if you have those).

Figure 49 illustrates that point with a practical example. And yes, we'd all prefer to run another 5k instead of going for that root canal treatment that we've been postponing for way too long.

That not only reminds you of the action ahead but also sends alerts when it's time to execute a Task. That is, if you use an electronic version of a diary, which we highly recommend. But nothing stops you from resorting to the paper version, if that's your thing. The automatic reminders are a lot less automatic, though.

Advanced thought: Some of us prefer to have a dedicated Personal OKR calendar, separate from their other calendars. You can use apps to show or hide individual calendars. This helps you avoid distractions. You can also display all the calendars at once. It's a good way to see if you've taken on too much. You don't want to miss important dates, like your wedding anniversary!

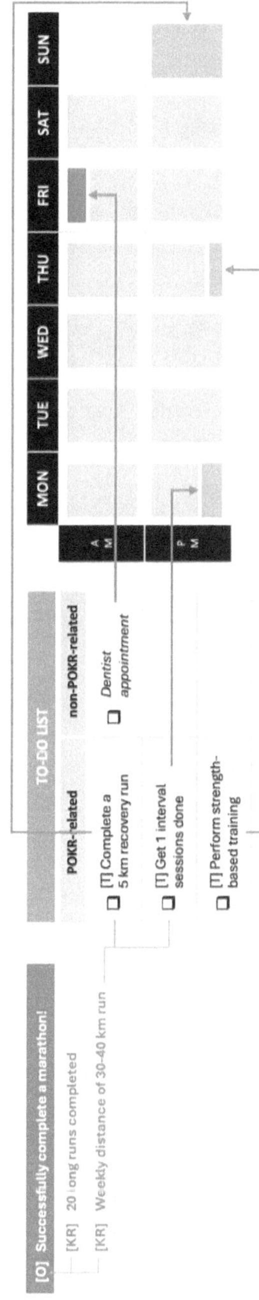

Figure 49. Show Integration of To-Do List with Calendar

WHEN IS A GOOD TIME?

The Energy–Time Connection

We have about 6 productive hours each day. Our peak happens 2 to 4 hours after waking, but this can vary based on your circadian rhythm.[7] This insight transforms how we should schedule our Personal OKR–related Tasks.

Elena, our novelist, discovered this principle through trial and error. Initially, she tried to write in the evenings after her day job. The results were disappointing: low word counts and frequent skipped sessions. Everything changed when she shifted her writing to early morning, dedicating the first 2 hours of each day to her novel. "It's like my brain knows that 6:00 to 8:00 a.m. is for writing, no questions asked," she explains. Her daily word count doubled, and more importantly, her consistency improved dramatically.

And if you are an "owl," the above timing might obviously differ quite a bit.

Context: The Missing Ingredient

One of the most powerful ways to integrate POKR with daily Tasks is through context-based organization. Think of context as the when, where, and how of Task execution. Let's say you aim at saving up some money for an upcoming vacation, as part of a travel Objective:

- **Morning Context**: Prepare homemade lunch to avoid extra spending (healthy, of course).

- **Evening Context**: Log daily spending into budget app (establishes a habit of tracking).

- **Weekend Context**: Review weekly budget figures (inspect and adapt in action).

This structured approach leads to an improvement in Task completion rates. Why? Because each Task had a natural home in your daily rhythm, making it more likely to get done.

Protect It!

Elena developed what she calls her "writer's firewall," a strict policy of no email or phone checks on Saturday mornings until she completes her daily writing quota. This simple rule transformed her writing from an "important but not urgent" Task into a "must-do-first" priority.

TIME TRACKING: YOU NEED TO FAIL FORWARD

We suggest tracking your time with tools or journals. This helps you see how you spend your time and spot patterns or inefficiencies. It allows you to gain awareness of time usage, and to take corrective action if we aren't too great at that, yet. Why would we want to do that?

No plan survives first contact with reality. Or in its original version, "No (battle) plan survives first-contact with the enemy," from Field Marshal Helmuth von Moltke the Elder.[8] The Prussians, such beautiful language. Meaning: We are horrible at estimating. Not you or us, but everyone is bad at it. On average. And the more uncertainty around, the worse it gets. The good news: It's normal. Life is hard. Stuff happens. So, let's simply acknowledge that. We tend to overestimate our abilities and underestimate complexity. It's known as the "planning fallacy".[9] Studies have shown that, on average, it takes three times longer to finish a Task than we think it will.

Now having that out of the way, let's see how we can get better at it. It's about finding patterns where we may be too optimistic or too critical in our estimates.

To make it clear on the outset: We are not advocating a formal time-tracking approach for implementing the POKR Method. Our experience shows that being too formal here can take a lot of time. It often results in mistakes, and we might overcompensate by simply adding (more) buffers for those future Tasks. But we still want to make sure we take stock of how well we did in planning, even though we keep it lean and pragmatic.

In Chapter 10, we discussed how frequent inspect-and-adapt steps help you review what you've achieved. They also allow you to look back on your processes. As part of the latter, you want to see if your assumptions about your Task breakdowns were good (enough). They will not be perfect, ever, but "directionally correct" is what you want to shoot for. When you go into your next planning cycle, make sure you spend some minutes contemplating how good or bad your estimates were in the past period.

When to do this exercise? You have a Retrospective routine on a quarterly and yearly level. That's a good opportunity to look into the rearview mirror. But feel free to do it more often, if you feel the need for it. Don't indeed wait until you have forgotten the root causes of the deviations. Hence, it is best to do it more frequently than not.

WHAT'S NEXT?

Calendar integration is one of multiple powerful visualization techniques that work great for those of us who prefer such spatial manifestations. Seeing is believing.

In the next chapter, we look at an alternative approach to bring Tasks to life, to turn them into a proper flow of action, for Personal OKRs and non-OKRs alike! Enter: Kanban Boards!

KEY TAKEAWAYS

1. For some of us, there's nothing like seeing your Tasks in your diary, front and center. This way, you can spot any potential conflicts with other non–Personal OKR activities right away.

2. To-Do Lists are a great foundation for adding Tasks to your calendar; it's almost a natural evolution from a flat list to a more time-driven grid.

3. Timeboxing has been proven to be one of the most effective productivity drivers out there, creating a "commitment device" that drives action in your day-to-day reality.

4. There is always room for things that are important, be it in the early morning, over lunch, in the evenings, or on the weekends. It oftentimes is just a matter of priority.

5. Keep time blocking simple; don't get annoyed if you can't come up with an estimate quickly, or if you need to move stuff around. That's normal.

6. We are awful at estimating activities to any degree of precision, and that's okay! We need to accept that. Directionally correct is the desired spirit.

7. Don't overdue task tracking, it's rarely worth the effort. But we can get better at it by regularly looking back at our past "performance" and learn from it for the next cycles.

THIRTEEN

KANBAN BOARDS
Visualize Task Flow

BRIDGING PERSONAL OKRs
AND PERSONAL KANBAN

MAGINE PAULINE, AN AVID RUNNER AND SELF-PROFESSED "goal junkie." Every New Year's Eve, she scribbles down resolutions on sticky notes: Learn to play the guitar, train for a mountaineering expedition, read a book a week, volunteer every month, and more. As the weeks pass, however, her enthusiasm fades:

- she can't seem to find time for guitar practice after work,
- her mountaineering training regimen fizzles out, and
- her volunteering goal gets buried under daily life.

By March, Pauline's once-exciting list of Objectives has become a source of frustration rather than motivation. And it's not for trying: She's been a good student and followed the POKR Method pretty well.

But something didn't quite work for her: If you ask her, she will probably tell you that she's more the "creative" type: doodling ideas down in journals, collecting tokens from vacations that turn into collages, going for vibe rather than stone-cold logic. In short: being very "visual" in life. Correspondingly, she's likely scoring high on "right brain" dimensions, showing a stronger inclination to decide intuitively, emotional, with a dislike for focusing on a single thing at a time.

We talked about the fact that most available productivity techniques are actually biased toward "left brain" individuals, who tend to be more analytical, ordered, and focused on doing one thing at a time. Those tend to love To-Do Lists, integrating activities into their calendars, being structured and orderly. But not Pauline.

This is where *Kanban* comes to the rescue, offering a visual and practical framework that provides more of a "flow" with flexibility to move things around, something that a flat To-Do List has trouble offering. Figure 50 gives you some examples of how that might look.

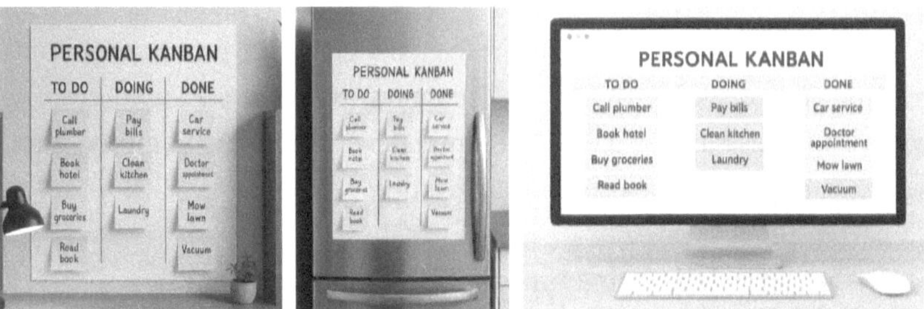

Figure 50. Examples of Personal Kanban Boards

By mapping her Personal OKRs onto a Kanban Board, Pauline finds herself transforming the "someday" target into daily, actionable steps that keep her moving forward with desired consistency, but with sufficient flexibility to change things around when needed. She doesn't have to sacrifice her ambition; with the POKR Kanban Board, she gains a clear map to make those ambitions real.

In this chapter, we'll look at how aligning Personal OKRs with a Kanban Board transforms goals, Objectives, and Key Results into an achievable, step-by-step process. By visualizing targets and managing progress in a concrete way, you can maintain both focus and flexibility on your personal development journey.

Figure 51 showcases where we are in the overall Execution context:

Figure 51. Execution Layer of POKR with Its Components

HOW KANBAN COMPLEMENTS PERSONAL OKRS

What Is Kanban?

Kanban is a visual workflow management method that makes your work visible while setting boundaries around what you tackle at any given time. It follows a number of core principles; the key ones in a simplified way are:

1. visualize your work ("visual management")
2. limit work in progress (WIP)
3. pulling work through the system

The Kanban system originated in Japan in the late 1940s, when Toyota engineer Taiichi Ohno developed it to streamline production. In Japanese, *kan* means "visual" and *ban* means "card," so Kanban translates to "signboard".[1]

The system was designed to prevent waste by ensuring that only necessary inventory was kept on hand; when supplies ran low, a Kanban card was sent to request more materials, which were then "pulled" through the production line as needed. This type of Kanban is also referred to as "Traditional" or "Manufacturing Kanban," largely focusing on inventory management, which isn't exactly why we want to talk about it here.

Over time, Kanban's principles of lean production found new applications beyond manufacturing, particularly in managing knowledge work. By the early 2000s, Kanban was being adapted for fields like software development,[2] and today it's used widely for personal task management.[3]

In personal productivity, Kanban Boards, whether they are physical or digital, help individuals visualize Tasks, manage workload, and limit multitasking, making it easier to progress through daily actions aligned with longer-term goals like Personal OKRs.

Kanban Boards tend to come in various flavors. It doesn't matter too much if you go for the whiteboard version on your office wall, the family fridge one, or purely digital incarnations. They largely all perform equally well, it's just a matter of personal preference (it's just that a digital Kanban app does not provide immediate context for urgent grocery shopping, to replace expired milk).

The visual nature of Kanban turns abstract Tasks into tangible, visible steps, helping you stay grounded in what's immediately important without feeling overwhelmed. Instead of relying on a long list of Tasks, Kanban provides a dynamic, visual system where you can see, prioritize, and manage your workflow at a glance.

How Do OKRs and Kanban Work Together?

Personal OKRs and Kanban Boards are like the GPS and dashboard of your personal development journey. Personal OKRs act as your destination and route planning system, while Kanban serves as your real-time dashboard, showing your current status, immediate next steps, and progress markers.

Cognitive psychology supports this dual approach: People do better with clear long-term goals and structured short-term feedback.[4] The POKR-Kanban combination offers this. It breaks down aspirational Objectives into measurable results (Key Results) and pairs them with a visual system for tracking daily progress.

Kanban complements Personal OKRs in four fundamental ways:

1. **Visibility**: While Personal OKRs provide the "what" and "why" of your targets, Kanban makes visible the "how" and "when" through its visual board system.

2. **Flow Control**: Personal OKRs help you set ambitious targets, while Kanban's WIP limits prevent you from becoming overwhelmed by keeping your daily workload manageable.

3. **Adaptability**: Personal OKRs provide quarterly and yearly directions, while Kanban offers the flexibility to adjust your daily and weekly tactics based on emerging priorities and constraints.

4. **Rationality and Feedback:** Pulling work on the Kanban Board through its different phases is an intentional process, providing kinesthetic feedback, which is a fancy way of saying that it feels good!

However, merging these systems isn't without its challenges. Many people struggle with:

- Maintaining separate systems for long-term goals and daily Tasks
- Balancing Personal OKR-related work with routine, reoccurring responsibilities
- Avoiding the trap of creating overly complex systems that become burdensome to maintain

In the following sections, we'll explore practical solutions to these challenges and show you how POKR integrates both approaches into a singular method. We'll start with the fundamental components of a Kanban system and then demonstrate how to overlay your Personal OKRs onto this visual framework effectively.

SETTING UP YOUR KANBAN SYSTEM

Remember Pauline from our opening story? Her first attempt at creating a Kanban Board involved meticulously creating categories for every possible type of Task, a common beginner's mistake. "I thought more structure meant better organization," she admitted, "but I ended up with a system so complex I avoided using it."

Let's learn from Pauline's experience and start with the essential components before adding layers of sophistication.

Essential Components of a Kanban Board

At its heart, Kanban rests on three fundamental principles:

1. **Make work visible:** By visualizing your tasks, Kanban provides a clear view of what's in progress, what's next, and what's completed. This visibility is key for maintaining focus and reducing cognitive overload.

2. **Limit WIP:** Setting limits on tasks in progress keeps you focused and prevents overcommitting. By concentrating on a few items, you can make meaningful progress and avoid mental fatigue.[5]

3. **Pulling work through the system:** Allowing you to selectively choose which tasks to focus on provides freedom of choice yet transparency on the overall ask at hand. Completing work creates a positive feedback loop for future iterations.

These principles might sound simple, but they're backed by solid cognitive science:

Visual task management systems significantly reduce cognitive load compared to traditional To-Do Lists.[6] Visual organization of tasks helps people resume work more quickly after interruptions and reduces the mental effort required to track multiple responsibilities.[7] When we can see our work laid out before us, our brains can more efficiently process, prioritize, and execute tasks.[8]

Creating Your Basic Board

Figure 52. A Basic Kanban Board

Conceptually speaking, your Kanban Board is to represent the flow of how you get stuff done, the process from beginning to end, like an assembly line, where you have multiple steps being done one after the other. Because that can quickly become very specific, let's start simple with these three essential columns:

1. To Do: Backlog of Tasks awaiting attention
2. Doing: Work actively in progress
3. Done: Completed Tasks

Figure 52 shows what such a typical Kanban Board filled with cards looks like, with work flowing from left ("To Do") to right ("Done").

This simple structure provides clarity while maintaining flexibility. "The simplest possible thing that could work should be your starting point" is the way to go.[9]

The Power of WIP Limits

One of the most crucial and often most challenging aspects of Kanban is setting and maintaining what's called a WIP limit. Think of a WIP limit as the guardrail that keeps you from veering off into the ditch of multitasking. It's the maximum number of Tasks that you're supposed to work on, at the same time.

Research has consistently shown that multitasking is largely a myth.[10] Heavy multitaskers are less productive and more susceptible to distractions than those who focus on one task at a time.[11]

Here are the simple rules:

- The "To Do" column represents your overall backlog (i.e., work that you just haven't been able to get to), hence there's no need to set a WIP limit. Sky is the limit for work that is ahead of you.

- For your "Doing" column, a WIP limit of two to three Tasks is appropriate for most people (there is actually a formula for this, but we'll spare you the specifics).

- Yes, this might feel restrictively low at first, but that's exactly the point. This constraint forces us to make active choices about our work rather than passively accepting every request that comes our way. The idea is that you can't pull more into "Doing" than your WIP limit. For example, if there are already two Tasks placed into this column, and your WIP limit is two, you can only pull from "To Do" when you've completed one of the Tasks first, having moved that one to "Done."

- The "Done" column, again, is not restricted by a WIP limit, given that it serves as the receiving bucket of all the great things that you have accomplished. Figure 53 visualizes this.

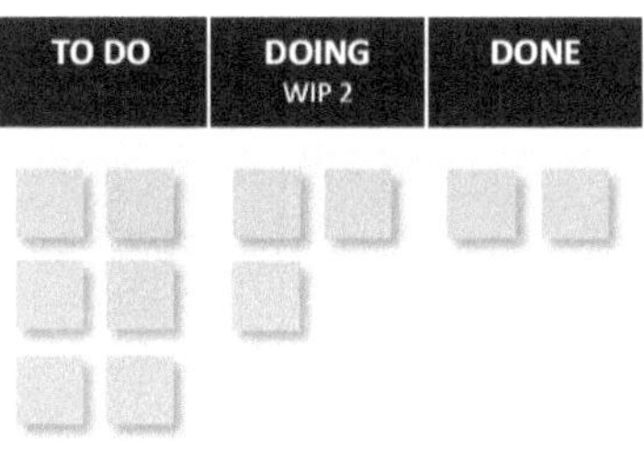

Figure 53. Kanban Board with WIP Limit

Customizing Your Board

Once you're comfortable with the basic setup, consider these additional columns to introduce some more nuance:

This Week

- **Purpose:** Medium-term planning and prioritization
- **Benefits:** Bridges the gap between immediate Tasks and longer-term goals
- **Source:** Pulled in from "To Do"
- **Timing:** During your Weekly Commitment routine

Today

- **Purpose**: High-priority Tasks for immediate attention
- **Benefits**: Helps focus daily efforts on most impactful work, without getting distracted with what is still in the "To Do" column
- **Source**: Pulled in from "To Do" or "This Week"
- **Timing**: When you do your Daily Check-In routine

Waiting

- **Purpose**: Tasks that are blocked or awaiting input from others. Placed in this column temporarily until the roadblock is removed, then moving them back to "Doing" or to "Done."
- **Benefits**: Makes dependencies visible and prevents false progress assumptions
- **Source**: Pulled in from "Doing"
- **Timing**: Whenever you hit a roadblock during "Doing." Make sure to regularly review this column, ideally every day as part of Daily Check-In.

Figure 54 shows an example of an evolved board structure with the additional columns just mentioned and a WIP limit on "Doing" of two:

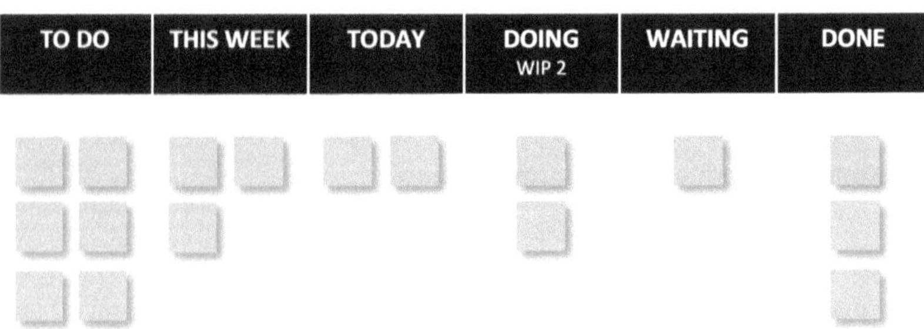

Figure 54. Evolved Kanban Board

We recommend starting simple, to get a feel for the "flow" and the "mechanics," first.

Remember that the columns represent the flow of how you get things done. It is tempting to add a lot of additional columns, but you might quickly hit a point where that creates too much specificity.

The type of things that you deal with via POKR can be very diverse. You usually deal with two to three Objectives from several Life Categories. For instance, "writing a book" has a very specific process flow compared to "prepare for a marathon." You don't want to end up with a Kanban Board tailored for each individual Objective. That would make the method rather cumbersome and overengineered.

Hence, it's best to keep the columns somewhat generic, to allow all types of work flowing on your board. But we don't want to stop you from iterating on this, so feel free to experiment!

A Word on Digital Versus Physical Boards

The original Kanban Boards were physical boards with physical cards being moved around. That also works well for your home, either on whiteboards, cardboards, or even just a fridge door. You can also craft a digital board in a Word document, a PowerPoint slide, a spreadsheet, or with Kanban software to display the same elements you'd see in a manual version.

Physical boards (using sticky notes) offer a tactile experience, while digital tools like Trello, Smartsheet, or Wrike provide remote access and automation features. Digital tools may work better for those who are constantly on the go, while physical boards are ideal for visual clarity at home.

While digital tools offer convenience and accessibility, don't dismiss the power of physical boards. Research demonstrates that physical interaction with work materials can enhance cognitive performance.[12] This suggests that the physical act of moving Task cards, whether on a physical or digital board, can help us better process and commit to our work. Consider these factors when choosing your medium:

Physical Boards
- **Pros**: Tactile engagement, always visible, no technical barriers
- **Cons**: Limited accessibility, not easily shared, can become messy

Digital Boards
- **Pros**: Accessible anywhere, easy to share, automated tracking
- **Cons**: Less tactile engagement, can be forgotten when out of sight

We personally use a digital version for our Kanban Boards, but this is really a matter of personal preference than anything else.

BRINGING IT ALL TOGETHER: THE POKR KANBAN BOARD

Let's return to Pauline's story. After establishing her basic Kanban Board, she faced a new challenge: "How do I make sure my daily Tasks actually move me toward my Personal OKRs, rather than just helping me stay busy?"

This is where a thoughtful POKR integration becomes crucial. The goal isn't just to manage Tasks efficiently, but to ensure those Tasks align with your broader Objectives. We want your new Kanban Board to avoid becoming an "untethered" artifact or just another visual management gimmick. It should become an essential part of your daily life.

Here's how that will work:

Mapping OKRs onto a Kanban Board

Let's bring back the POKR Canvas from a previous chapter. You still remember how we visualized Objectives and Key Results across the various Life Categories in a yearly grid, but we want to get to a Task level here. So, let's take it a level down. Our top choice here is to use multiple swim lanes, one for each Objective. Essentially, we zoom into the current quarter of your POKR Canvas to provide a Kanban perspective of underlying Tasks. That will show POKRs you're tracking right now:

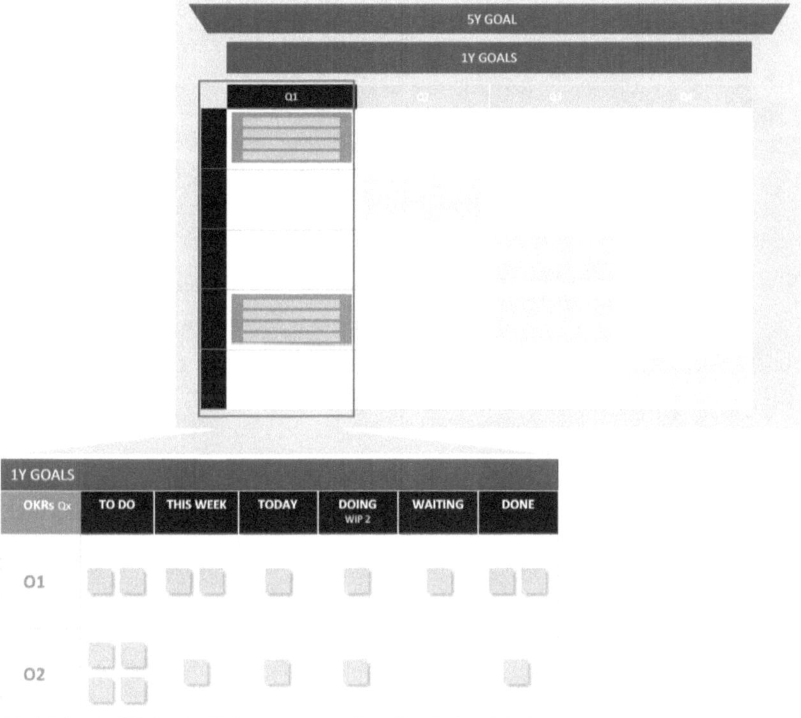

Figure 55. POKR Canvas Meets Kanban Board, for the Current Quarter

Given that you'll never deal with more than two to three Objectives per quarter, this becomes a rather manageable visual. And your Kanban Board will always just represent that current quarter, never going beyond it. (How would it? You only have Personal OKRs for the current quarter anyway.)

Think of your Personal OKRs and Kanban Tasks in the usual hierarchical relationship, as an example:

1. *Objective Level* (*Quarter/Year*)

   [o] **Become a recognized thought leader in AI ethics.**

2. *Key Results Level* (*Monthly*)

    [KR] Published 3 peer-reviewed articles in at least one top-tier journal

3. *Task Level* (*Daily/Weekly*)

    [T] *Complete literature review for article number one*
    [T] *Draft methodology section*

Not only does that organize the work more sensibly, it also always keeps your Personal OKRs visible. Furthermore, we recommend keeping your Yearly Goal(s) visible above the board, to constantly remind you why you're doing all the good stuff underneath.

How to Show Routine and Reoccurring Tasks?

Your Kanban Board can include both Personal OKR–focused Tasks and other daily responsibilities. That is particularly important for "stuff" that is reoccurring in nature, which is something you typically wouldn't manifest as Personal OKRs. This is often referred to as "Business as Usual" (BAU) or "keep the lights on" activities.

Life is not always a creative space of discrete, exciting pieces of work. It might have a more mundane angle to it at times, too. Examples:

- Weekly football practice for the kids (if not modeled by OKRs)
- That Thursday evening commitment with friends (watching Premier League?)
- Biweekly lawn mowing or seasonal yard maintenance
- Refilling prescriptions/managing medications (yours or family member's)
- Daily dog walk (a nonnegotiable with your four-legged accountability coach)
- Daily school drop-off and pick-up duties (a.k.a. "Dad/Uber mode")
- Paying monthly utility bills (because electricity is still considered essential)

You get the idea.

Now why do we propose to map these routine activities out as well? Well, they might actually consume a considerable amount of bandwidth, which in turn is not available anymore for Personal OKR work. So, it can help you in judging POKR commitments better if you have a visual representation of routine and reoccurring Tasks on the same board as your Personal OKR action.

Given that routine and reoccurring Tasks aren't really "moving" on a board as beautifully as "discrete" work, that swim lane needs to look rather different: It shows the Task, but you'd simply tick it off on the day that it took place. A weekly pattern is the classical way to model this:

RE-OCCURING	MON	TUE	WED	THU	FRI	SAT	SUN
	✓						
		✓					

Figure 56. Kanban Swim Lane for Reoccurring Tasks

Sarah gained accountability by connecting with a native Italian speaker for weekly chats. These scheduled sessions made her feel the need to practice daily. After all, no one wants to arrive unprepared for such a conversation.

You could also do that for a monthly pattern, but given that we "reset" this Kanban Board every quarter anyways, this might not be necessary. But again, feel free to experiment!

We therefore advise to keep these types of routine activities visible. Do these activities "consume" your WIP limit? Probably not. So, you want to keep them excluded from that.

What about non-OKR-related Tasks?

Using a Kanban Board lets you manage both Personal OKR and non–Personal OKR Tasks in one place. If work and personal responsibilities demand attention, you could either:

1. Create a multi-board setup, one for professional OKRs and another for personal commitments. Not ideal, given that you must switch between them all the time to judge your overall level of commitment. Doable, but there's a better way:

2. Simply add another (set of) swim lane(s) to your existing board, where you track those activities that aren't related to POKRs and are not reoccurring by nature.

The complete piece of art in a single, "composite" POKR Kanban Board, hung on the wall, based on Pauline's Personal OKRs for the current quarter:

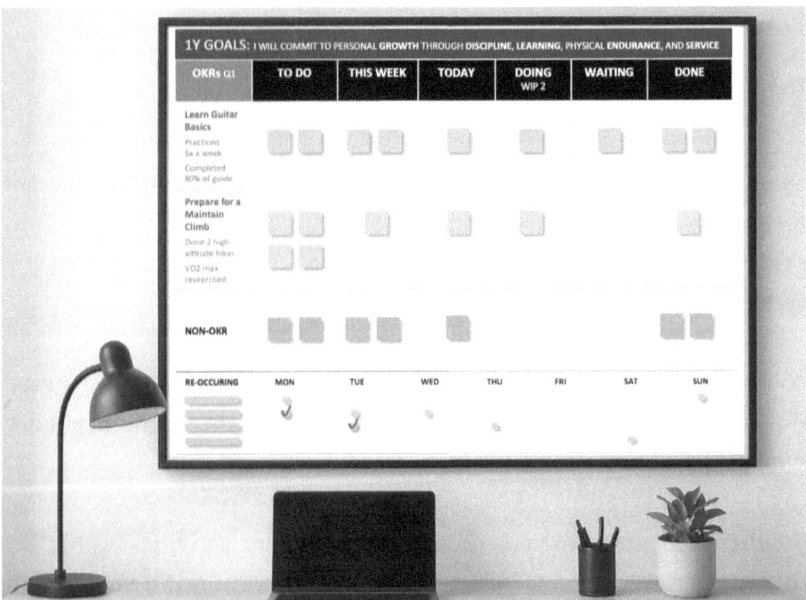

Figure 57. POKR Kanban Board, Example

Make It Colorful!

If you want to use different colors for different types of Tasks, go for it! That's also a nifty hack for digital tools that don't allow swim lanes; simply use different color codes to indicate the various Objectives.

Doing this with software is easy (all tools offer this capability), by either tagging a Task or changing its color. The same is true for physical boards: Use different-colored Post-it notes, plus colored sticky dots. Alternatively: Invest in some multicolored pens and draw a bit!

Adapting the System for Continuous Improvement

Kanban encourages celebrating each small win. When Tasks reach the "Done" column, pause to recognize your progress. Each completed Task represents a step forward, building confidence and motivation toward larger Personal OKRs.

Retrospectives, which are a common practice in Agile ways of working, offer insights into which aspects of your Kanban setup are working and which need tweaks. As we recommend, please run a Quarterly Retrospective at the tail end of each (quarterly) Personal OKR cycle. You only will get better over time if you make this a conscious step in the journey. It is tempting to skip it, but that would remove one of the most powerful learning opportunities that POKR offers you.

Use these reflections to refine the structure of your Kanban Board. Your "Done" column, by the way, should be nicely filled by the end of the quarter. Using accomplished Tasks as an input into both Retrospectives and Review is good practice.

Plus: Before you start a new cycle, clear the "Done" column. Just take a photo so that you can revisit at a later point.

WHAT'S NEXT?

This chapter concludes the "visual" part of POKR.

But before we go on, remember that helpful swim lane on reoccurring Tasks? The actions you plan to repeat regularly, some just monthly, but others weekly or even daily? Oftentimes, we try to establish new behaviors, or unlearn those that we feel are hindering us, by simply using Tasks on a Kanban Board.

And there's nothing wrong with that. But we might have a better idea. Why not use the power of POKR by more directly establishing new habits? Let's discuss the science and mechanics of habit forming in Chapter 14.

KEY TAKEAWAYS

1. **Start Simple**: Begin with a basic Kanban Board layout that includes only essential columns like "To Do," "Doing," and "Done." Focus on the core principles of visualizing work and limiting WIP. Add complexity, such as additional columns or labels, only as your needs evolve, ensuring you're not overwhelmed by too many features at the start.

2. **Stay Flexible**: Adapt the Kanban system to your unique needs. Embrace change and experiment with new approaches, being open to modifications that can make the system more effective for you. Don't hesitate to let go of elements that aren't working.

3. **Top-Down Approach**: Use your POKR Canvas as the starting point, which shows your total year, and "zoom in" to the current quarter for more details for your POKR Kanban Board.

4. **Maintain Alignment**: Keep your Personal OKRs visible and central on your POKR Kanban Board to maintain focus on your Objectives for the current quarter. Conduct regular alignment checks to ensure your daily Tasks are progressing toward these targets.

5. **Trust the Process**: Give yourself time to see the benefits of this visual approach. Recognize that results may take a while to show and treat any failures as opportunities to learn and improve. Celebrate each milestone or inchstone, however small, as they reinforce motivation and confidence in your process.

Remember Pauline? Her final insight was perhaps the most valuable: "The real power of combining Personal OKRs and Kanban isn't in the system itself, but in how it helps you to think differently about your targets, because you can literally watch them getting done!"

FOURTEEN

HABIT FORMATION WITH POKR

A Match Made in Productivity Heaven!

THE INTERSECTION OF OKRS AND HABITS

WHEN WE INTRODUCED KEY RESULTS, WE HAD EXAMPLES like "Exercise for 30 minutes, 5 days a week" or "Read one book per month." You're not wrong if you're scratching your head thinking, *Wait a minute; aren't these just habits in disguise?*

Let's talk about the elephant in the room: How do Personal OKRs relate to habit formation?

HABITS 101: NOT JUST YOUR MORNING COFFEE RITUAL

Before we dive deeper, let's get our definitions straight. Habits, as James Clear, author of *Atomic Habits*, would tell you, are the compound interest of self-improvement.[1] They're those automatic behaviors we perform without thinking much. These actions are the building blocks of our daily lives.

Figure 58. Execution Layer of POKR with Its Components

Charles Duhigg, who wrote *The Power of Habit*, says habit formation has four key elements:

1. **Cue:** The trigger that initiates the behavior
2. **Craving:** The motivation or desire to act
3. **Response:** The actual habit or behavior
4. **Reward:** The benefit gained from performing the habit[2]

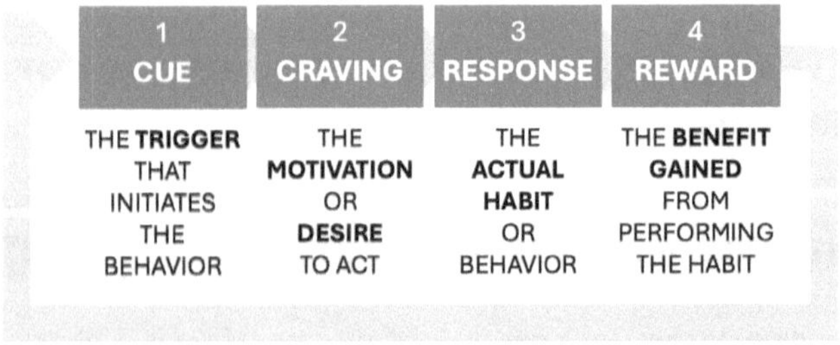

Figure 59. Process Loop for Habit Formation

Consider Suki, who wants to start a daily meditation practice. She places her meditation cushion next to her bed (cue), so she sees it first thing each morning. The sight of the cushion reminds her how calm and centered she feels after meditating (craving). Each morning, she'd sit for just two minutes of mindful breathing (response), a small commitment that feels achievable.

Afterward, she rewards herself with her favorite morning coffee, savoring it in that peaceful post-meditation state (reward). Within weeks, the meditation-then-coffee routine becomes as natural as brushing her teeth.

Now, contrast this with Ian's smoking habit. The sight of his coworkers heading out for a smoke break (cue) triggers a craving for both nicotine and social connection. He joins them outside (response), getting not just the chemical hit from the cigarette but also 10 minutes of relaxed socializing (reward).

This powerful combination of chemical and social rewards makes the habit particularly sticky. Knowing this can help Ian stop his habit. He can find new ways to socialize and handle stress. This will break the cycle that has held him for years.

In both cases, habits continue due to the reward and the brain's link between the cue and response. To change or form habits, grasping this loop is key. For positive habits, design cues and rewards that support your goals. To break negative habits, try changing your response. For example, Nicotine Replacement Therapy (NRT) is an approach to reduce withdrawal symptoms and thus break the cue–reward linkage.[3] You can also try linking the cue or trigger (work breaks) to something else altogether (e.g., use this time to stretch, meditate, or chat with a nonsmoking colleague).[4]

Suki purposefully crafted her habit loop to meet her desires. In contrast, Ian's habit loop developed without intention and harmed his long-term well-being. As Clear would say, make good habits obvious, attractive, easy, and satisfying, and make bad habits invisible, unattractive, difficult, and unsatisfying.

Or phrased differently: To build a good habit, remove friction. For habits you want to avoid, add friction.

Here's the twist: The two habit experts don't mention OKRs in their popular books. It's like hosting a party with two celebrities who have never met before. Awkward, maybe. But it's also a chance to make a productive introduction. So, let's explore how.

OKRS AND HABITS: COMPLEMENTARY OR CONFLICTING?

At first glance, Personal OKRs and habits might seem to operate in different domains. Personal OKRs set bold Objectives and track progress. Habits focus on making behaviors automatic. However, a closer examination reveals some interesting points of convergence.

Personal OKRs give you structure and clarity. They help turn vague intentions into trackable actions. Think of it as an organized system for your habits. This approach lets you quantify progress, for example by saying "meditate 10 minutes daily" instead of "become more mindful." It also includes regular check-ins to keep you accountable.

Perhaps most importantly, connecting daily habits to larger life Objectives provides meaningful motivation; suddenly, that daily flossing routine becomes part of your greater journey toward optimal health.

However, Personal OKRs can make habit formation more complicated than it needs to be. Sometimes, you just need to act instead of overthinking it. Focusing too much on numbers can be risky. For instance, you might mistakenly care more about hitting a step count than living an active lifestyle.

Also, the quarterly cycle of Personal OKRs often clashes with the messy reality of habit formation. Progress can be like "two steps forward, one step back." This pattern may not fit neatly into your Key Results. While consistency is important, too much rigidity can hinder lasting change. Recent research, including a study conducted at Google, illustrates how cultivating flexibility within routines leads to more robust and adaptable habits.[5] Being able to adjust a routine to different circumstances is key to building habits that endure.

FINDING THE RIGHT BALANCE

So, should you use Personal OKRs to form habits? You absolutely can and should!

Using Personal OKRs can indeed help establish good habits. Their structure, accountability, and clear motivation can greatly help you build habits. With POKR, you've already laid the groundwork for making systematic changes in your life.

Now, we can use that foundation to design, manage, and track your habits. This is a crucial step that many habit experts might miss! There are two popular ways to use POKR for habit formation:

1. Directly as an Objective (if it's *really* important)
2. Indirectly via a Key Result, supporting an Objective

Let's see both concepts in action.

Directly as an Objective

The obvious way to do this is having your target habit as an Objective. That's a good choice for really important ones, where you want to spend a considerable amount of time "fixing" something that is bothering you. The classical one: how you might drop a bad habit of doomscrolling on your phone:[6]

> [o] **Reduce my compulsion to doomscroll to foster a healthier relationship with my environment**
>
> [kr1] Used the built-in screen time features to cap my usage of key apps to 30 minutes/day[7]
>
> [kr2] Followed 10 accounts that promote well-being, reducing distressing content[8]
>
> [kr3] Applied Cognitive Behavioral Therapy (CBT), practicing one technique/day[9]
>
> [kr4] Replaced scrolling with exercise, stretching, taking a walk instead, at least once every day

Now, you'd "lose" an Objective slot on your POKR Canvas (remember to not have more than three per quarter), so you'd be careful about what Objectives you'd do that with.

Indirect as a Key Result

If the above is "elevating" the habit too much, and you'd rather go for smaller steps, maybe placing habit-forming elements underneath the Objective is the more appropriate way to go:

> [o] **Boost my energy and productivity at work**
>
> [kr1] Established a consistent sleep schedule (in bed by 10:00 p.m., up by 6:00 a.m.) 5 days a week
>
> [kr2] Meditated for 10 minutes daily, 6 days a week
>
> [kr3] Increased water intake to eight glasses per day, on average

This way, the habits serve a larger purpose and are more likely to stick. It's like promoting your habits. They become more than just habits; they turn into Key Results!

Mixing Personal OKRs with habits forms a powerful system for personal growth. It's like having a personal development Swiss Army knife: you've got all the tools you need in one package.

Remember, the key to success is finding the right balance for you.

Go ahead and set your Objectives, track your Key Results, and develop those habits. And don't forget to floss, even if it's not part of your Personal OKRs. Your Future-Self will thank you and might even give you a perfect Personal OKR score.

WHAT'S NEXT?

With the previous suggestions on habit formation, we conclude *Part IV of Execution*. We'll shift gears next with *Part V* to go *Beyond the Mechanics,* to talk about balancing personal projects with family priorities in Chapter 15.

You might wonder why we need to discuss this. The thing is, it's easy to get carried away with a new method. You could end up treating family members like they're part of a corporate board. But there's a better approach. Let's explore how.

KEY TAKEAWAYS

1. Habit formation is a simple process: cue, craving, response, and reward. This creates a loop between reward and cue, driving both positive and negative habits.

2. Popular habit formation methods often lack the needed system. They don't provide clear recommendations on how to make them stick.

3. POKR is a strong way to build new habits or drop old ones. It focuses on practical steps and clear routines.

4. Using habits as Key Results under Objectives is a simple way to get to that new personal growth target!

BEYOND THE MECHANICS

"Prioritize what matters. You can't be everywhere, do everything, and have everything."

—OPRAH WINFREY

FIFTEEN

BALANCING PERSONAL PROJECTS AND FAMILY TIME

WHEN THE PICNIC BECOMES THE PROJECT

PICTURE THIS: MIGUEL, A DEDICATED PROJECT MANAGER, decides to bring his workplace skills into family life. Why? To organize the "best family picnic ever." He sets ambitious Personal OKRs:

[O] **Achieve the ultimate family picnic**

[KR1]   Five gourmet dishes prepared

[KR2]   50 Instagram-worthy photos captured

[KR3]   10 new followers gained by showcasing family happiness

The day arrives. The artisanal sandwiches are wilting in the sun. His kids are staging a rebellion against the seventh "candid" photo shoot. His spouse is wondering if their family memories now require a social media strategy. By sunset, the supposedly idyllic picnic has become a running family joke, and Miguel is left wondering: what went wrong?

This story shows an important truth: Our families aren't just Key Results. Instead, our personal Objectives should fit into family life, not take it over. Trying to make family interactions too rigid can raise stress and lower satisfaction for everyone involved.

Balancing personal goals with family needs takes teamwork, flexibility, and focus, not metrics and milestones. POKR is giving you the tool set to strike the right balance in theory, but you're still in the driver's seat, having to make the *right* decisions along the way.

WEAVING PERSONAL GOALS INTO FAMILY LIFE

Balancing personal ambitions and family commitments often feels like walking a tightrope. When you overemphasize personal targets, guilt or resentment can quickly creep in. Focusing too much on family duties can stall your dreams. This might leave you feeling frustrated or even burned out.

Take Simone, a passionate amateur photographer who set an ambitious goal to build her portfolio. She dedicated every weekend to photo walks and editing sessions, determined to make progress. Three months in, she realized she had missed her daughter's soccer games and her son's music recital. The gorgeous landscapes she captured couldn't make up for the family moments she'd lost. The guilt was affecting not just her mood but her creative work as well.

Then there's Marcus, who went to the opposite extreme. After getting feedback that he wasn't present enough for his family, he put his dream of designing his own board game completely on hold. He threw himself into being the "perfect" dad: coaching teams, helping with homework, handling every household chore. Six months later, he found himself sketching game mechanics on napkins after everyone had gone to bed. He felt frustrated with his slow progress and resented not being able to pursue his passion openly.

These examples show how either extreme can create tension. The sweet spot lies somewhere in the middle, where personal ambitions and family life don't compete but complement each other. The key is finding ways to pursue your goals while staying connected to your loved ones.

Predictably, studies show that over 50% of working parents struggle to balance work and family.[1] Adding personal projects makes this challenge even harder.

However, there is an opportunity here. Everyday moments can become meaningful family interactions when we approach them mindfully.[2] When done right, integrating personal targets into family life creates a virtuous cycle. Pursuing your passions enhances your well-being, which in turn makes you a more engaged and happier partner or parent. Involving your family in your ambitions adds their unique views and strengthens your bonds.

BUILDING BRIDGES, NOT WALLS

Balancing personal projects with family life needs strategies that focus on connection, not division. This includes open communication, setting boundaries, cocreating your Objectives, and adopting health-focused habits that support everyone's well-being.

Open Communication

Transparent communication is the foundation of a harmonious family life. Sharing your goals with your family builds trust and fosters collaboration. Explaining why your personal projects matter helps others understand your values. This approach encourages understanding instead of resistance.

Family meetings are a great way to align schedules and address concerns. Regular check-ins, whether at dinner or during a casual walk, ensure everyone feels heard and included. Transparency isn't just good practice; it's essential for family harmony. Open communication strengthens family relationships and reduces conflict.[3]

Consider Emma, a writer working on her first novel. Instead of hiding away with her manuscript, she shares her writing milestones with her teenage daughter. Their talks on character development have grown into deeper chats about setting and reaching life goals. Her personal challenge has become a teaching tool for ambition and perseverance.

Cocreate Objectives

As discussed in previous chapters, you don't have to be alone on this journey. Coming up with well-balanced Personal OKRs is a bit more art than science and requires patience; failure is absolutely priced in! But you don't have to suffer through this on your own. Remember the different Life Categories of Personal OKRs that we proposed? One was "Family," wasn't it?

How about we codesign Personal OKRs in that swim lane? You include your personal ecosystem, like your partner and kids. The other categories might be exclusively yours to formulate, but the *Family* one offers an opportunity to cocreate them. What would that do? Well, participation in the creative process directly creates ownership and desire in the outcomes. That can dramatically increase the likelihood for that particular Personal OKR to get done!

It can also become a family routine. High-priority family matters can be set as Personal OKRs and managed using the familiar POKR Method. If you have to brief your family anyway on your Personal OKRs, why not have them join in the crafting process itself?

Setting Boundaries

Clear boundaries are crucial for balancing personal and family life. Set specific times for your initiatives and stick to family activities. This way, you won't neglect either one. This isn't specific to POKR, but a good practice in any case. Wolfram spends his early mornings on deep work. This keeps his evenings free for family time, starting with dinner.

Flexibility is just as important, especially with young children or teenagers. If you're parenting young kids, shorter, adaptable focus blocks during nap times or play sessions can make a big difference. Parents of teenagers might collaborate with them on schedules, respecting their growing independence. Sebastian uses the time that his son is going for various cocurricular activities (CCA) to work on personal projects. There's always a coffee shop nearby with good enough Wi-Fi.

Health Metrics and Habits

Family well-being often sits outside traditional Personal OKRs, but it is an essential component of balance. Keeping an eye on habits, such as having three family dinners weekly, doing emotional check-ins with family members, or attending 80% of school events, helps prioritize relationships.

Kenji, a tech entrepreneur, uses a habit-tracking app. He tracks family dinners and game nights, seeing these times as sacred. These practices focus on building habits that show the shared values of your home, not on strict metrics.

And you know already that establishing new habits with POKR is a real thing!

INSPIRING THROUGH ACTION

Personal OKRs can inspire your family when you include everyone and plan with purpose. When they align with family priorities, they show values, create shared experiences, and encourage meaningful growth.

Role Modeling

Your actions set a powerful example for your family. Showing resilience in tough times teaches perseverance. Also, keeping a balanced schedule proves that personal growth can happen without sacrificing family priorities.

By living your values, you encourage your loved ones to embrace discipline, purpose, and optimism in their own endeavors. Children who see their parents chasing meaningful goals learn to set better goals themselves.[4] And yes, cracking that high score in *Call of Duty* qualifies, absolutely!

Creating Opportunities for Participation

When families get involved, personal ambitions become chances to bond rather than compete for time. For instance:

- A parent training for a marathon can create family "fun runs." Have the offspring accompany you on the first stretch of a slow, long run, for example. A great warm-up exercise!

- An aspiring photographer can teach basic photography skills during family outings

- A business project can become a family learning experience about entrepreneurship

These shared moments deepen relationships and enrich your goals with fresh perspectives.

Family as Accountability Partners

As discussed in Chapter 8, family members, especially spouses, are important Accountability Partners. They see your daily habits, share your motivations, and have a personal stake in your success. A spouse might help reinforce your commitment to unplug from work by 6:00

p.m., while your kids can cheer you on as you pursue a fitness milestone. Making your Personal OKR journey a team effort turns it into a celebration of support and encouragement.

THE JOY OF IMPERFECTION

Balancing personal projects with family time isn't about achieving perfection; it's about striving for harmony. By fostering open communication, setting intentional boundaries, and embracing shared experiences, you can pursue personal growth while deepening your relationships.

Remember, life isn't about creating the perfect picnic but about savoring the journey together. And if the gourmet dishes burn or the photos turn out blurry? Those missteps are just seasoning for the family storybook.

WHAT'S NEXT?

Chapter 16 will explore how to handle setbacks. It will also focus on refining your strategies when life doesn't go as planned. Because let's face it, not every attempt to blend personal projects with family life will go smoothly. But as we'll explore, those hiccups are where real learning happens.

KEY TAKEAWAYS

1. **Integrate your goals with family life**: Personal OKRs should support family, not take over. Too much structure in family interactions can cause stress instead of harmony.

2. **Find a balance between personal goals and family duties**: Focusing too much on personal ambition can cause guilt and distance. On the other hand, neglecting them can lead to frustration and resentment. The key is blending both in a way that enhances well-being and relationships.

3. **Talk and work together to find balance**: Discussing goals with family builds trust and encourages everyone to join in. Cocreating family Personal OKRs ensures alignment and shared ownership of priorities.

4. **Set clear boundaries and make time for what matters**: Define family time that you won't change. Also, create space for your personal interests. Flexibility is key, especially with young children or teenagers.

5. **Make Personal OKRs family bonding time**: Get your family involved in your goals. For example, let your kids join your workouts or creative hobbies. This way, you turn competing priorities into fun, shared experiences.

6. **Use family as Accountability Partners**: They can offer daily support and motivation. This helps reinforce your Personal OKRs and builds stronger relationships.

SIXTEEN

THE JOURNEY AHEAD

STRAIGHTFORWARD, BUT NOT EASY

THE PRINCIPLES BEHIND PERSONAL OKRS AND THE POKR Method might seem deceptively simple. Set inspiring Objectives; define measurable results; track progress; adjust as needed. What could possibly go wrong? As it turns out, quite a bit, and that's perfectly normal.

Here are our own stories to illustrate: Wolfram first worked on Personal OKRs during his gardening leave at the end of 2020, between two consulting jobs, amid the COVID-19 pandemic.

Like many professionals juggling multiple responsibilities, I was drawn to the clarity and structure that OKRs promised. My first quarter was... well, let's call it "a learning experience."

Channeling my newfound energy and marveling at what I could possibly achieve in 3 months, I set six Objectives: start an online business, get training certificates in three different topics, learn Chinese, learn to play guitar, get that elusive six-pack, and sort out all my financials. I also made my Key Results far too ambitious, pushed ahead by myself without aligning first with my wife and friends, and forgot to schedule regular check-ins. The result: I kicked off a lot, got many things done, but nothing really got completed. I simply ran out of time and then started my new job, which diverted energy.

To contrast, Sebastian wanted to finish a full marathon in 2023. He had one goal for the year, but it lacked detail. What could go wrong here? You can't just wing it for a 42-kilometer race in 32°C heat and 120% humidity. Why is that surprising? Just running kilometer after kilometer was not only dull but also ineffective. If you need proof, google "anaerobic versus aerobic training." It might put you to sleep though.

"I didn't get where I wanted to be, and almost lost the fun in running altogether," he remembers. "I had no system to help me find a good rhythm. I needed a way to balance this health Objective with my other priorities as a working professional and family man."

But here's where our stories get interesting. Instead of abandoning our slightly misguided OKR endeavors entirely, we both took a step back to analyze what went wrong. "I realized I was treating OKRs like a To-Do List on steroids," Wolfram recalls, "rather than a way to create real change."

COMMON SETBACKS AND HOW TO OVERCOME THEM

If your first try with Personal OKRs didn't work out, you're not alone. Even John Doerr, who brought OKRs to Google, says it takes time and practice to get it right.[1]

Trying to Change Everything, Everywhere, All at Once

One of the biggest pitfalls with Personal OKRs is setting too many ambitious Objectives at once.

Tackling several lifestyle changes at once is possible. It can even be effective because there can be self-reinforcing effects between the different changes you want to make.[2] For example, it's easier to drink less coffee if at the same time you get more sleep. But this reinforcement happens between related activities or habits you want to implement. This we take as evidence that having several, related, and reinforcing Key Results for one Objective is the way to go.

But when people try to make multiple significant changes simultaneously, that is, having major Objectives in the way we define them in this book, their chance of success drops dramatically for each additional target. Remember we are talking about bigger goals here: writing-a-book, running-a-marathon, building-a-house type of goals. Those quickly become too big to handle alongside each other. It's like juggling while learning to ride a unicycle; it's possible, but why complicate things?

Objectives should inspire you, but Key Results must be realistic. The aim is to challenge yourself while staying motivated. Avoid setting impossible targets that can lead to discouragement.

The solution: Pick one or maximum two meaningful Objectives that genuinely excite you. It's better to fully achieve one important target than to make little progress on three. Use the confidence level test for your Key Results we discussed earlier. If you're more than 80% confident you'll achieve the Key Result, it's too easy. Less than 50% confident? It's probably too ambitious. Aim for that sweet spot in between.

Not Having an Integrated System

The secret to sticking with Personal OKRs isn't just willpower. It's about having a system that helps you succeed. Without a system, you're essentially trying to navigate with your eyes closed. You heard the common saying, "What gets measured gets managed." We would rather say, "What gets measured mindfully gets improved." Not everything that matters can be measured. Not everything that we can measure matters. The key to successful Personal OKRs is in the mindful choice of Objectives and relevant Key Results, and the approaches to keep track of these.

The solution: Choose a tracking method that fits naturally into your existing routine. Whether it's a simple notebook, a digital app, or a wall calendar, the best system is the one you'll actually use. But make sure that Personal OKRs are grounded in your day-to-day reality.

Trying to Go It Alone

Holding yourself accountable is like trying to tickle yourself: It seldom works. Rich Roll's journey in Chapter 8 highlights the strength of public accountability. As we learned, having an Accountability Partner can increase your success rate significantly.[3] This is more than just reporting to someone; it's about forming a support network for your journey.

The solution: Share your Objectives with someone who can provide both encouragement and honest feedback. This could be a mentor, friend, spouse, or even a dedicated Personal OKR buddy.

Forgetting to Review and Adjust

Personal OKRs need regular attention. They aren't a "set it and forget it" system. Without review sessions, even well-crafted goals can get lost in daily life.

The solution: Create and follow standard routines. Set weekly check-ins and monthly reviews. Add them to your calendar and treat them like any important appointment.

Not Celebrating Progress

We often focus on the end target and forget to celebrate our progress. Acknowledging small wins releases dopamine in your brain.[4] This boosts positive behaviors and keeps us motivated. Still, many of us overlook this important step and keep looking ahead to the next milestone.

The solution: Include celebration steps in your Key Results. You can treat yourself to a favorite activity, share your progress with your support network, or take a moment to acknowledge your growth. Make celebration a formal part of your Personal OKR process. It is so much easier to achieve success with a bit of self-love.

The Mindset Shift

Implementing Personal OKRs requires more than just learning a new system; it demands a fundamental shift in how we think about target setting and progress. As Alfred Pennyworth wisely noted in *Batman Begins*, "Why do we fall? So, we can learn to pick ourselves up."[5] This isn't just a catchy movie quote; it encapsulates the growth mindset essential for Personal OKR success.

Individuals with a growth mindset (those who view challenges as opportunities to learn) are significantly more likely to achieve their targets.[6] When facing setbacks with Personal OKRs, ask yourself:

- What can I learn from this experience?
- How can I adjust my approach?
- What small win can I celebrate, even in apparent failure?

Starting Over, Starting Smarter

So, here's your reset strategy in a nutshell, in case you need one (handily abbreviated as 5 S's):

- **Simplify**: Choose one meaningful Objective that genuinely excites you.
- **Structure**: Set up a simple but consistent tracking system.
- **Support**: Share your Objectives with someone who can provide accountability.
- **Schedule**: Block time for weekly reviews.
- **Success**: Acknowledge progress, no matter how small.

These reset strategies aren't just theoretical suggestions; they're practical steps backed by research and real-world experiences. When you apply them thoughtfully and systematically, you're not just starting over; you're starting smarter.

POKR = YOUR LIFE OS!

We've promised you more than just another target-setting framework. Why? Because whatever we throw at you needs to be a well-integrated method that combines good practices and aligns with your regular life.

In the earlier chapters, we shared our reasons for needing POKR. We believe it truly can impact your universe as well, as it did for us:

1. Tie Personal OKRs to a **compelling Mission** (your longer-term goal, your *why*).
2. Follow solid Personal OKR **mechanics**, particularly around prescriptive yet lean routines (inspect and adapt as a concept, the ability to pivot).
3. Bring it into your **everyday life** by linking it to your preferred task and time management tools and approaches (the *what*, Task-level details).
4. Develop an ability to **form new habits** (that's what we often try to do but fail at it without proper "mechanics").

What do you think? How did we do?

THE JOURNEY *IS* THE DESTINATION

As we conclude this book, remember that implementing Personal OKRs is a journey, not a destination in itself. Every quarter brings new opportunities to refine your approach and deepen your practice. As the author James Clear notes, "You do not rise to the level of your goals. You fall to the level of your systems."[7] Focus on *implementing* the system, and the results will follow.

Think of each setback as data, not defeat. Each "failure" provides valuable information about what works for you and what doesn't. As Thomas Edison famously said, "I have not failed. I've just found 10,000 ways that won't work."[8]

The beauty of POKR lies not in its perfection but in the ability to guide us toward meaningful progress. It provides a method for turning our aspirations into reality, one quarter at a time. When setbacks occur (and they will), reconnect with why you started this journey. Your *why* is what holds you steady in tough times. It guides you as you advance your career, improve your health, or follow a passion project.

Start small, stay consistent, and be patient with yourself. Remember the authors' journey? You're holding this book because we've learned from our experiences. We adapted our Personal OKRs and found balance in our work and personal lives. Our secret? We stopped aiming for perfection and focused on being consistent.

Welcome to the start of your Personal OKR success story. You have the tools and understand the principles. You know setbacks are not just normal; they are opportunities for growth.

The path ahead is clear, though not easy. But then again, was anything worth achieving ever easy?

ACKNOWLEDGMENTS

First and foremost, to our families: Thank you for your patience, perspective, and persistent questioning whether this whole "productivity thing" was just elaborate avoidance of doing actual work. To Tracy, Vicky, Alexander, Niklas, and Steven: This book was written during stolen hours that rightly belonged to you. Thank you for letting us steal them anyway. Our midlife crisis needed this. You'll understand, someday.

To our parents: Thanks for being the original productivity coaches, long before we knew what OKRs, KPIs, or even calendars were. To all the friends, colleagues, and casual contacts that we pitched the idea to, who confirmed our suspicion that we might be on to something and encouraged us to actually put the idea down on paper.

To the team at Scribe Media: We're grateful for your guidance, encouragement, and heroic attempts to keep us on track, especially when we declared that the "POKR Burger" was a legitimate metaphor. You didn't flinch.

Special thanks for all the rounds of editing that made our many semicolons, dashes, and yes, our love of overlong sentences, barely readable.

You've helped turn our sprawling, post-vomit-draft collection of ideas into something that resembles a book (and even a good one, if you squint at the references). We offer the sincerest compliment a pair of control freaks can give: We couldn't have done it better ourselves.

Finally, to all the readers embarking on your own journey of Personal OKRs: May your Objectives be bold, your Key Results measurable, and your Accountability Partners just nagging enough to keep you going. You've got this!

To the beautiful chaos of coauthoring: Writing a book together really means endlessly debating whether this paragraph is the way of the Jedi (focused and serene) or drifting dangerously toward the Dark Side of academic references. (Do or do not. There is no rough draft.) Thanks for being the best arguing partner a coauthor could ask for. It was a really entertaining journey!

ABOUT THE AUTHORS

You might be wondering: *Who are these guys, and why should I trust them with my personal goals?* Fair question! We're not self-help gurus who discovered the secret to life while meditating on a mountaintop. We're seasoned business consultants who spent decades helping organizations achieve extraordinary results through our consulting work, only to realize we were terrible at applying the same principles to our own lives.

This book is our attempt at honest transparency: Here's who we are, what we've learned the hard way, and why we believe the POKR Method can work for you too.

SEBASTIAN VOSS

Transformation Coach | Digital Entrepreneur | Agility Realist | People Whisperer

Sebastian's career spans close to 30 years of enterprise transformation, digital entrepreneurship, and professional and Agile coaching. Think of him as someone who's been in the trenches of technology and organizational change management long enough to know what works, what doesn't, and what makes people want to hide under their desks.

He cut his teeth as a project and program manager for various global enterprise clients (SAP, BMW, BHP, etc.), discovering that getting hands-on with delivery can be hugely rewarding! Leading multimillion-dollar transformation programs and training more than 2,000 people in project management, Scrum, Kanban, and Design Thinking skills taught him that the best frameworks are worthless without the right people applying them. A stint as a tech entrepreneur was super exciting, but that venture didn't succeed. It was a humbling experience that became surprisingly valuable when he later became a transformation leader for enterprises, where those past experiences (including the failures) came in handy.

Working as a trainer and professional coach thereafter made it clear over and over that in the end, it's always about people, people, people, and the systems they work in. Whether he was coaching executives to improve employee engagement, implementing Agile and lean ways of working in highly regulated industries, or managing global SAP rollouts, the common denominator was always human behavior and motivation. Through Delta Evolutions, his Singapore-based consulting practice, he's been quietly catalyzing change from the inside out.

Lots of different angles, with a common theme and desire to have a meaningful impact on people, processes, and systems. What worked great in a professional setting didn't translate to his private life, though: POKR is, in many ways, his own response to a life that once blurred the line between progress and burnout. It's a method he uses himself to stay grounded, sane, and purpose driven, without treating life like a never-ending project plan.

Sebastian holds an Executive MBA from the University of Maryland's R.H. Smith School of Business and completed executive education at INSEAD Business School in Singapore. He's certified as a Professional Coach (ICF-ACC), Professional Scrum Master, Product Owner, and Project Management Professional, among others.

When he's not transforming organizations or writing about personal effectiveness, you'll find him mentoring startups or trying that next endurance event in a way-too-humid climate.

WOLFRAM HEDRICH

Risk Strategist | Sustainable Finance Enthusiast | Recovering Perfectionist | AI Music Producer

Wolfram has spent nearly 30 years advising banks, insurers, regulators, and sovereign wealth funds around the world. A former partner at global consulting firms Oliver Wyman and Ernst & Young, he built a reputation for turning complex risk and sustainability questions into clear strategies and measurable actions. He's led hundreds of consulting projects across four continents, most recently helping financial institutions stress-test for climate risk and embed sustainability, and trained senior leaders on everything from ESG governance to AI oversight.

If you've ever wondered what it takes to guide major financial institutions through complex transformations while juggling several consulting projects across three continents, Wolfram has learned a thing or two about staying focused and productive under pressure. Along the way, he tested many productivity tools on himself. He's coached hundreds of new consultants in the dark arts of strategy consulting, and hundreds of clients on performance measurement and management. His research work has been featured in numerous publications, and he somehow found time to become a frequent public speaker with, at one point, 50-plus engagements per year.

Like Sebastian, Wolfram found himself succeeding professionally but feeling stuck when it came to making progress on personal goals. The irony wasn't lost on him; here he was, helping organizations achieve results through structured approaches, yet his personal guitar remained largely un-played, and his Mandarin textbooks gathered dust. When a rare 3-month sabbatical came, he dove into long-postponed goals, only to overcommit and finish none. Sound familiar? This led him to rethink the way he planned for personal goals, and to test OKRs for personal use. This book is the result of that journey.

He holds graduate degrees in business administration from the Beisheim Graduate School of Management (WHU Koblenz) and ESC Lyon, with a stint at the University of Michigan's Ross School of Business. He's a certified Financial Risk Manager (FRM) and CFA ESG investment certified. Currently, he serves as adjunct faculty at Singapore Management University, teaching sustainability risk.

When he is not trying to do his bit to save the planet, he is producing AI music with his sons under the artist's name *LangDaRen*. And yes, the carbon footprint of AI is a concern here, and dutifully offset.

TAKE THE NEXT STEP WITH US!

Want to bring POKR to your team or event? Sebastian and Wolfram regularly deliver keynote talks, workshops, and corporate training sessions on how to apply Personal OKRs and sustainable productivity in real life and real work.

We both spent the last three decades outside of our native Germany, with longer stays in China and other Asia Pacific countries. Singapore is home away from home, but we love to travel.

If you're interested in bringing the POKR approach to your organization, team off-site, or conference, reach out to us at *contact@dreamsand deadlines.com*. We'd love to hear from you.

TEMPLATES AND WORKBOOKS

Chapter 5. **Power of Purpose: The 5+1 Approach**

Begins on next page...

STEP 1: ENVISION YOUR *5Y FUTURE-SELF*

FAMILY & OTHER RELATIONSHIPS
What kind of relationships will I cultivate?

HEALTH & FITNESS
What would my ideal health look like?

PERSONAL FINANCES
How do I want my finances to develop?

PERSONAL DEVELOPMENT
Which item(s) on my bucket list will I have achieved?

CAREER DEVELOPMENT
Where do I want my career to go?

1-LINER FOR *5Y FUTURE-SELF*

STEP 1: ENVISION YOUR *5Y FUTURE-SELF*

STEP 2: **IMAGINE A *5Y FEARED FUTURE***

FAMILY & OTHER RELATIONSHIPS
What might my relationships become without intervention?

HEALTH & FITNESS
What could my health look like if I don't address the warning signs?

PERSONAL FINANCES
How do I want my finances to develop?

PERSONAL DEVELOPMENT
What opportunities might I miss if I don't make time for personal growth?

CAREER DEVELOPMENT
How might my career stagnate if I don't evolve?

1-LINER FOR *5Y FEARED FUTURE*

STEP 3: RECONCILE *5Y FUTURE-SELF* WITH *5Y FEATURE FUTURE*	
FUTURE-SELF	**FEARED FUTURE**

STEP 4: **DISTIL INTO *1-YEAR GOAL(S)***

What specific outcomes across different areas of life would make me feel accomplished in one year?

Which parts of my Future Self can I realistically start working toward this year?

What actions would have the greatest leverage across multiple life areas?

What skills do I need to develop first to enable my longer-term Goals?

How will these 1-Year Goals help me avoid my Feared Future?

FAMILY & OTHER RELATIONSHIPS

HEALTH & FITNESS

PERSONAL FINANCES

PERSONAL DEVELOPMENT

CAREER DEVELOPMENT

1-LINER FOR *1-YEAR GOAL(S)*

PERSONAL OKR CANVAS

	Q1	Q2	Q3	Q4
5Y GOAL				
1Y GOAL(S)				
FAMILY				
HEALTH				
FINANCES				
DEVELOPMENT				
CAREER				

Chapter 8: **Holding Yourself Accountable**

Weekly Check-In with Accountability Partner(s)
If you are pressed for time, a simple email summary to your Accountability Partner(s) can be a useful way to keep you tethered to them and vice versa. It's typically sent at the end of the week, to provide a quick summary of what you've accomplished (or not).

It provides transparency to broadcast your judgment on how likely you're able to get there (confidence factor X out of 10) and might spell out where you need help.

Hi <Accountability Partner> -

Just to keep you posted on what I got done this week, and where I might need your help.

Regards,
<POKR User>

PERSONAL OKR STATUS
O1: <title>
KR1: <title> <x/10>
KR2: <title> <x/10>
KR3: <title> <x/10>
O2: <title>
KR1: <title> <x/10>
KR2: <title> <x/10>

HIGHLIGHTS OF LAST WEEK
- <task 1>
- <task 2>
- ...

PRIORITIES FOR NEXT WEEK

- <task 1>
- <task 2>
- ...

HELP NEEDED

- <item 1>
- <item 2>

Chapter 10: **Cadence Makes Productivity Sustainable**

ROUTINE	LENGTH	TIMING	INPUTS	OUTCOMES
YEARLY				
Yearly Goal Setting	~2hrs	first week of the year	• Mission (5+1 Goal) • Past Years OKRs • Lessons learned	Defined & committed Goal(s) across relevant Categories
Yearly Review	~1hr	last week of the year	Performance data from just the completed Year	• Goal results reviewed & scored, visualized • Lessons observed
QUARTERLY				
Quarterly POKRs Planning	~1hr	first week of the quarter	• Goal (1Y) • Review Findings from past Quarter • Lessons learned from past Quarter	• Defined Objectives & Key Results (OKRs) for the current Quarter • Defined "Candidate Objectives" beyond the current Quarter (optional)
Monthly Review	~30min	last week of the month	Performance data from the month so far	Monthly interim results assessed
Quarterly Review	~30min	last week of the quarter	Performance data for current quarter	• Quarterly Interim results assessed • Lessons observed

ROUTINE	LENGTH	TIMING	INPUTS	OUTCOMES
WEEKLY				
Start of Week: Commitment	~30min	first day of the week (maybe a calm Sunday morning?)	OKRs for current quarter	• Commitment made of what to focus on for the upcoming week • Tasks defined/ refined & scheduled for the upcoming week (top 2–3 priorities)
End of Week: Celebration	~30min	last day of the week (maybe a calm Saturday morning?)	• OKRs for current quarter • Tasks from the past week	• Updated tasks with progress • Updates to Accountability Partner(s) • Celebreate progress!
DAILY				
Daily Check-In (optional)	~15min	(recommended to be early morning before any other action)	Tasks for the current day (via Calendar or To Do List)	• Awareness of what is scheduled for today (your top 2–3 key actions) • Possible roadblocks

Head over to our website to download these directly into your calendar (https://www.dreamsanddeadlines.com/).

Retrospective

A simple template to list lessons that you observed, and those that you actually learned (an important distinction), as a shared tracker across all retrospective events (quarterly and yearly):

RETROSPECTIVE ITEM & DESCRIPTION	DATE	STATUS
START DOING		
STOP DOING		
CONTINUE TO DO		

POKR GLOSSARY

5S Strategy: Our five-step method to regain clarity and order when things go off the rails. It stands for Stop, Scan, Simplify, Schedule, and Start, like hitting the productivity reset button when life turns into a hot mess.

5+1 Approach: A deceptively simple shortcut for personal clarity: Your 5-Year Goal sets your compass (your longer-term life direction), while your 1-Year Goal translates that mission into something you can act on now. It's like plotting a transatlantic voyage but packing your carry-on for the first leg. Used as the POKR Method's "Mission" bun.

Accountability Partner: Like a gym buddy for your goals. An Accountability Partner checks in, cheers you on, and gently calls you out when Netflix beats your To-Do List. In POKR, they help you follow through without feeling like you're doing it all alone.

Cadence: The steady drumbeat of your Personal OKRs practice. In POKR, cadence means committing to a regular rhythm: weekly check-ins, quarterly resets, and the occasional life reevaluation jam session. Like a fitness class with just enough structure to keep you coming back (but no yelling spin instructor).

Committed Objectives: A special type of Objective that isn't just aspirational; it's nonnegotiable. These are the "must-do" items on your life menu, often tied to responsibilities or deeply held values. You don't dabble in Committed Objectives, you deliver on them.

Execution: The daily doing of it all, where lofty goals meet reality (and your calendar). Execution is where most systems break down, but POKR keeps it simple with weekly check-ins, calendar syncing, and task planning that fits your life. It's not about working harder; it's about making meaningful progress with less chaos.

Feared Future: A visualization exercise in which you imagine what life might look like if you don't change your current trajectory. It's the "ghost of goals unachieved" and can be a powerful motivator when your present self feels too comfy to grow.

Future-Self: The version of you who's benefitted from your progress: stronger, wiser, and maybe with better posture. Visualizing your Future-Self helps align today's actions with tomorrow's aspirations.

GTD (Getting Things Done): the productivity method by David Allen that's famous for capturing every task, thought, or errand in a trusted system so your brain can finally chill. While GTD can be beautifully geeky, POKR is the friendly cousin that shows up with a plan, a burger metaphor, and a focus on goals that matter, without needing a PhD in list management.

Habits: In POKR, habits are defined as "recurring behaviors that become part of your weekly or daily life, ideally automatic and rewarding." They're the foundation of sustainable progress, turning intentions into identity over time. Think of them as the behavioral scaffolding for your life's construction project. Small, steady, and compounding.

Ikigai: A Japanese concept that roughly means "reason for being." It's the intersection of what you love, what you're good at, what the world needs, and what you can be paid for. POKR gives you tools to explore your Ikigai without falling into a philosophical rabbit hole.

Kanban Boards: A visual task management system that helps you see your workflow at a glance. Based on columns like "To Do," "In Progress," and "Done," Kanban Boards turn abstract plans into tangible progress. They're like whiteboards for your goals: intuitive, flexible, and oh-so-satisfying when you move a task card to "Done."

Key Results: The measurable outcomes that tell you if you're on track to achieve your Objective. Think of them as the road signs that say, "Yep, still heading in the right direction!" Each Key Result must be specific, time-bound, and something you can actually control. No points for "waited for someone else to approve it." Ideally, you want three to five per Objective to avoid turning your life into a metrics spreadsheet.

KISS: Short for "Keep It Simple, Stupid." A cheeky reminder that over-complicating things kills momentum. Whether you're crafting Key Results or managing your To-Do List, POKR follows the KISS rule: simple scales, complex fails.

Life Categories: The five big slices of your life that POKR helps you manage: Family and Relationships, Health and Fitness, Finances, Career Development, and Personal Development and Passion Projects. These ensure you're not just killing it at work while your health and social life quietly burn in the background. They also help you balance your Objectives, one delicious layer at a time, like slicing a burger vertically instead of flattening it with a mallet.

Life OS: Your all-in-one personal operating system, the combination of strategies, tools, and habits that keep your goals, routines, and calendar playing nice together. It's like a digital (or analog) HQ for your brain, heart, and hustle. With POKR, your Life OS gets a major upgrade: less chaos, more clarity.

Mission (POKR Definition): We define "Mission" as a preestablished and self-imposed, strongly felt goal, aim, ambition, calling, or purpose. Or in simple terms: an overarching sense of direction.

Mission Layer: The top of the POKR Burger, your overarching purpose or direction. It includes your 5-Year Goal, your 1-Year Goal, and any other vision-type statement that helps you know where you're heading. We call it a "layer" because it holds everything else together, like the bun does for a burger (without it, you just have chaos and condiments).

Mission Statement: A short, meaningful declaration of your life direction. It captures your deeper values and helps you stay grounded when life gets busy. It's not set in stone; you're allowed to revise it as you grow.

Objectives: The "what" of your quarter. These are aspirational, qualitative targets that keep your fire lit and your compass pointing true. They're meant to stretch you, not stress you. Phrased to inspire action, like "Build a creative father-son project" rather than "Be a better dad" (what does that even mean?). Limit yourself to one to three per quarter; remember, you're building focus, not a buffet.

OKRs: Short for Objectives and Key Results, this is the core structure POKR builds on. Born in the corporate world but reimagined here for real humans with jobs, kids, hobbies, and that endless pile of laundry. Objectives define where you're headed; Key Results tell you how you'll measure progress. The magic is in how they connect. With POKR, we make OKRs personal, meaningful, and (dare we say it) fun.

PDCA: Short for Plan-Do-Check-Act, this classic improvement loop is like the productivity version of rinse and repeat. You set a plan, give it a shot, check what worked (or didn't), and then adjust. In POKR, we borrow PDCA to frame our weekly and quarterly rhythms; it keeps us from just grinding and helps us learn from how things go.

Personal OKRs: Your very own version of OKRs, adapted from the workplace into your living room, yoga mat, inbox, or whatever else life throws at you. Personal OKRs are short, focused cycles of intentional change: one to three motivating Objectives with three to five measurable Key Results each. It's like a GPS for the life you want, not just the one you're defaulting into.

POKR Burger: Our house special, and the main metaphor for the method. Picture a delicious productivity burger: the Mission layer on top (your long-term direction), the Objectives and Key Results in the juicy middle (your quarterly Strategy), and Tasks at the bottom (your daily Execution). Add your favorite condiments, like accountability and routines, and you've got a system that's tasty and transformational.

POKR Canvas: Your one-pager playbook for each quarter. It holds your Objectives, Key Results, and supporting routines in one easy-to-scan place. Like a dashboard for your personal strategy: minimalist but mighty.

POKR Kanban Board: A visual way to track your progress, one sticky note at a time. POKR's Kanban approach helps you see your Tasks and Execution flow, from To Do to In Progress to Done. It's productivity meets project board, with a side of dopamine for every card you move.

POKR Method: Short for Personal OKR, this is the full framework the book teaches. It combines strategy, structure, and just enough fun to help you then follow through. It includes the 5+1 Goal setting, OKRs, Life

Categories, habit routines, and check-ins, all laid out like a productivity burger. It's OKRs, but made for messy, multidimensional, glorious real life.

Purpose Statement: Closely related to your Mission Statement, but more emotionally driven. It answers the question: "Why am I doing this?" Useful when you're staring down tough Tasks and wondering if it's all worth it.

Quarterly Objectives: The 3-month version of your bigger aspirations. These help you make meaningful progress without the overwhelming pressure of planning your entire life. Why a quarter? Because it's short enough to create urgency, long enough to get real stuff done, and just right for building momentum. Think of it as your personal "season of change."

Self-Evaluated Key Results: A gentle blend of metrics and mindfulness. These Key Results let you rate your own progress with structured self-reflection; think "80% effort on language learning" or "7/10 satisfaction with morning routine." It's still measurable, just more "you" than "spreadsheet."

SMART Goals: A classic framework for goal setting that stands for Specific, Measurable, Achievable, Relevant, and Time-bound. While POKR prefers the flexibility of Key Results, SMART criteria are still helpful for sanity-checking your metrics.

Standard Routines: POKR's built-in productivity rituals. These are the recurring habits that keep the engine humming, like weekly reviews, Task planning, and quarterly reflections. Think of them as the seasoning in your burger: easy to skip, but everything tastes better with them.

Task Prioritization Techniques: POKR draws from classics like the Eisenhower Matrix, Ivy Lee Method, and timeboxing to help you tame your To-Do List. It's not just about doing more; it's about doing the right things, in the right order, without losing your mind.

Tasks: The action layer at the bottom of the POKR Burger. Tasks are what you do today or this week to make progress toward your Key Results. They live in your To-Do List, calendar, or Kanban Board. Tasks are flexible, fast-changing, and bite-sized. Key Results stay consistent over the quarter, but Tasks shift and move with your daily life.

Timeboxing: The art of assigning fixed time slots to your Tasks. It's like speed dating for your To-Do List; you give each item a chance but keep things moving. Helps you stay focused, avoid perfectionism, and actually finish what you start.

To-Do Lists: The humble, ever-present list of Tasks we love to hate and hate to live without. In POKR, To-Do Lists are made powerful by tying them directly to your Key Results, turning random errands into intentional actions.

Vision Statement: A broad, aspirational picture of your ideal future. It's like the skyline in the distance; you may not be there yet, but it shapes your path. In POKR, your Vision inspires your Mission, which then powers your 1-Year Goals and Quarterly Objectives.

Why Statement: This is your "fire in the belly" phrase. A personal reminder of why a goal matters to you, deep down. It helps you power through the slog and stay motivated beyond the initial burst of enthusiasm.

Yearly Goal: Your 1-Year Goal is the smaller but serious cousin of your Mission. It brings focus and urgency to your broader vision, giving you a tangible 12-month target that bridges today with your longer-term aspirations.

REFERENCE NOTES

Disclaimer

The following references and explanations in this book are provided for informational purposes only. They do not constitute medical, mental health, financial, or legal advice. Readers should consult a qualified professional for personalized guidance regarding health, wealth, and well-being.

Introduction: **Why Dreams Need Deadlines**

This section relied entirely on life experience, questionable metaphors, and caffeine. No references were harmed (or used) in the making of this section.

Chapter 1: **Why Objectives and Key Results for Personal Use?**

1   Andrew S. Grove, *High Output Management* (Random House, 1983).

2   John Doerr, *Measure What Matters: How Google, Bono, and the Gates Foundation Rock the World with OKRs* (Portfolio, 2018).

3   Jeff Weiner, "The Management Framework that Propelled LinkedIn to a $20 Billion Company," *First Round Review*, accessed October 1, 2025, https://review.firstround.com/the-management-framework-that-propelled-linkedin-to-a-20-billion-company.

4   "Spotify KPIs and OKRs," Comparably, accessed May 12, 2025, https://www.comparably.com/companies/spotify/kpi-okr.

5   Doerr, *Measure What Matters*. See Chapter 11.

6   Agata Krzysztofik, "Ex-Googler's Tips on How to Write OKRs [+ OKR Examples & Templates]," Piktochart, updated May 3, 2024,, https://piktochart.com/blog/how-to-write-okrs/.

7   James Clear, *Atomic Habits: An Easy & Proven Way to Build Good Habits & Break Bad Ones* (Avery, 2018).

8   Christina Wodtke, *Radical Focus: Achieving Your Most Important Goals with Objectives and Key Results* (Cucina Media, 2016).

9   Christina Wodtke, "Personal OKRs, Three Years Later," Medium, December 30, 2016 https://cwodtke.medium.com/personal-okrs-three-years-later-7616e60574a4; Christina Wodtke, "Personal OKRs," Eleganthack, January 16, 2013, https://eleganthack.com/personal-okrs/.

10 Aaron Aiken, "The Benefits of Using OKRs to Purposefully Focus Your Personal Life," Medium, February 12, 2018, https://medium.com/@aaronaiken/the-benefits-of-using-okrs-to-purposefully-focus-your-personal-life-47f6d6553512.

11 Doerr, *Measure What Matters*, 17.

Chapter 2: **The Essentials for Making POKR Work**

All insights in this chapter were home-grown. No academic studies were consulted, yet somehow, it works.

Chapter 3: **What We Learned from Corporate OKRs**

1   John Doerr, *Measure What Matters: How Google, Bono, and the Gates Foundation Rock the World with OKRs* (Portfolio, 2018), 1–20; Bryan Schuldt, "27 Companies that Use OKRs and Success Stories," *Tability*, March 19, 2024, https://www.tability.io/odt/articles/companies-that-use-okrs-and-success-stories; Jeff Weiner, "The Management Framework that Propelled LinkedIn to a $20 Billion Company," *First Round Review*, accessed October 1, 2025, https://review.firstround.com/the-management-framework-that-propelled-linkedin-to-a-20-billion-company.

2   Jules Cook, "7 Reasons Why OKRs Won't Last," LinkedIn, September 16, 2021, https://www.linkedin.com/pulse/7-reasons-why-okrs-wont-last-julian-cook.

3   "10 Reasons Why OKRs Fail," OKR International, January 6, 2025, https://okrinternational.com/10-reasons-why-okrs-fail/.

4   Henrik Kniberg, "Spotify Rhythm—How We Get Aligned (Slides from My Talk at Agile Sverige)," *Crisp* (blog), June 8, 2016, https://blog.crisp.se/2016/06/08/henrikkniberg/spotify-rhythm; Johanna Bolin Tingvall, "Why Individual OKRs Don't Work for Us," *HR Blog*, Spotify, August 15, 2016, https://hrblog.spotify.com/2016/08/15/our-beliefs.

5   Susan Fowler, *Whistleblower: My Journey to Silicon Valley and Fight for Justice at Uber* (Viking, 2020). See also: Susan Fowler, "Reflecting on One Very, Very Strange Year at Uber," *Susan Fowler* (blog), February 19, 2017, https://www.susanjfowler.com/blog/2017/2/19/reflecting-on-one-very-strange-year-at-uber.

6   Brian Vannoy, "Top 5 Reasons Why We Failed at OKRs," LinkedIn, January 4, 2020, https://www.linkedin.com/pulse/top-5-reasons-why-we-failed-okrs-brian-vannoy.

7   OKR International, *OKRs State of the Industry: Connecting Research to Performance* (2023), https://okrinternational.com/okrs-soir/.

8   Bob Lutz, *Car Guys vs. Bean Counters: The Battle for the Soul of American Business* (Portfolio, 2011). See also Steven Jurczak, "Sandbagging OKRs: Why Teams Under Promise and Over Deliver," *What Matters*, accessed October 2, 2025, https://www.whatmatters.com/faqs/sandbagging-under-promise-deliver-okrs.

9   OKR International, *OKRs State of the Industry* (2023).

10 Mangalindan, J. P. (2012, April 13). What it's really like to work at Zynga. *Fortune.* https://fortune.com/2012/04/13/what-its-really-like-to-work-at-zynga.

11 Spencer Reynolds, "Sears—The Collapse of a Company from Within," Technology and Operations Management MBA Student Perspectives, Harvard Business School, December 6, 2015, https://d3.harvard.edu/platform-rctom/submission/sears-the-collapse-of-a-company-from-within/; Michal Rozworski and Leigh Phillips, "Failing to Plan: How Ayn Rand Destroyed Sears," excerpt from *The People's Republic of Walmart: How the World's Biggest Corporations are Laying the Foundation for Socialism* (Verso, 2019), Verso Books, July 18, 2019, https://www.versobooks.com/blogs/news/4385-failing-to-plan-how-ayn-rand-destroyed-sears.

12 Satya Nadella, *Hit Refresh: The Quest to Rediscover Microsoft's Soul and Imagine a Better Future for Everyone* (Harper Business, 2017); Kurt Eichenwald, "Microsoft's Lost Decade," *Vanity Fair* (August 2012), https://www.vanityfair.com/news/business/2012/08/microsoft-lost-mojo-steve-ballmer.

13 Tuomo Peltonen, "Case Study 4: The Collapse of Nokia's Mobile Phone Business," in *Towards Wise Management: Wisdom and Stupidity in Strategic Decision-Making* (Palgrave Macmillan, 2019), 163–188, https://doi.org/10.1007/978-3-319-91719-1_6.

14 Iulia, "Why 'Demolition Man', Fab.com's Former CEO Should Have Studied TOM (at GSB) Before Running His Company into the Ground,"

Technology and Operations Management MBA Student Perspectives, Harvard Business School, December 9, 2015, https://d3.harvard.edu/platform-rctom/submission/why-demolition-man-fab-coms-former-ceo-should-have-studied-tom-at-gsb-before-running-his-company-into-the-ground/.

15   Jeffrey K. Liker, *The Toyota Way: 14 Management Principles from the World's Greatest Manufacturer* (McGraw-Hill, 2004).

16   Jacquie McNish and Sean Silcoff, *Losing the Signal: The Untold Story Behind the Extraordinary Rise and Spectacular Fall of BlackBerry* (Flatiron Books, 2015).

Chapter 4: **Setting Your Direction**

1   Stephen R. Covey, *The 7 Habits of Highly Effective People: Powerful Lessons in Personal Change* (Free Press, 1989).

2   Stephen R. Covey, A. Roger Merrill, and Rebecca R. Merrill, *First Things First: To Live, to Love, to Learn, to Leave a Legacy* (Free Press, 1994). To simplify things, Franklin Covey provides an online tool that you can use to quickly generate a personal mission statement. You can think of it as the "CliffsNotes" for creating the ultimate personal mission statement. https://msb.franklincovey.com/.

3   Simon Sinek, *Start with Why: How Great Leaders Inspire Everyone to Take Action* (Portfolio, 2009).

4   Simon Sinek, David Mead, and Peter Docker, *Find Your Why: A Practical Guide for Discovering Purpose for You and Your Team* (Penguin Books, 2017).

5   The King Center, "About Dr. Martin Luther King, Jr," accessed May 12, 2025, https://thekingcenter.org/about-tkc/martin-luther-king-jr/.

6   Oprah Winfrey, "Every Person Has a Purpose," Oprah.com, accessed May 12, 2025, https://www.oprah.com/spirit/how-oprah-winfrey-found-her-purpose. Note that Oprah herself uses calling, purpose, and divine assurance to describe this. Others have labeled this mission. See, for example, Stephanie Vozza, "Personal Mission Statements of 5 Famous CEOs (And Why You Should Write One Too)," *Fast Company*, February 25, 2014, https://www.fastcompany.com/3026791/personal-mission-statements-of-5-famous-ceos-and-why-you-should-write-one-too. Again, it just shows that these concepts are all being used interchangeably in practice.

7   Rachel Hollis, "I promised myself in my 30s that I would run a half marathon before I turned 40 and a full marathon before I turned 50!,"

Facebook post, April 5, 2014, accessed May 12, 2025, https://www.facebook
.com/photo.php?fbid=10156477940891259&id=99908631258&set=a
.199476321258.

8   Laura A. King, "The Health Benefits of Writing about Life Goals,"
Personality and Social Psychology Bulletin 27, no. 7 (July 2001): 798–807,
https://doi.org/10.1177/0146167201277003.

9   Sakurako S. Okuzono et al., "Ikigai and Subsequent Health and Wellbeing
Among Japanese Older Adults: Longitudinal Outcome-Wide Analysis," *The
Lancet Regional Health—Western Pacific* 21, no. 100391 (April 2022), https://
doi.org/10.1016/j.lanwpc.2022.100391; Juni Miyazaki et al., "Purpose in Life
(Ikigai) and Employment Status in Relation to Cardiovascular Mortality:
The Japan Collaborative Cohort Study," *BMJ Open* 12, no. 10 (2022):
e059725, https://doi.org/10.1136/bmjopen-2021-059725.

10   Nick Kemp, host, *The Ikigai Podcast*, episode 28, "The Health Benefits of
Ikigai with Dr. Yasuhiro Kotera," July 28, 2021, https://ikigaitribe.com/
podcasts/podcast28/.

11   Christopher Peterson and Martin E.P. Seligman, *Character Strengths and
Virtues: A Handbook and Classification* (Oxford University Press, 2004).

12   Barbara K. Searight, and Russell Searight, "The Value of a Personal Mission
Statement for University Undergraduates," *Creative Education* 2, no. 3
(August 2011): 313–315, https://doi.org/10.4236/ce.2011.23043.

13   Peterson and Seligman, *Character Strengths and Virtues.*

Chapter 5: **Power of Purpose**

1   Hal E. Hershfield et al., "Increasing Saving Behavior Through Age-
Progressed Renderings of the Future Self," *Journal of Marketing Research* 48,
no. 2011 (2011): S23–S37, http://www.jstor.org/stable/23033463.

2   Gabriele Oettingen, *Rethinking Positive Thinking: Inside the New Science of
Motivation* (Penguin Random House, 2014).

3   Dana Zeif and Eldad Yechiam, "Loss Aversion (Simply) Does Not
Materialize for Smaller Losses," *Judgment and Decision Making* (January
2023), https://doi.org/10.1017/s193029750000930x; Yuling Liu, "The Review
of Loss Aversion," *Advances in Education, Humanities and Social Science
Research* 7, no. 1 (2023), https://doi.org/10.56028/aehssr.7.1.428.2023.

4   Laura A. King, "The Health Benefits of Writing about Life Goals,"
Personality and Social Psychology Bulletin 27, no. 7 (July 2001): 798–807,
https://doi.org/10.1177/0146167201277003.

Chapter 6: Setting Powerful Objectives

1   Richard Wiseman, "New Year's Resolution Project," Quirkology, accessed October 3, 2025, http://www.richardwiseman.com/quirkology/new/USA/ Experiment_resolution.shtml; Ray Williams, "Why New Year's Resolutions Fail and What to Do about It," Ray Williams, December 26, 2022, https:// raywilliams.ca/why-new-years-resolutions-fail-and-what-to-do-about-it/.

2   The quote "How to eat an elephant? Bite by bite." is often attributed to Nelson Mandela, although there is some debate about its exact origin. It's also sometimes linked to Creighton Abrams, a US Army general during the Vietnam War. The phrase emphasizes tackling large, overwhelming tasks by breaking them down into smaller, more manageable steps.

3   Christina Wodtke, "Personal OKRs: Three Years Later," Medium, December 30, 2016, https://cwodtke.medium.com/personal-okrs-three-years-later-7616e60574a4.

4   Christina Wodtke, "Personal OKRs," Elegant Hack, July 16, 2013, https:// eleganthack.com/personal-okrs/.

5   Brian P. Moran and Michael Lennington, *The 12 Week Year: Get More Done in 12 Weeks than Others Do in 12 Months* (John Wiley & Sons, 2013).

6   Aaron Aiken, "The Benefits of Using OKRs to Purposefully Focus Your Personal Life," Medium, Februrary 12, 2018, https://medium.com/@ aaronaiken/the-benefits-of-using-okrs-to-purposefully-focus-your-personal-life-47f6d6553512.

7   GV (Google Ventures), "How Google Sets Goals: OKRs / Startup Lab Workshop," posted May 14, 2013, YouTube, https://www.youtube.com/ watch?v=mJB83EZtAjc.

8   John Doerr, *Measure What Matters: How Google, Bono, and the Gates Foundation Rock the World with OKRs* (Portfolio, 2018).

9   Michael Bungay Stanier, *How to Begin: Start Doing Something That Matters* (Page Two Books, 2022).

10   Stanier, *How to Begin.*

11   Doerr, *Measure What Matters*; Christina Wodtke, *Radical Focus: Achieving Your Most Important Goals with Objectives and Key Results* (Cucina Media, 2016).

12   Robert Waldinger and Marc Schulz, *The Good Life: Lessons from the World's Longest Scientific Study of Happiness* (Simon & Schuster, 2023).

13   Katie Bohn, "Love Actually, Americans Agree on What Makes People Feel Loved," Penn State University, news release, November 6, 2017, https:// www.psu.edu/news/research/story/love-actually-americans-agree-what-makes-people-feel-love.

14	April Eldemire, "How to Make and Keep New Year's Resolutions for Your Relationship," The Gottman Institute, December 30, 2024, https://www.gottman.com/blog/how-to-make-and-keep-new-years-resolutions-for-your-relationship/; Kelsey Down, "Make New Year's Resolutions a Family Affair," The Gottman Institute, January 8, 2025, https://www.gottman.com/blog/make-new-years-resolutions-family-affair/.

15	*Relationships First: Creating Connections that Help Young People Thrive* (Search Institute, 2017), https://www.search-institute.org/wp-content/uploads/2017/12/2017-Relationships-First-final.pdf.

16	Lisa Damour, *The Emotional Lives of Teenagers: Raising Connected, Capable, and Compassionate Adolescents* (Ballantine Books, 2023).

17	Dan Buettner and Sam Skemp, "Blue Zones: Lessons from the World's Longest Lived," *American Journal of Lifestyle Medicine* 10, no. 5 (Sep–Oct 2016), https://doi.org/10.1177/1559827616637066, retrieved from https://www.academia.edu/86289746/Blue_Zones; Nazanin Rajai et al., "Association Between Social Isolation with Age-Gap Determined by Artificial Intelligence-Enabled Electrocardiography," *JACC: Advances* 3, no. 9 pt. 2 (March 2024), https://doi.org/10.1016/j.jacadv.2024.100890.

18	Dominika Kwasnicka et al., "Theoretical Explanations for Maintenance of Behaviour Change: A Systematic Review of Behaviour Theories," *Health Psychology Review* 10, no. 3 (March 2016): 277–296, https://doi.org/10.1080/17437199.2016.1151372.

19	Peter Attia, "#342—Aging Well: Peter Shares Strategies for Improving Longevity with Residents at a Senior Living Center," *The Drive* (podcast), accessed October 28, 2025, https://peterattiamd.com/agingwell/.

20	Peter Attia, *Outlive: The Science and Art of Longevity* (Harmony Books, 2023).

21	Michelle Segar, *No Sweat: How the Simple Science of Motivation Can Bring You a Lifetime of Fitness* (AMACOM, 2015).

22	Michelle L. Segar et al., "Type of Physical Activity Goal Influences Participation in Healthy Midlife Women," *Women's Health Issues* 18, no. 4 (July–August 2008):281–91, https://doi.org/10.1016/j.whi.2008.02.003.

23	Michael Kitces and Carl Richards, hosts, *With Kitces & Carl*, podcast, episode 75, "Crafting a Statement of Financial Purpose to Find the Client's Financial Why," December 16, 2021, https://www.kitces.com/blog/statement-of-financial-purpose-advice-achieving-goals-financial-planning/; Sarah Newcomb, *Loaded: Money, Psychology, and How to Get Ahead Without Leaving Your Values Behind* (Wiley, 2016).

24 Lyndsay Bryan-Podvin, "How to Set Money Goals You'll Actually Achieve This Year," *SELF Magazine*, January 3, 2023, https://www.self.com/story/ values-based-financial-goals; Lindsay Bryan-Podvin, *The Financial Anxiety Solution: A Step-by-Step Workbook to Stop Worrying about Money, Take Control of Your Finances, and Live a Happier Life* (Ulysses Press, 2020).

25 Richard H. Thaler and Cass Sunstein, *Nudge: Improving Decisions about Health, Wealth, and Happiness* (Penguin Books, 2017).

26 Teresa Amabile and Steven Kramer, *The Progress Principle: Using Small Wins to Ignite Joy, Engagement, and Creativity at Work* (Harvard Business Review Press, 2011); Melissa Russell, "Why Celebrating Small Wins Matters," *Harvard Summer School Blog*, May 30, 2024, https://summer.harvard.edu/ blog/why-celebrating-small-wins-matters.

27 Steven Capasso, "Turning Financial Goals into Achievable Milestones," *IAPDA Blog*, December 8, 2023, https://iapda.org/blog/ financial-goals-into-achievable-milestones.

28 Andrea E. Abele and Bettina S. Wiese, "The Nomological Network of Self-Management Strategies and Career Success," *Journal of Occupational and Organizational Psychology* 81, no. 4 (December 2010): 73–749, https://doi. org/10.1348/096317907X256726.

29 Ryan Bradshaw, "15 Important Networking Statistics Everyone Should Know," Apollo Technical, March 29, 2025, https://www.apollotechnical. com/networking-statistics/; LinkedIn, "Eighty Percent of Professionals Consider Networking Important to Career Success," news release, June 2, 2017, https://news.linkedin.com/2017/6/eighty-percent-of-professionals-consider-networking-important-to-career-success.

30 University of Waterloo Work-Learn Institute, "Framing Future-ready Talent," Insight Newsletter, April 2022, https://uwaterloo.ca/ work-learn-institute/insight-newsletter/framing-future-ready-talent.

31 Douglas T. Hall and Philip H. Mirvis, "The New Career Contract: Developing the Whole Person at Midlife and Beyond," *Journal of Vocational Behavior* 47, no. 3 (December 1995):269–289 https://doi.org/10.1006/ JVBE.1995.0004.

32 Wodtke, "Personal OKRs Three Years Later."

33 Carol Dweck, *Mindset: The New Psychology of Success* (Random House, 2006).

34 E. A. Locke, and G. P. Latham, "Building a Practically Useful Theory of Goal Setting and Task Motivation: A 35-year Odyssey," *American Psychologist* 57, no. 9 (2002): 705–717, https://doi.org/10.1037/0003-066X.57.9.705.

Chapter 7: **Crafting Impactful Key Results**

1   Benjamin Harkin et al., "Does Monitoring Goal Progress Promote Goal Attainment? A Meta-Analysis of the Experimental Evidence," Psychological Bulletin 142, no. 2 (February 2016): 198–229, https://doi.org/10.1037/bul0000025. Refer to this APA announcement for background: American Psychological Association, "Frequently Monitoring Progress Towards Goals Increases Chance of Success," news release, October 28, 2015, https://www.apa.org/news/press/releases/2015/10/progress-goals?form=MG0AV3.

2   The quote "What gets measured gets managed" is widely attributed to management guru Peter Drucker, but it seems like he never said it. There is also some debate about whether this point is valid. For a good summary of this debate, check out this illuminating article by Danny Buerkli: Danny Buerkli, "'What Gets Measured Gets Managed'—It's Wrong and Drucker Never Said It," Centre for Public Impact, Medium, April 8, 2019, https://medium.com/centre-for-public-impact/what-gets-measured-gets-managed-its-wrong-and-drucker-never-said-it-fe95886d3df6.

3   George T. Doran, "There's a S.M.A.R.T. Way to Write Management's Goals and Objectives," Management Review 70, no. 11 (1981): 35–36. The SMART goal-setting framework originated from management and planning practices in the business world. The concept was first introduced by George T. Doran in 1981. Doran's article aimed to provide a practical method for organizations to improve goal setting and achieve better results. The acronym SMART was designed to guide managers in creating clearer, more actionable goals. Though some variations of what each letter stands for have appeared over time, Doran's original version has endured as the most recognized.

4   Michael Jensen, "Paying People to Lie: The Truth about the Budgeting Process," European Financial Management 9, no. 3 (January 2001), 379–406, https://doi.org/10.2139/ssrn.267651.

5   Robert Trivers, The Folly of Fools: The Logic of Deceit and Self-Deception in Human Life (Basic Books, 2011); William von Hippel and Robert Trivers, "The Evolution and Psychology of Self-Deception," Behavioral and Brain Sciences 34, no. 1 (February 2011): 1–16, https://doi.org/10.1017/S0140525X10001354.

6   C.A.E. Goodhart, "Problems of Monetary Management: The U.K. Experience," in Monetary Theory and Practice (Palgrave, 1984), 91–121, https://doi.org/10.1007/978-1-349-17295-5_4. Rationalization theory

explains that people justify their actions after the fact to align with their desired self-image, even if their behavior didn't match their original intent. For instance, someone might convince themselves that breaking down a simple task into many smaller ones is still "progress" because it feels more satisfying to check off tasks, even if the core goal remains unmet.

7   Piers Steel, "The Nature of Procrastination: A Meta-Analytic and Theoretical Review of Quintessential Self-Regulatory Failure," Psychological Bulletin 133, no. 1 (January 2007): 65–94, https://doi.org/10.1037/0033-2909.133.1.65.

8   Leon Festinger, *A Theory of Cognitive Dissonance* (Row, Peterson, 1957). Festinger's Cognitive Dissonance Theory shows that when there is a mismatch between expectations and reality, people will often adjust their perceptions or behaviors to restore psychological comfort. In the case of self-imposed targets, this could mean lowering the bar or focusing on easier, measurable metrics that give the appearance of progress.

9   Teresa Amabile and Steven Kramer, *The Progress Principle: Using Small Wins to Ignite Joy, Engagement, and Creativity at Work* (Harvard Business Review Press, 2011).

10 Doran, "There's a S.M.A.R.T. Way to Write Management's Goals and Objectives."

Chapter 8: Holding Yourself Accountable

1   Rich Roll. "Rich's Story," *Rich Roll* (blog), accessed October 6, 2025, https://www.richroll.com/bio/.

2   Rich Roll, "The MF 25," *Rich Roll* (blog), accessed October 6, 2025, https://www.richroll.com/blog/the-mf-25/. Also: Mark Lelinwalla, "The World's Fittest Vegan Is a 51-Year-Old Ultra-Endurance Athlete," *Men's Health*, March 19, 2018, https://www.menshealth.com/fitness/a19460422/rich-roll-workout-vegan-diet/.

3   Rich Roll, *Finding Ultra: Rejecting Middle Age, Becoming One of the World's Fittest Men, and Discovering Myself* (Harmony Books, 2012).

4   Gail Matthews, "Goal research summary," conference presentation, Dominican University Goals Research Symposium, 2015, https://www.dominican.edu/sites/default/files/2020-02/gailmatthews-harvard-goals-researchsummary.pdf?form=MG0AV3.

5   Bluma Zeigarnik, "Über das Behalten von erledigten und unerledigten Handlungen [On Finished and Unfinished Tasks],"*Psychologische Forschung* 9 (1927): 1–15, https://gwern.net/doc/psychology/willpower/1927-zeigarnik.pdf.

6   Barrett Wissman, "An Accountability Partner Makes You Vastly
    More Likely to Succeed," *Entrepreneur*, March 20, 2018, https://www.
    entrepreneur.com/leadership/an-accountability-partner-makes-you-vastly-
    more-likely-to/310062?form=MG0AV3.

7   Robert B. Cialdini, ed., *Influence: Science and Practice*, 5th edition (Pearson
    Education, 2009).

8   Roll, *Finding Ultra*.

9   Michael Bungay Stanier, *How to Begin: Start Doing Something That Matters*
    (Page Two Books, 2022). The concept of the "Spouse-ish" person is
    discussed in Chapter 2.

10 Benjamin Hardy, "Accountability Partners Are Great. But 'Success'
    Partners Will Change Your Life," *Medium*, January 17, 2019, https://medium.
    com/@benjaminhardy/accountability-partners-are-great-but-success-
    partners-will-change-your-life-8850ac0efa04.

11 Leon Festinger, "A Theory of Social Comparison Processes," *Human Relations*
    7, no. 2 (May 1954): 117–140, https://doi.org/10.1177/001872675400700202.
    Leon Festinger's social comparison theory posits that individuals have
    an inherent drive to evaluate their abilities and opinions by comparing
    themselves to others. This comparison can motivate individuals to
    improve their performance, especially when they perceive themselves as
    lagging behind their peers. Such dynamics can cultivate a blend of support
    and competition within groups, as members strive to align with or surpass
    the standards set by their peers.

12 Cathy Liska, "Measuring Coaching ROI," *ATD Blog*, December 10, 2013,
    https://www.td.org/content/atd-blog/measuring-coaching-roi.

13 Merrill C. Anderson, *Executive Briefing: Case Study on the ROI of
    Executive Coaching* (MetrixGlobal LLC, 2001), https://researchportal.
    coachingfederation.org/Document/Pdf/681.pdf; Work/Life Solutions,
    "Executive coaching yields return on investment of almost six times
    its cost!," news release, January 4, 2011, https://researchportal.
    coachingfederation.org/Document/Pdf/689.pdf.

14 Kim Scott, *Radical candor: Be a Kick-Ass Boss Without Losing Your Humanity*,
    revised and updated ed. (Macmillan, 2019).

Chapter 9: **Execution Matters**

1   The quote "Vision without execution is hallucination" is widely
    attributed to Thomas Edison, but there is no direct source or text

from Edison himself that confirms he used this exact wording. The quote is often referenced in various articles and discussions about Edison's philosophy on innovation and execution, but a primary source from Edison has not been identified. See for example: Bryan Stolle, "Vision Without Execution is Just Hallucination," *Forbes*, July 23, 2014, https://www.forbes.com/sites/bryanstolle/2014/07/22/vision-without-execution-is-just-hallucination/?form=MG0AV3.

2 The quote "Everyone has a plan until they get punched in the face" is widely attributed to Mike Tyson, but the actual words were "Everybody has a plan until they get hit." He famously said this before his fight with Evander Holyfield when asked if he was worried about his opponent's plans. Many years later in an interview with the *South Florida Sun Sentinel* he said this about the quote: "People were asking me [before a fight], 'What's going to happen?' They were talking about his style. 'He's going to give you a lot of lateral movement. He's going to move, he's going to dance. He's going to do this, do that.' I said, 'Everybody has a plan until they get hit. Then, like a rat, they stop in fear and freeze.'" Mike Berardino, "Mike Tyson Explains One of His Most Famous Quotes," *South Florida Sun Sentinel*, November 9, 2012, https://www.sun-sentinel.com/2012/11/09/mike-tyson-explains-one-of-his-most-famous-quotes-3/.

3 David Allen, *Getting Things Done: The Art of Stress-Free Productivity* (Viking, 2001).

4 For more information on the various personality assessment tools, please refer to: James M. Butcher, *Clinical Personality Assessment: Practical Approaches*, 2nd ed. (Oxford University Press, 2002); Jane Simkus, "Myers-Briggs Type Indicator (MBTI): 16 Personality Types," *Simply Psychology*, updated March 19, 2025, https://www.simplypsychology.org/the-myers-briggs-type-indicator.html; Annabelle G.Y. Lim, "Big Five Personality Traits: The 5-Factor Model of Personality," *Simply Psychology*, updated March 20, 2025, https://www.simplypsychology.org/big-five-personality.html; Courtney E. Ackerman, "Big Five Personality Traits: The OCEAN Model Explained," October 4, 2020, https://www.marottaonmoney.com/wp-content/uploads/2020/08/Big-Five-Personality-Traits.pdf.; Jeremy Sutton, "Using the Big Five Personality Traits (OCEAN) in Practice," *Positive Psychology*, May 2, 2025, https://positivepsychology.com/big-five-personality-theory/; The Enneagram Institute, "The Nine Enneagram Type Descriptions," *The Enneagram Institute*, accessed February 26, 2025, https://www.enneagraminstitute.com/type-descriptions/; DiSC Profile, "What is

DiSC?" DiSC Profile, accessed February 26, 2025, https://www.discprofile.com/what-is-disc.

5   Olivia Guy-Evans, "Lateralization of Brain Function & Hemispheric Specialization," Simply Psychology, updated May 2, 2025, https://www.simplypsychology.org/brain-lateralization.html; Eagle Gamma, "Left Brain vs. Right Brain: Hemisphere Function," *Simply Psychology*, October 20, 2023, https://www.simplypsychology.org/left-brain-vs-right-brain.html.

6   Jared A. Nielsen et al., "An Evaluation of the Left-Brain vs. Right-Brain Hypothesis with Resting State Functional Connectivity Magnetic Resonance Imaging," *PLOS One* 8, no. 8 (August 2013): e71275, https://doi.org/10.1371/journal.ponc.0071275.

7   Robert H. Shmerling, "Right Brain/Left Brain, right?," Harvard Health Publishing, Harvard Medical School, March 24, 2022, https://www.health.harvard.edu/blog/right-brainleft-brain-right-2017082512222.

8   Edward T. Hall, *The Silent Language* (Doubleday, 1959). The term monochronic comes from Edward Hall's cultural time orientation theory, where he distinguishes between: Monochronic cultures which focus on one task at a time. They follow schedules and work in a structured, linear way.Polychronic cultures which are more flexible, dealing with multiple things simultaneously and prioritizing relationships over rigid schedules.

9   Wikipedia, "Chronemics," last modified August 16, 2025, accessed October 6, 2025, https://en.wikipedia.org/wiki/Chronemics. Allen Bluedorn, Carol Felker Kaufman, and Paul M. Lane concluded that "developing an understanding of the monochronic/polychronic continuum will not only result in a better self-management but will also allow more rewarding job performances and relationships with people from different cultures and traditions." See: Allen Bluedornet al., "How Many Things Do You like to Do at Once? An Introduction to Monochronic and Polychronic Time," *Executive* 6, no. 4 (November 1992), 17–26, https://www.jstor.org/stable/4165091. Other researchers have examined that predicting someone's polychronicity plays an important role in productivity and individual well-being. See: Jichul Jang and R. Thomas George, "Understanding the Influence of Polychronicity on Job Satisfaction and Turnover Intention: A Study of Non-supervisory Hotel Employees," *International Journal of Hospitality Management* 31, no. 2 (June 2012): 588–595, https://doi.org/10.1016/j.ijhm.2011.08.004.

10 J.P. Guilford, *The Nature of Human Intelligence* (McGraw-Hill, 1967). Guilford identified these two types of human responses to problems,

where convergent thinking involves finding a single correct solution, and divergent thinking involves generating multiple possible solutions. Convergent thinking focuses on finding the best solution to a problem. It is systematic and aimed at making decisions. This contrasts with divergent thinking, which is open-ended, exploratory, and creative, generating multiple possibilities. Also see: Olga M. Razumnikova" Divergent Versus Convergent Thinking," in *Encyclopedia of Creativity, Invention, Innovation and Entrepreneurship*, ed. Elias G. Carayannis (Spring, Cham, 2020), 759–765, https://doi.org/10.1007/978-3-319-15347-6_362.

11   "KISS, an acronym for "Keep it simple, stupid!", is a design principle first noted by the US Navy in 1960. First seen partly in American English by at least 1938, KISS implies that simplicity should be a design goal. The phrase has been associated with aircraft engineer Kelly Johnson. The term "KISS principle" was in popular use by 1970. Variations on the phrase (usually as some euphemism for the more churlish "stupid") include "keep it super simple," "keep it simple, silly," "keep it short and simple," "keep it short and sweet," "keep it simple and straightforward," "keep it small and simple," "keep it simple, soldier," "keep it simple, sailor," "keep it simple, sweetie," "keep it stupidly simple," or "keep it sweet and simple." Wikipedia "KISS principle," last modified August 24, 2025, accessed October 6, 2025, https://en.wikipedia.org/wiki/KISS_principle.

12   Anxious Minds, "CBT Tools—Activity Scheduling and Prioritisation," *Anxious Minds Blog*, accessed February 25, 2025, https://www.anxiousminds. co.uk/cbt-tools-activity-scheduling/?form=MG0AV3; Tiger Management Institute, "How Do You Stop Cognitive Load? 10 Ways to Reduce," Tiger Management Institute, accessed February 25, 2025, https://www.tigermi. com/learning-center/stop-cognitive-owerload?form=MG0AV3.

13   Select books on habit formation we would recommend include: James Clear, *Atomic Habits: An Easy & Proven Way to Build Good Habits & Break Bad Ones* (Avery, 2018); Charles Duhigg, *The Power of Habit: Why We Do What We Do in Life and Business* (Random House, 2012); Stephen Guise, *Mini Habits: Smaller Habits, Bigger Results* (CreateSpace Independent Publishing Platform, 2013); B.J. Fogg, *Tiny Habits: The Small Changes that Change Everything* (Houghton Mifflin Harcourt, 2019); Gretchen Rubin, *Better Than Before: Mastering the Habits of Our Everyday Lives* (Crown, 2015); Stephen R. Covey, *The 7 Habits of Highly Effective People: Powerful Lessons in Personal Change* (Free Press, 1989). Here some TED talks on habit formation, as of February 25, 2025, from www.ted.com: Christine Carter, "The 1-Minute

Secret to Forming a New Habit," TEDxMarin, September 2020, https://www.ted.com/talks/christine_carter_the_1_minute_secret_to_forming_a_new_habit; Jude Aburdan, "The Power of Habit," TEDxSafirSchool, March 2021, https://www.youtube.com/watch?v=F8nPv7Alrw4; Marco Badwal, "The Science of Habits," TEDxFS, December 2017, https://www.ted.com/talks/marco_badwal_the_science_of_habits; James Clear, "How to Develop the Habits You Want—and Get Rid of the Ones You Don't," *TED Original Podcast*, April 2024, https://www.ted.com/talks/how_to_be_a_better_human_how_to_develop_the_habits_you_want_and_get_rid_of_the_ones_you_don_t_w_james_clear; Charles Duhigg, "The Power of Habit," TEDxTeachersCollege, February 2013, https://www.youtube.com/watch?v=OMbsGBlpP30.

Chapter 10: **Cadence Makes Productivity Sustainable**

1   Anil K Gupta, "The Road to Success is Paved with the Roadkill of Good Intentions," Lecture on Business Strategy, Executive MBA Class of 2007, Smith School of Business.

2   Masaaki Imai, *Kaizen: The Key to Japan's Competitive Success* (Random House, 1986).

3   Nancy R. Tague, ed., *The Quality Toolbox*, 3rd ed. (ASQ Quality Press, 2024).

4   Christina Wodtke, *Radical Focus: Achieving Your Most Important Goals with Objectives and Key Results* (Cucina Media, 2016), 166; Marty Cagan and Chris Jones, *Empowered: Ordinary People, Extraordinary Products* (Wiley, 2020).

5   Hengchen Dai et al., "Put Your Imperfections Behind You: Temporal Landmarks Spur Goal Initiation When They Signal New Beginnings," *Psychological Science* 26, no. 12 (November 2015): 1927–1936, https://doi.org/10.1177/0956797615605818.

6   Michael Hyatt and Daniel Harkavy, *Living Forward: A Proven Plan to Stop Drifting and Get the Life You Want* (Baker Books, 2015). The quote "What gets scheduled gets done" is often attributed to productivity expert Michael Hyatt. He has emphasized the importance of intentional planning and time management in his books and teachings. The idea is that by deliberately scheduling tasks, you are more likely to follow through and achieve your goals.

7   Bluma Zeigarnik, "Über das Behalten von erledigten und unerledigten Handlungen [On Finished and Unfinished Tasks]," *Psychologische Forschung* 9 (1927): 1–15, https://gwern.net/doc/psychology/willpower/1927-zeigarnik.pdf.

8   Teresa Amabile and Steven Kramer, *The Progress Principle: Using Small Wins to Ignite Joy, Engagement, and Creativity at Work* (Harvard Business Review Press, 2011).

9   Chad Stahelski, dir., *John Wick* (Summit Entertainment, 2014).

Chapter 11: **To-Do Lists**

1   Brigitte J. C. Claessens et al., "Things to Do Today…: A Daily Diary Study on Task Completion at Work," *Applied Psychology* 59, no. 2 (February 2010): 273–295, https://doi.org/10.1111/J.1464-0597.2009.00390.X.

2   TimeWatch, "Time Management Statistics (New Research in 2024), TimeWatch, September 30, 2024, https://www.timewatch.com/blog/time-management-statistics/; Acuity Training, "Time Management Statistics: Original Independent Research," Acuity Training, March 26, 2025, https://www.acuitytraining.co.uk/news-tips/time-management-statistics-research/.

3   B. Zeigarnik, "On Finished and Unfinished Tasks," *Psychologische Forschung* 9 (1927): 1–85, https://doi.org/10.1007/BF02409636; E.J. Masicampo and R.F. Baumeister, "Consider It Done! Plan Making Can Eliminate the Cognitive Effects of Unfulfilled Goals," Journal of Personality and Social Psychology 101, no. 4 (2011): 667–683, https://doi.org/10.1037/a0024192; Sarah Schrager and Emily M. Sadowski, "Getting More Done: Strategies to Increase Scholarly Productivity," *Journal of Graduate Medical Education* 8, no. 1 (2016): 10–13, https://doi.org/10.4300/JGME-D-15-00165.1.

4   Microsoft, "Survey Shows Increasing Worldwide Reliance on To-Do Lists," Microsoft News Center, January 14, 2008, https://news.microsoft.com/source/2008/01/14/survey-shows-increasing-worldwide-reliance-on-to-do-lists.

5   Michael K. Scullin et al, "The Effects of Bedtime Writing on Difficulty Falling Asleep: A Polysomnographic Study Comparing To-Do Lists and Completed Activity Lists," *Journal of Experimental Psychology: General* 147, no. 1 (2018): 139–46, https://doi.org/10.1037/xge0000374.

6   Ralph Ryback, "The Science of Accomplishing Your Goals," *Psychology Today*, October 3, 2016, https://www.psychologytoday.com/us/blog/the-truisms-wellness/201610/the-science-accomplishing-your-goals.

7   Daniel Markovitz, "To-Do Lists Don't Work," *Harvard Business Review*, January 25, 2012, https://hbr.org/2012/01/to-do-lists-dont-work.

8   Barry Schwartz, *The Paradox of Choice: Why More Is Less* (HarperCollins, 2004); Barry Schwartz, "The Tyranny of Choice," *Scientific American*, April 2004, https://bschwartz.domains.swarthmore.edu/Sci.Amer.pdf.

9   Sheena Iyengar, *The Art of Choosing* (Twelve, 2011).

10   Stephen J. Dubner and Steven D. Levitt, "The Stomach-Surgery Conundrum," *New York Times*, November 18, 2007, https://www.nytimes.com/2007/11/18/magazine/18wwln-freakonomics-t.html; Wikipedia, "Commitment Device," last modified September 25, 2025, accessed October 6, 2025, https://en.wikipedia.org/wiki/Commitment_device.

11   Marc Zao-Sanders, "How Timeboxing Works and Why It Will Make You More Productive," *Harvard Business Review*, December 12, 2018, https://hbr.org/2018/12/how-timeboxing-works-and-why-it-will-make-you-more-productive.

12   Robert N. Kraft, "10 Benefits of Making Lists," Psychology Today, May 7, 2021, https://www.psychologytoday.com/us/blog/defining-memories/202105/10-benefits-making-lists.

13   Timo Kiander, "How to Create an Effective To-Do List," Lifehack, updated May 31, 2025, https://www.lifehack.org/articles/productivity/how-to-create-a-to-do-list-that-makes-you-smile.html; Damon Zahariades, *To-Do List Formula: A Stress-Free Guide to Creating To-Do Lists That Work!* (Independently published, 2016); Allison Rimm, "Taming the Epic To-Do List," *Harvard Business Review*, March 26, 2018, https://hbr.org/2018/03/taming-the-epic-to-do-list.

14   ActiveCollab, "What Is ABCDE Method—Guide For Efficient Time Management," ActiveCollab, March 11, 2025, https://activecollab.com/blog/project-management/abcde-method.

15   Steven Lam, "The POSEC Method of Time Management," Planarty, 2004, https://www.planarty.com/blog/posec-method.

16   James Clear, "The Ivy Lee Method: The Daily Routine for Peak Productivity," James Clear, accessed May 29, 2025, https://jamesclear.com/ivy-lee.

17   Sarah Laoyan, "Understanding the Pareto Principle (The 80/20 Rule)," Asana, March 5, 2025, https://asana.com/resources/pareto-principle-80-20-rule.

18   Sigma US, "The Power of the Action Priority Matrix in Project Management," Sigma US, July 24, 2024, https://www.6sigma.us/six-sigma-in-focus/action-priority-matrix-eisenhower-matrix/.

19   Eisenhower did say this quote in a 1954 speech to the Second Assembly of the World Council of Churches, but he was quoting someone else, most likely referencing Dr. J. Roscoe Miller, rather than claiming it as his own original thought.

20   Stephen R. Covey, *The 7 Habits of Highly Effective People: Powerful Lessons in Personal Change* (Free Press, 1989). The Eisenhower Matrix focuses on urgency and importance to prioritize tasks, while the Covey Matrix expands on it by aligning tasks with personal values and long-term goals to emphasize proactive, principle-centered living.

21   Hannah Bratterud et al., "The Sung Diagram: Revitalizing the Eisenhower Matrix," Diagrammatic Representation and Inference: 11th International Conference, Diagrams 2020, *Lecture Notes in Computer Science* 12169 (August 2020), https://doi.org/10.1007/978-3-030-54249-8_43; TimeWatch, "Time Management Statistics (New Research in 2024), TimeWatch, September 30, 2024, https://www.timewatch.com/blog/time-management-statistics/. Although just 1% of respondents in this survey say they use the Eisenhower Matrix, a further 92% are actually using some elements of this system (to-do list, scheduling, doing what feels important), offering the possibility that with a little extra effort they could improve their time management with the full Eisenhower time management system.

22   Agile Business Consortium, "MoSCoW Prioritisation," *DSDM Project Framework* (Agile Business Consortium), accessed May 29, 2025, https://www.agilebusiness.org/dsdm-project-framework/moscow-prioririsation.html.

23   Kelsey Alpaio, "I Tried 4 To-Do List Methods. Here's What Worked," *Harvard Business Review*, January 14, 2021, from https://hbr.org/2021/01/i-tried-4-to-do-list-methods-heres-what-worked.

24   Damon Zahariades, *To-Do List Formula: A Stress-Free Guide to Creating To-Do Lists That Work!* (Independently published, 2016).

25   David Allen, *Getting Things Done: The Art of Stress-Free Productivity* (Viking, 2001).

26   Allison Rimm, "Taming the Epic To-Do List," *Harvard Business Review*, March 26, 2018, https://hbr.org/2018/03/taming-the-epic-to-do-list.

27   James Clear, *Atomic Habits: An Easy & Proven Way to Build Good Habits & Break Bad Ones* (Avery, 2018).

28   Timothy J. Smoker et al., "Comparing Memory for Handwriting versus Typing," *Proceedings of the Human Factors and Ergonomics Society Annual Meeting* 53, no. 22 (October 2009): 1744–1747, https://doi.org/10.1177/154193120905302218; Abraham Flanigan et al., "Typed Versus Handwritten Lecture Notes and College Student Achievement: A Meta-Analysis," *Educational Psychology Review* 36 (July 2024):78, https://doi.org/10.1007/s10648-024-09914-w; Pam A. Mueller and Daniel M.

Oppenheimer, "The Pen Is Mightier than the Keyboard: Advantages of Longhand over Laptop Note Taking," *Psychological Science* 25, no. 6 (April 2014): 1159–1168, https://doi.org/10.1177/0956797614524581.

29   Mona Haraty et al., "How Personal Task Management Differs Across Individuals," *International Journal of Human-Computer Studies* 88 (April 2016): 13–37, https://doi.org/10.1016/J.IJHCS.2015.11.006; Amirrudin Kamsin et al., "Personal Task Management: My Tools Fall Apart When I'm Very Busy!," *CHI'12 Extended Abstracts on Human Factors in Computing Systems* (May 2012): 1369–1374, https://doi.org/10.1145/2212776.2212457.

30   Anna Havron, "To-Do Lists for Visual Thinkers," Anna Havron, accessed May 30, 2025, https://www.annahavron.com/blog/to-do-lists-for-visual-thinkers.

31   Lea Nobbe et al., "Smartphone-Based Study Reminders Can Be a Double-Edged Sword," *NPJ Science of Learning* 9 (2024): 40, https://doi.org/10.1038/s41539-024-00253-7.

32   Allen, *Getting Things Done*.

33   Cal Newport, "Getting (Unremarkable) Things Done: The Problem with David Allen's Universalism," Cal Newport, December 21, 2012, https://calnewport.com/getting-unremarkable-things-done-the-problem-with-david-allens-universalism.

Chapter 12: **Calendar Integration**

1   The quote is often attributed to the ancient Greek philosopher Heraclitus, though his original phrasing was slightly different: "No man ever steps in the same river twice, for it's not the same river and he's not the same man." His philosophy emphasized the constant flow and change in life, suggesting that everything is in a state of flux.

2   TimeWatch, "Time Management Statistics (New Research in 2024), TimeWatch, September 30, 2024, https://www.timewatch.com/blog/time-management-statistics/; Filtered, *Definitive 100 Most Useful Productivity Hacks* (Filtered, 2018); https://learn.filtered.com/hubfs/Definitive%20100%20Most%20Useful%20Productivity%20Hacks.pdf.

3   Daniel Markovitz, "To-Do Lists Don't Work," *Harvard Business Review*, January 24, 2012, https://hbr.org/2012/01/to-do-lists-dont-work.

4   Marc Zao-Sanders, *Timeboxing: The Power of Doing One Thing at a Time* (St. Martin's Press, 2024).

5   Gwendolyn D. Galsworth, *Visual Workplace Visual Thinking: Creating Enterprise Excellence Through the Technologies of the Visual Workplace*, 2nd ed. (Productivity Press, 2017).

6   Got your interest, right? That one is from us. We tried to find someone famous to credit for "Your calendar is your best to-do list"; we really did. Searched high and low, checked blogs, books, productivity cults... nada. So, we're taking the liberty. Call it poetic license. Or just a really good Tuesday. Wolfram & Sebastian, authors, calendar nerds, and to-do list skeptics.

7   Mariah D. R. Evans, Paul Kelley, and Jonathan Kelley, "Identifying the Best Times for Cognitive Functioning Using New Methods: Matching University Times to Undergraduate Chronotypes," *Frontiers in Human Neuroscience* 11 (April 19, 2017): 188, https://doi.org/10.3389/fnhum.2017.00188.

8   The quote originates from Helmuth von Moltke the Elder, a Prussian field marshal. His original phrasing in an 1871 essay on military strategy was: "No plan of operations extends with any certainty beyond the first encounter with the main enemy forces." Over time, this statement was paraphrased into the more commonly cited version: "No battle plan survives first contact with the enemy." Wikiquote, "Helmuth von Moltke the Elder," last modified May 31, 2024, accessed May 30, 2025, https://en.wikiquote.org/wiki/Helmuth_von_Moltke_the_Elder.

9   Roger Buehler et al., "The Planning Fallacy: Cognitive, Motivational, and Social Origins," *Advances in Experimental Social Psychology* 43 (201): 1–62, https://doi.org/10.1016/S0065-2601(10)43001-4; Roger Buehler et al., "Exploring the 'Planning fallacy': Why People Underestimate Their Task Completion Times," *Journal of Personality and Social Psychology* 67, no. 3 (1994): 366–381, https://doi.org/10.1037/0022-3514.67.3.366.

Chapter 13: **Kanban Boards**

1   Taiichi Ohno, *Toyota Production System: Beyond Large-Scale Production* (Productivity Press, 1988).

2   David J. Anderson, *Kanban: Successful Evolutionary Change for Your Technology Business* (Blue Hole Press, 2010).

3   John Coleman et al., "The Kanban Guide," Kanban Guides, updated May 1, 2025, accessed October 7, 2025, https://kanbanguides.org/english/.

4   Edwin A. Locke and Gary P. Latham, "Building a Practically Useful Theory of Goal Setting and Task Motivation: A 35-Year Odyssey," *American Psychologist* 57, no. 9 (September 2002): 705–717, https://doi.org/10.1037//0003-066x.57.9.705.

5   Nadja Damij and Talib Damij, "An Approach to Optimizing Kanban Board Workflow and Shortening the Project Management Plan," *IEEE Transactions on Engineering Management* 71 (2024): 13266–13273, https://doi.org/10.1109/TEM.2021.3120984.

6   Abdulrahman K. Eesee et al., "Impact of Work Instruction Difficulty on Cognitive Load and Operational Efficiency," *Scientific Reports* 15 (2025): 11028, https://doi.org/10.1038/s41598-025-95942-7; Merve Ekin et al., "Prediction of Intrinsic and Extraneous Cognitive Load with Oculometric and Biometric Indicators," *Scientific Reports* 15 (2025): 5213, https://doi.org/10.1038/s41598-025-89336-y.

7   Katherine Labonté and François Vachon, "Resuming a Dynamic Task Following Increasingly Long Interruptions: The Role of Working Memory and Reconstruction," *Frontiers in Psychology* 12 (June 2021): 659451, https://doi.org/10.3389/fpsyg.2021.659451.

8   Jim Benson and Tonianne DeMaria, *Personal Kanban: Mapping Work | Navigating Life* (Modus Cooperandi Press, 2011); "11 Advantages of Visual Task Boards," Week Plan, December 11, 2024, https://weekplan.net/advantages-visual-task-boards.

9   Anderson, *Kanban*.

10   Neil Baum, "The Myth of Multitasking," *Healthcare Administration Leadership & Management Journal* 2, no. 3 (2024): 127–128, https://doi.org/10.55834/halmj.3391135898.

11   L. Mark Carrier et al., "Causes, Effects, and Practicalities of Everyday Multitasking," *Developmental Review* 35 (March 2015): 64–78, https://doi.org/10.1016/J.DR.2014.12.005.

12   Frédéric Vallée-Tourangeau et al., "Interactivity Mitigates the Impact of Working Memory Depletion on Mental Arithmetic Performance," *Cognitive Research: Principles and Implications* 1 (2016): 26, https://doi.org/10.1186/s41235-016-0027-2; Gaëlle Vallée-Tourangeau et al., "Interactivity Fosters Bayesian Reasoning Without Instruction," *Journal of Experimental Psychology: General* 144, no. 3 (June 2015): 581–603, https://doi.org/10.1037/a0039161.

Chapter 14: **Habit Formation with POKR**

1   James Clear, *Atomic Habits: An Easy & Proven Way to Build Good Habits & Break Bad Ones* (Avery, 2018).

2   Charles Duhigg, *The Power of Habit: Why We Do What We Do in Life and Business* (Random House, 2012).

3   "Know Your Triggers," Australian Government Department of Health, Disability, and Aging, updated December 22, 2023, https://www.health.gov.au/topics/smoking-vaping-and-tobacco/how-to-quit/know-your-triggers.

4   Monday Campaigns, "8 Ways to Conquer Mindless Smoking Triggers this Monday," Quit and Stay Quit Monday, accessed October 7, 2025, https://www.mondaycampaigns.org/quit-stay-quit/8-ways-conquer-mindless-smoking-triggers-monday.

5   Katy Milkman, "A Flexible Routine Can Help You Change for Good," *Strategy+business*. May 6, 2021, https://www.strategy-business.com/article/A-flexible-routine-can-help-you-change-for-good.

6   Robert West, *Stop Doomscrolling: How to Break the Cycle to Relieve Stress, Decrease Anxiety, and Regain Your Life* (Hentopan Publishing, 2020).

7   Claire Spencer, "7 Strategies to Combat Doomscrolling in Teens and Young Adults," *Go Aro* (blog), September 25, 2024, https://www.goaro.com/blog/7-strategies-to-combat-doomscrolling-in-teens-and-young-adults.

8   Cerebral, "What is Doomscrolling, and How Do You Stop?," *Cerebral*, May 23, 2024, https://www.resiliencelab.us/thought-lab/doomscrolling; Jeffrey Davis, "Breaking out of the Doomscrolling Cycle," *Psychology Today*, June 9, 2022, https://www.psychologytoday.com/us/blog/tracking-wonder/202206/breaking-out-of-the-doomscrolling-cycle.

9   Kevin H, "13 Ways to Stop Doomscrolling & Protect Your Mental Health," SoCal Mental Health, accessed October 7, 2025, https://socalmentalhealth.com/13-ways-to-stop-doomscrolling.

Chapter 15: Balancing Personal Projects and Family Time

1   *Modern Parenthood: Roles of Moms and Dads Converge as They Balance Work and Family* (Pew Research Center, March 14, 2013), https://www.pewresearch.org/social-trends/2013/03/14/modern-parenthood-roles-of-moms-and-dads-converge-as-they-balance-work-and-family/.

2   Tamar Kremer-Sadlik and Amy L. Paugh, "Everyday Moments: Finding 'Quality Time' in American Working Families," *Time & Society* 16, no. 2–3 (September 2007): 287–308, https://doi.org/10.1177/0961463X07080276.

3   John M. Gottman and Nan Silver, *The Seven Principles for Making Marriage Work: A Practical Guide from the Country's Foremost Relationship Expert* (Harmony Books, 2015). Also see: Janet Bayramyan, "Deepening Connections," The Gottman Institute., updated March 4, 2024, https://www.gottman.com/blog/deepening-connections-gottman-and-ifs/?form=MG0AV3.

4   Albert Bandura, *Social Learning Theory* (Prentice Hall, 1976).

Chapter 16: **The Journey Ahead**

1   John Doerr, *Measure What Matters: How Google, Bono, and the Gates Foundation Rock the World with OKRs* (Portfolio, 2018). Refer to chapter "Resource 4: In Sum" for the key takeaways of his approach.

2   Michael D. Mrazek et al., "Pushing the Limits: Cognitive, Affective, and Neural Plasticity Revealed by an Intensive Multifaceted Intervention," *Frontiers in Human Neuroscience* 10 (March 2016), https://doi.org/10.3389/fnhum.2016.00117.

3   The American Society of Training and Development. Referenced in Barrett Wissman, "An Accountability Partner Makes You Vastly More Likely to Succeed," *Entrepreneur*, March 20, 2018, https://www.entrepreneur.com/leadership/an-accountability-partner-makes-you-vastly-more-likely-to/310062?form=MG0AV3.

4   Meg Selig, "The Amazing Power of Small Wins," Psychology Today, July 18, 2012, https://www.psychologytoday.com/us/blog/changepower/201207/the-amazing-power-of-small-wins. For more scientific background on dopamine, refer to R. A. Bressan and J.A. Crippa, "The Role of Dopamine in Reward and Pleasure Behaviour—Review of Data from Preclinical Research, *Acta Psychiatrica Scandinavica* 111, no. s427 (May 2005): 14–2,. https://doi.org/10.1111/j.1600-0447.2005.00540.x.

5   Christopher Nolan, dir., *Batman Begins* (Warner Bros. Pictures, 2005). While most quoted as "Why do we fall? So, we can learn to pick ourselves up," the screenplay actually contains the sentence "And why do we fall, Master Bruce? So that we might better learn to pick ourselves up."

6   Carol Dweck, *Mindset: The New Psychology of Success* (Random House, 2006).

7   James Clear, *Atomic Habits: An Easy & Proven Way to Build Good Habits & Break Bad Ones* (Avery, 2018).

8   The quote "I have not failed. I've just found 10,000 ways that won't work" is often attributed to Thomas Edison, but its precise source is not well-documented. It is widely cited in various books and articles, but there is no definitive original source for this exact wording.